ON THE ROAD

— THE OFFICIAL —

MOVIE COMPANION

PENGUIN BOOKS

PENGUIN BOOKS

Published by the Penguin Group
Penguin Group (USA) Inc., 375 Hudson Street, New York, New York 10014, USA
Penguin Group (Canada), 90 Eglinton Avenue East, Suite 700, Toronto,
Ontario M4P 2Y3, Canada (a division of Pearson Penguin Canada Inc.)
Penguin Books Ltd, 80 Strand, London WC2R 0RL, England
Penguin Ireland, 25 St Stephen's Green, Dublin 2,
Ireland (a division of Penguin Books Ltd)
Penguin Group (Australia), 707 Collins Street, Melbourne, Victoria 3008,
Australia (a division of Pearson Australia Group Pty Ltd)
Penguin Books India Pvt Ltd, 11 Community Centre,
Panchsheel Park, New Delhi – 110 017, India
Penguin Group (NZ), 67 Apollo Drive, Rosedale, Auckland 0632,
New Zealand (a division of Pearson New Zealand Ltd)
Penguin Books, Rosebank Office Park, 181 Jan Smuts Avenue,
Parktown North 2193, South Africa
Penguin China, B7 Jaiming Center, 27 East Third Ring Road North,
Chaoyang District, Beijing 100020, China

Penguin Books Ltd, Registered Offices:
80 Strand, London WC2R 0RL, England

First published in France by MK2 Agency 2012
Published in Penguin Books 2012

1 3 5 7 9 10 8 6 4 2

Copyright © MK2 Agency, 2012
All rights reserved

ISBN 978-0-14-312384-2

Printed in the United States of America

ALWAYS LEARNING   PEARSON

✳CONTENTS✳

CREATED AND PRODUCED FOR THE PENGUIN GROUP BY
Trois Couleurs and MK2 Agency
55 rue Traversière, 75012 Paris
+33 (0)1 44 67 30 00

EDITORIAL DIRECTOR
Elisha Karmitz (elisha.karmitz@mk2.com)

EDITOR IN CHIEF
Aureliano Tonet (aureliano.tonet@mk2.com)

DEPUTY EDITORS-IN-CHIEF
Juliette Reitzer (juliette.reitzer@mk2.com)
Etienne Rouillon (etienne.rouillon@mk2.com)

REPORTERS
Clémentine Gallot (clementine.gallot@mk2.com)
Laura Tuillier (laura.tuillier@mk2.com)

ART AND DESIGN DIRECTOR
Sarah Kahn (hello@sarahkahn.fr)
in collaboration with Tom Bücher

ENGLISH EDITION
Anita Conrade
Lucy Bergeret

FRENCH EDITION
Jérémy Davis (jeremy.davis@mk2.com)

COPY EDITOR
Laura Hugo Westerhout

PHOTO EDITOR
Juliette Reitzer

INTERNS
Quentin Grosset, Isaure Pisani-Ferry

CONTRIBUTORS
Ève Beauvallet, Yves Buin, Arnaud Contreras,
Anastasia Lévy, Gladys Marivat, Laura Pertuy,
Bernard Quiriny, Éric Vernay, Anne-Lou Vicente

TRANSLATORS
Audrey Concannon, Anita Conrade, Jennifer
Gay, Catherine Guesde, Carol Shyman, Alex
Wynne Hauet, Laura Hugo Westerhout

GENERAL DIRECTOR
Elisha Karmitz

THANKS
Gordon Ball, Bernard Benoliel,
Jean-Jacques Bonvin, Michel Bulteau, Ray Carney,
Charles Carmignac, Carolyn Cassady, Jerry Cimino,
John Cohen, Carlos Conti, Bradley D. Cook,
Roman Coppola, Christophe Cousin, Peter Coyote,
Marie-Laure Dagoit, Maria Teresa Davis,
Philippe Djian, Galerie Frank Elbaz,
Philippe Garnier, Eric Gautier, Isaac Gewirtz,
Barry Gifford, Charles Gillibert, Cindy Guagenti,
Helen Hall, Robert Hastings, Al Hinkle,
Joyce Johnson, Hettie Jones, Jami Kandel,
Nathanaël Karmitz, Jean-Jacques Lebel,
Alain Lefèvre-Utile, Jeffrey Lewis, Paul Marion,
James McKee, Barry Miles, Dave Moore,
Gilles Mouëllic, Jon Nix, F. J. Ossang, Claude Pélieu,
Stefanie Posavec, Richard Prince, Emmanuel Proust,
Ed Ruscha, Walter Salles, John Sampas,
Gustavo Santaolalla, Stephen Shore, Yves Simon,
L. Parker Stephenson, Catherine Thieck,
Todd Tietchen, UNI Studios, Anne Waldman,
Saul Williams, Rebecca Yeldham,
www.beatbookcovers.com Documents
and photographs from the Jack Kerouac archives
at the New York Public Library are reproduced
with permission from John Sampas. All images
taken from On the Road and photos from the set,
unless otherwise indicated: ©Gregory Smith

Cover photo © MK2/Photo: Gregory Smith

THE ROAD REGAINED

BY AURELIANO TONET | TRANSLATED BY ANITA CONRADE

n 2004, when Francis Ford Coppola asked Walter Salles to direct a film version of *On the Road*, Salles confessed he didn't feel ready. Before tackling the hazardous task of reconstituting the epic work of Yankee prose, he made a documentary *"to improve his understanding"* of Kerouac's novel and its context. Its working title, *Searching for On the Road*, contains echoes of *Remembrance of Things Past*, the title of Proust's saga. Despite countless obstacles and challenges, Salles has finished his *On the Road*. It, too, gives off a whiff of Proust's spirit. The characters are continually passing a copy of *Swann's Way* from hand to hand like a fetish, as if Proust's masterpiece conferred a special vision of life.

To the neophyte, the Kerouac-Proust parallel may seem absurd. Outwardly, the two writers are total opposites. Proust's aristocrats *"go to bed early"* (and with little enthusiasm). Prisoners of convention, compared to Kerouac's *"mad ones, the ones who never yawn,"* fascinated by the fringes of American society – hobos, loose women, hicks, working stiffs. Debussy's piano poems and impressionist visions form the cohesive and harmonious charm of the *Search for Lost Time*. *On the Road* bops along, its breathless sentences spinning an ecstatic, syncopated trance. For one, time is like a folded fabric; for the other, an endless highway. Grandmother Europa versus teenage America, parlors versus the Great Plains. Proust and Kerouac inhabit two different planets!

But the writer Kerouac, whose mother tongue was French, always acknowledged his debt to Proust: *"I decided to do just like Proust, only fast." "My work* comprises one vast book like Proust's except that my remembrances are written on the run instead of afterwards in a sick bed."* Protected throughout his cirrhosis-shortened life by Mémère, "Ti-Jean" Kerouac identified with Marcel, who couldn't bear being separated from *maman*. Ceaselessly rewriting, correcting, and reinventing, both embarked on literature as if upon a long inner journey, tuning the language to suit their convoluted psyches, blazing sublime and unconventional trails. Kerouac, who urged his contemporaries to write *"the book movie, the movie in words, the visual American form,"* was especially enamored of the translucent descriptions shimmering in Proust's prose - for example, *"the transparent but closed screen that separated us from the beach, while allowing us to see everything, so suffused with sunlight that the azure sky seemed to be the same color as the windows, and its white clouds, a defect in the glass."* The prism operates to the same cinegenic effect as Kerouac's windshield, rendered magnificently onscreen by Walter Salles.

This companion to the film is an imperfect Proustian *madeleine*. It took a year to bake the cake – far less, of course than the time it took for the *Search* (15 years), *On the Road* (9 years), or the film version (8 years). All our probing, peregrination, and palaver has led us to one observation: the journeys of a man, a book, and film can share the same horizon. *"Real life, life at last discovered and brightened and, consequently, the only life really lived, is literature,"* suggested Proust. *"The road is life,"* added Kerouac, in a novel that was initially written on an endless ribbon, scrolling through the typewriter like a paper road, a dream coming true in reel, an inky river at the mouth of which a person ends up finding himself, exhausted but alive. ●

> ## "THE TRUE JOURNEY OF DISCOVERY CONSISTS NOT IN SEEKING NEW SCENERY, BUT IN HAVING NEW EYES."
>
> MARCEL PROUST

---

[1] His *Belief & Technique for Modern Prose - List of Essentials* recommends, *"Like Proust, be an old teahead of time,"* an injunction that unfortunately reduces to a painful pun when translated into French ("Comme Proust, pars à la recherche du joint perdu.")

Words followed by the sign (*) are explained in a glossary page 228.

GUEST

YVES BUIN[1] | CAROLYN CASSADY[2] | ARNAUD CONTRERAS[3]
JÉRÉMY DAVIS[4] | QUENTIN GROSSET[5] | HETTIE JONES[6]

BY ISAURE PISANI-FERRY AND QUENTIN GROSSET

TRANSLATED BY CAROL SHYMAN

1. It was the bebop style of *On the Road* that attracted Yves Buin, poet, psychiatrist, and author of a biography on Thelonious Monk. He wrote a biography of Jack Kerouac, and a preface to an anthology of Kerouac's work published by Gallimard, as well as an essay on the documentary *King of the Beats*. On **page 33,** he analyzes the links between jazz and the Beat Generation – a question of tempo.

2. The blond Carolyn, alias Camille in *On the Road,* met the *"mystical wanderer"* of the Beat Generation, Neal Cassady, on the campus of the University of Denver. She became his wife and the mother of his children, as well as one of the closest witnesses of the life and values of the budding beatniks: Kerouac, Ginsberg, Burroughs, among others. Her priceless assistance and exactness make her the godmother of this special issue.

3. In 2011, director, photographer, and radio producer Arnaud Contreras made an audio documentary entitled *Kerouac, The Brittany Obsession,* in which he refers to the writer's trip to France in search of his origins. Much to our pleasure, Contreras agreed to recount this French journey, part of the Kerouac saga, on **page 48,** and includes several photos taken during his investigation.

4. A copy editor, who smokes an electronic cigarette and prefers organized travel with specific destinations. No, not particularly Beat in style, but a great corrector with a diploma in languages and English literature, as well as an avid fan of Bukowski.

5. A specialist in teen movies (he completed his dissertation on Gregg Araki), Quentin began reading Kerouac at the age of 18 and took off... for India, a mystical version of *On the Road.* But instead of 'dharma bums', he mainly ran into tourists along the way. He was more than happy to travel around France to pick up a family portrait of the French Beat cousins, as shown on **page 88.**

6. Hettie Jones knew the Beat Generation well. Together with her husband Leroi Jones, she launched the magazine called *Yugen,* in which Allen Ginsberg and Gregory Corso's writings were published. She herself wrote a collection of poems called *Drive,* as well as her memoirs, in which she describes the beat scene during the fifties. She talks openly on **page 72** about her steadfast beliefs on the ambivalent relations between the Beat Generation and minority groups.

* *

LIST

GLADYS MARIVAT[7] | BARRY MILES[8] | ISAURE PISANI-FERRY[9]
WALTER SALLES[10] | ÉRIC VERNAY[11] | AURELIANO TONET[12]

7. Gladys discovered the works of Kerouac in high school, headed to California via Highway 101 in a truck, and finally arrived at the café Vesuvio with a group of old beatniks. Today she is a versatile journalist, working for magazines *Trois Couleurs* and *Technikart*, and radio channels RFO and France Inter. Her curiosity fuels the articles on the wild adventures of Kerouac **(on page 41)**, how the book was received **(on page 63)** and his Americana **(on page 66)**.

8. A figure of Swinging London, Miles was the first to give a space cake to Paul McCartney, as stated in the biography he wrote about him (*Paul McCartney: Many Years from now*). The beat clan also visited Miles on more than one occasion. Known for spreading the name of Beat writers across England, he shared his thoughts on the ambivalent relations Kerouac maintained with minority groups **(on page 71)**. His book *Beat Hotel* provides description of the French Beats **(on page 88)**.

9. Isaure came to the project with a negative take on Kerouac, which reversed as she read through the background documents while bumming around in the Romanian mountains. Won over by the down-to-earth humility of *On the Road*, she plunged into the archives in order to paint a picture of the nine years leading up to the book, on **page 54**.

10. Who other than the director of *The Motorcycle Diaries* could bring to the screen the American mythical work *On the Road*? Since *Foreign Land* and *Central Do Brasil* (recipient of the Golden Bear in Berlin in 1998), he has continually been reigniting Brazilian cinema, and certainly extolled the value of road adventures. Besides giving us valuable advice on several occasions, he also agreed to an extensive interview. The 8 pages can be read on **page 160**.

11. Music and film journalist for *Slate.fr, Fluctuat.net* and *Premiere.fr*, Éric Vernay says he was very moved by Kerouac, as well as other American writers gravitating around the Beat Generation (Hubert Selby Jr., Charles Bukowski, John Fante...). The musical quality of *On the Road* and its constant concern for man's quest for freedom naturally led him to explore the beat influence on rock music, on **page 78**.

12. With origins from Normandy and Brazil, Aureliano devoured *On the Road* aged 15, fifteen years ago, and walked away with memories as exciting as his first visit to Le Havre. After having worked with publications such as *Chronic'art, Libération, Les Inrockuptibles* and *Grazia*, he was chief editor at *Trois Couleurs* from 2007 to 2012, when he left to work at *Le Monde*.

A TRAVELER'S GUIDE

THE PROTAGONISTS OF THE BEAT GENERATION EACH HAD THEIR ALTER EGOS IN KEROUAC'S BOOK *ON THE ROAD*. THESE CHARACTERS ARE NOW PORTRAYED BY ACTORS IN THE ADAPTATION OF THE BOOK FOR THE BIG SCREEN. A LOOK AT THE IMPRESSIVE CAST.

| TRANSLATED BY CAROL SHYMAN

REALITY / BOOK / MOVIE

★

LUANNE HENDERSON REALITY

PHOTO COURTESY OF ANNE-MARIE SANTOS AND GERALD NICOSIA

MARYLOU BOOK

Luanne married Neal Cassady at the age of 15 and divorced him soon after but remained his mistress for many years. She was with Dean and Sal as they travelled across the USA, experimenting with drugs, alcohol and other antics, often crude in nature. LuAnne is Marylou in *On the Road*. *"I am not at all like her,"* proclaimed the actress Kristen Stewart who, before *Twilight*, embodied as another muse, sensually pouting in the open spaces and along the roads of *Into the Wild* by Sean Penn. **J. R.**

KRISTEN STEWART MOVIE

CAROLYN CASSADY REALITY

© CAROLYN CASSADY

CAMILLE BOOK

Played by the evanescent Kirsten Dunst (*Virgin Suicides, Marie Antoinette, Melancholia*), Carolyn Cassady, Camille in *On the Road*, is eighty-eight years old today. She answered our questions by email, freely elaborating on her adventures with Jack Kerouac and didn't mind giving us a grammar lesson at the same time. She was a courageous mother who raised her children fathered by Neal Cassady, while he would often hit the road on escapades with other young women. **J. R.**

KIRSTEN DUNST MOVIE

| NEAL CASSADY — REALITY | DEAN MORIARTY — BOOK | GARRETT HEDLUND — MOVIE |

Dean is the perfect guy for the road

The iconic beat poet Neal Cassady was charming but burned out, avidly chasing after freedom, road miles and women. Kerouac travelled with him to some very out-of-the-way spots in the United States; these wild adventures are narrated in *On the Road*, where Neal becomes Dean Moriarty, the charismatic adventurer who intimidates Sal Paradise. The role could have been given to Marlon Brando or Brad Pitt, but is finally played by the cheeky Garrett Hedlund *(Troy, Tron: Legacy)*. **Q. G.**

| JACK KEROUAC — REALITY | SAL PARADISE — BOOK | SAM RILEY — MOVIE |

I was only myself, Sal Paradise, sad, strolling in this violet dark

The "King of the Beats" Jack Kerouac was a vagabond angel whose spontaneous prose placed him among some of the most important literary giants of the 20th century. In his masterpiece work, *On the Road*, he portrays himself as Sal Paradise, a slightly withdrawn young man fascinated by Dean Moriarty, who takes him under his wing as they take off across country. Following his role as Ian Curtis in *Control*, Sam Riley embodies Paradise, another counterculture icon. **Q. G.**

WILLIAM S. BURROUGHS REALITY

OLD BULL LEE BOOK

" **We'd all learned from HIM** "

VIGGO MORTENSEN MOVIE

The junkie guru Williams S. Burroughs was the oldest and gloomiest of the original beat clan. Considered his most symbolic work, *Naked Lunch* suggests a metaphor of the human condition enhanced by drug addiction. Old Bull Lee, his avatar in *On the Road*, is totally irresponsible and keeps trying to enlighten Sal and Dean in their carefree lives. A paradoxical role for Viggo Mortensen (*Lord of the Rings, The Road*), who was reportedly surprised at the lack of mystical spirit in the writings of his character. "*To me, his work feels much more cold-blooded, surgical, clean than the ones of Kerouac and Ginsberg.*" **Q.G.**

ALLEN GINSBERG REALITY

CARLO MARX BOOK

Tom Sturridge, a 26 year old Brit, could have played the vampire in the film series *Twilight*, if it hadn't been that Robert Pattinson had already signed the contract. Seen in *The Boat that Rocked*, he takes on the aura of the luminary poet Allen Ginsberg, one of the pillars of the Beat Generation. The fervent author of *Howl*, baptized Carlo Marx in the book, was to become a collateral victim of the tormented love affairs of Sal and Dean. A coveted role, recently portrayed by James Franco in a film entitled *Howl* and soon to be played by Daniel "*Harry Potter*" Radcliffe. **C.G.**

TOM STURRIDGE MOVIE

JOAN VOLLMER REALITY

JANE BOOK

Before becoming William Burroughs' girlfriend, Joan Vollmer was already one of the founding members of the beat circle in New York. During her studies she shared an apartment with the intellectual Edie Parker, Jack Kerouac's first wife. Joan Vollmer died a tragic death in Mexico when Burroughs accidentally killed her while playing William Tell. The red-headed Amy Adams (*Julie & Julia, The Muppets*) becomes Jane, notably in a couple of very intoxicated scenes in New Orleans as the battered hostess. **C.G.**

AMY ADAMS MOVIE

HELEN HINKLE REALITY

GALATEA DUNKEL BOOK

Al Hinkle's wife, who died in 1994, provided for her husband while he completed his studies. At the time they were living in San Jose, California, not far from the home of their longtime friends, the Cassadys. Renamed Galatea in the book, this stubborn young bride is left along the way by her husband and Dean. After a forced stay at Old Bull Lee's in Louisiana, the gang is reunited and the occasion calls for a stretch of lively fun. Elisabeth Moss, the ingenious Peggy from the *Mad Men* series, livens up this comedy scene with the right touch. **C. G.**

ELISABETH MOSS MOVIE

AL HINKLE REALITY

ED DUNKEL BOOK

Ed Dunkel was a tall, calm, **unthinking fellow** who was completely **READY** to do anything Dean **asked him**

"

DANNY MORGAN MOVIE

Born in 1926, Al Hinkle is one of the rare male survivors of the Beat Generation. He first met Cassady then Kerouac, who instilled in him a determination and thirst for learning. *"To my friends, freedom was worth all they went through to celebrate it,"* he said. His biggest regret was to not have been able to predict the premature death of Cassady in 1968. Danny Morgan, 29, new to the world of films after several appearances on television in the UK, takes on the role of Ed Dunkel, the chubby road chum. **C. G.**

BEA FRANCO REALITY

TERRY BOOK

Kerouac scrawled *"Terry, the Mexican girl in Road"* on several letters he received from Bea in 1947, following a short love affair in the cotton fields of California. She was a young and single mother and hoped to join him in New York. In one letter she poignantly said *"if only I had been born a man"*, and slipped this photo of herself in the envelope. Brazilian actress Alice Braga, seen in *City of Gods* and *Predators*, brings her serious and kindly touch to the screen. **J. R.**

ALICE BRAGA MOVIE

TIMELINE

BY QUENTIN GROSSET, ISAURE PISANI-FERRY AND JÉRÉMY DAVIS
TRANSLATED BY CAROL SHYMAN

THE KEROUAC FAMILY CIRCA 1930

1720's

Urbain-François Le Bihan, a landowner in Kervoac, leaves Brittany and heads to New France (today's Quebec). At the end of the 19th century, one of his descendants - Jack Kerouac's grandfather - settles in the United States.

MARCH 12, 1922

March 12, 1922 Jean-Louis Kerouac, nicknamed Ti-Jean, is born in Lowell, Massachusetts. Son of Léo-Alcide and Gabrielle-Ange (Mémère), he is the youngest of three children, preceded by brother Gerard and sister Caroline.

JUNE 1926

Jack's adored brother, Gerard, dies of rheumatic fever. His passing is a deep trauma for Jack Kerouac and inspires the novel *Visions of Gerard* in 1955-1956.

1927-1936

He studies in two parish primary schools in Lowell, then attends Bartlett Junior High School. A good student, Kerouac shows an early interest in reading and writing, and skips the sixth grade.

1933

Miss Mansfield, Kerouac's literature teacher, guides him in his reading choices and encourages him to write his first stories. In 1965, she is mentioned by the author as Miss Dineen in *Satori in Paris*.

1936-1939

Kerouac takes up football while studying at Lowell High School. His grades are good and so are his skills in sports, earning him a scholarship to attend university. He discovers jazz music during this period.

1939

Kerouac moves to New York. He attends the Horace Mann college preparatory school where he meets Frenchman Henri Cru (Remi Boncoeur in *On the Road*). Has a love affair with Mary Carney (Maggie Cassady, eponymous heroine of the book written in 1953).

JACK KEROUAC, 1940

1939-1940

Kerouac hangs out in Harlem jazz clubs. He spends much of his time with Sebastian Sampas, a childhood friend from Lowell, who introduces Kerouac to the writings of Thomas Wolfe and convinces him to become a writer. Meets Edie Parker through Henri Cru.

SEPTEMBER 1940

He begins studies at Columbia University on a scholarship awarded for his football skills. However, he fractures his tibia during the second game. He gives up on a football career and devotes himself to his studies.

1941

He continues to delve into the jazz scene, becoming a regular at Minton's Playhouse club in Harlem, where he meets Dizzy Gillespie who records a version of *Exactly Like You* entitled *Kerouac*. In October he drops out of Columbia University.

1942

Kerouac joins the United States Merchant Marines and goes to sea on the S.S. *Dorchester* heading for Russia. It was his own personal log kept while on board that became his first book, *The Sea is My Brother*. It was not published in its entirety until 2011.

LÉO AND GABRIELLE KEROUAC

1943

In February, Kerouac joins the US Navy, and then sails to Liverpool on the S.S. *George Weems*. He visits London. In September, he receives an honorable discharge on psy-chiatric grounds.

1944

In March, Sebastian Sampas dies during a troop landing in Italy. Kerouac meets Lucien Carr (Damion in *On the Road*), Allen Ginsberg (Carlo Marx) and William S. Burroughs (Old Bull Lee). He writes extensively.

LOWELL HIGH

1944 (2)

In August, Carr kills David Kammerer. Kerouac is considered an accomplice, and goes to jail for 2 weeks. He marries Edie Parker, whose parents are willing to pay bail. In December, he sets up house with Parker, Vollmer, Carr, Ginsberg and Burroughs on 115th Street.

1946

Kerouac's father dies in May. Edie Parker asks for an annulment in September. In December, Kerouac meets Neal Cassady (Dean Moriarty) who played a decisive role in his life from then on. He begins work on *The Town and the City*, strongly influenced by Thomas Wolfe.

LÉO KEROUAC IN 1925

1947

In March, Cassady leaves New York. In July, Kerouac also leaves and sets out on his first road trip across the United States: New York – Denver – San Francisco – Los Angeles. He returns to New York in October.

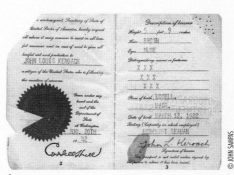

JACK'S PASSPORT, ISSUED IN 1942

1948

In the spring, Kerouac finishes writing *The Town and the City*. He meets John Clellon Holmes (Tom Saybrook in *On the Road*). In November, he has a title and first version of *On the Road*, which narrates his first road trip.

1949

In the winter, a second trip: Rocky Mount, N.C. – New York – New Orleans – San Francisco – New York, travelling with Neal, LuAnne Henderson (Marylou) and Al Hinkle (Ed Dunkel). In spring, the third trip: New York – Denver – San Francisco – Detroit – New York.

1950

In March, *The Town and the City* is published. In the spring, the last trip: New York – Denver – Mexico, and a visit to Burroughs. He spends two months totally intoxicated on drugs, then returns to NY. In November, he meets and marries Joan Haverty.

1951

In April during three weeks, Kerouac writes a new version of *On the Road* on one long roll of typewriter-fed paper. Joan and Kerouac separate even though she is pregnant. Some elements of the first draft of *On the Road* are used in *Visions of Cody*.

AN OLD FACTORY IN LOWELL

JANUARY. - MAY 1952

During a long stay in San Francisco at the Cassady home, Kerouac has a love affair with Carolyn Cassady, Neal's wife (Camille in *On the Road*.) Carolyn later wrote her version of their adventures in *On my Road*.

FEBRUARY 1952

Joan Haverty gives birth to Janet (Jan) Michelle, who Kerouac refuses to acknowledge as his own daughter despite their strong resemblance. Joan also became a writer, up until her death in 1996.

JACK AND AL HINKLE

SUMMER OF 1952

A productive visit to the Burroughs in Mexico. Kerouac works on the novel *Doctor Sax* and *Visions of Cody*. He begins jotting down his dreams in *Book of Dreams*, publish nine years later.

1953

Kerouac works a little for the Southern Pacific Railroad, and then as a waiter on board the S.S. *William Caruth*, bound for Korea, but gets off in New Orleans. He writes *Maggie Cassady* and *The Subterraneans*.

JACK DURING A POETRY READING

1953 (2)

City Lights, the "Beat" bookstore and publishing house, opens in San Francisco. The founder Lawrence Ferlinghetti publishes *Howl and other Poems* in 1956 written by Ginsberg, and soon after is jailed and tried for obscenity.

FACE OF BUDDHA, DRAWING BY JACK, 1958

1954

Kerouac lives with the Cassadys in San Jose, California. There he writes the poems that make up *San Francisco Blues* and the beginning of his *Book of Dreams*. He discovers Asian writings and develops an interest in Buddhism.

1955

Meeting with Gary Snyder and the other San Francisco poets. the *Paris Review* publishes an excerpt from *On the Road*. In August, he meets Esperanza Villanueva (Tristessa) in Mexico and writes the first part of *Tristessa* and *Mexico City Blues*.

DESOLATION PEAK

OCTOBER 7, 1955

Kerouac attends the famous public readings at Six Gallery in San Francisco, notably the reading of the long poem *Howl* by Ginsberg. This event is a milestone in the growing popularity of the Beat Generation.

1956

Kerouac finishes his book *Visions of Gerard*. He spends some time at Gary Snyder's home in Mill Valley, California. In May, he works on *The Scripture of the Golden Eternity* and *Old Angel Midnight*.

1956 (2)

From June to September, Kerouac works as a forest ranger at Desolation Peak, in Washington state. He begins writing *Angels of Desolation*. In December, Viking Press agrees to publish *On the Road*.

1957

In February, he travels to Tangiers, where he meets William Burroughs. In April, he goes to Paris and London. *On the Road* is published on September 5th by Viking Press. Kerouac spends November and December writing *The Dharma Bums*.

1957 (2)

Jack Kerouac writes to young Marlon Brando asking him to buy the screen rights to *On the Road*. Jack wants to write the screenplay and play the role of Sal Paradise; Brando would play the role of Dean Moriarty. Brando does not respond.

1958

In February, Grove Press publishes *The Subterraneans* and later in spring the screenplay adaptation is bought up by MGM Studios. Tri-Way Productions buys *On the Road*, but then goes bankrupt. In October, Viking Press publishes *The Dharma Bums*.

FEBRUARY 1959

Based on his play *The Beat Generation*, Kerouac writes a screenplay for a short film, *Pull My Daisy*, directed by Robert Frank and Alfred Leslie. Kerouac supplies the voice-over, while Allen Ginsberg, Peter Orlovsky and Gregory Corso play themselves.

END OF 1959

Kerouac releases the record *Poetry for the Beat Generation*, on which he recites his poems accompanied by Steve Allen on the piano, and also *Blues and Haikus* about jazz saxophonists Al Cohn & Zoot Sims. In November, *Mexico City Blues* is published.

1959 (2)

Bob Dylan discovers *On the Road*. *"... (it was) like a bible for me... I fell into that atmosphere of everything Kerouac was saying... and I felt like I fit right into that bunch"*, he writes in his autobiography *Chronicles* published in 2005.

JACK IN 1959

1960

Tristessa is published by Avon, *The Scripture of the Golden Eternity* is published by Jones' Totem Press, *Book of Dreams* by City Lights, and the screen adaptation of *The Subterraneans* is released. Yves Saint Laurent presents the scandalous fashion collection *Beat Look*.

JOHN SAMPAS AND JACK, 1968

1961-1963

In 1961, Kerouac writes the second part of *Desolation Angels* in Mexico, and *Big Sur* in Orlando. *Big Sur* is published in September 1962 by Farrar, Straus and Cudahy. One year later, the same publishing house publishes *Visions of Gerard*.

1963

Closing days of the shabby hotel on 9 rue Gît-le-Cœur in the Latin Quarters, nicknamed the "Beat Hotel" by Corso, Ginsberg and Burroughs and where they were frequent lodgers when in Paris from 1957. Today it is a 4-star hotel.

1964

In February, Jim Morrison reads *On the Road* and sets off on his own cross-country tour of the United States. Last meeting with Neal Cassady. Kerouac continues traveling, sinking deeper into alcohol and drugs, and looses sight of his friends from the 40s.

1965

In May, *Desolation Angels* is published by Coward-McCann. In June, Kerouac leaves for Paris and Brittany in search of his roots. In July, he writes *Satori in Paris*. He travels up and down the East Coast.

JACK AND STELLA SAMPAS, 1968

1966

Kerouac marries Stella Sampas, the sister of his childhood friend Sebastian, so that she can care for his ailing mother, Mémère. *Satori in Paris* is published by Grove Press in spring. He works on *Vanity of Duluoz*.

1968

On February 4th, Neal Cassady dies in Mexico. On February 6th, *Vanity of Duluoz* is published by Coward-McCann. In May, Kerouac takes off for a tour of Europe with Nick and Tony Sampas. In August, he meets up with Carr and Burroughs once again in New York.

JACK'S GRAVE IN LOWELL

1969

In May, Kerouac sells *Pic* to his publisher, one of the first versions of *On the Road* written in 1951, in order to pick up a little money. In September, he publishes his last text, in the *Chicago Tribune*, an article entitled *After Me the Deluge*.

JULY 1969

The cult film *Easy Rider* directed by Dennis Hopper is released, starring Peter Fonda and Jack Nicholson. This road movie portrays the adventures of three friends drinking and doing drugs as they cross the county, a Harley Davidson version of *On the Road*.

OCTOBER 21, 1969

Jack Kerouac passes away at the age of 47 of complications due to cirrhosis. He dies penniless but leaves behind archives worth an estimated value of 10 million dollars.

JACK, AL HINKLE AND HIS SON, WITH THE CASSADY CHILDREN

1970's

Pic is published in 1971, and *Visions of Cody* in 1972. In 1973, a first biography of Kerouac written by Ann Charters is published. In 1975, Allen Ginsberg and Bob Dylan visit Kerouac's grave in Lowell and read poems from *Mexico City Blues*.

1974

Allen Ginsberg and Anne Waldman found the Jack Kerouac School of Disembodied Poetics at the Naropa (Buddhist-inspired) University in Boulder, Colorado, attempting to perpetuate the beat approach to poetry for future generations.

1978

Barry Gifford and Lawrence Lee collect interviews from all those who knew Kerouac and put together *Jack's Book: An oral biography of Jack Kerouac*, which is still considered a reference book and continues to be republished regularly.

1980

Heart Beat, a film by John Byrum with Nick Nolte and Sissy Spacek is released, supposedly based on the ménage à trois Kerouac, Neal Cassady and his wife Carolyn. Carolyn, sole survivor, denounces the film as untrue and demeaning.

THE HUDSON IN THE FILM

1990

Carolyn Cassady, Neal's wife and ringside witness to the Beat Generation, publishes her own version, *Off the Road*, retracing the twenty years of tormented life alongside Neal Cassady, Jack Kerouac and Allen Ginsberg.

1990's

In 1990, Tom Waits sings *Jack & Neal* in homage to Kerouac and Cassady. In 1995, Gap features Kerouac in an ad campaign. In 1997, poets, writers and musicians record the spoken word tribute album *Kerouac: Kicks Joy Darkness*.

KERVOAC, IN BRITTANY

1994

Barry Gifford, who wrote the novel and screenplay of *Sailor & Lula* directed by David Lynch, finishes the screenplay of *On the Road* for Francis Ford Coppola. Gus Van Sant is in the wings to helm the film, but the project is shelved.

2001

Kerouac's archives are sold. The New York Public Library buys numerous manuscripts, journals and notebooks. The paper roll on which he wrote *On the Road* is privately purchased at auction for 2.5 million dollars.

JACK'S LAST HOME IN LOWELL

NEAL CASSADY AND JACK IN 1952

2003

Jerry Cimino, businessman and fan of Kerouac and cohorts, founds the Beat Museum in Monterey, California, which was later moved to San Francisco. Letters, photographs and original publications are on display.

2007

For the 50th anniversary of *On the Road*, Viking Press publishes *The Original Scroll*, the original uncensored manuscript written in 1951. In 1957, Kerouac's publisher had forced him to tone it down.

2011

The film *Dharma Guns* by F. J. Ossang, implying reference to *The Dharma Bums* by Kerouac., is released. In the late 90s, the director had worked on an adaptation of *On the Road*, with a pinch of *Visions of Cody* and *The Dharma Bums*, but once again the project was shelved.

NOVEMBER 2011

Kerouac's very first book is published: *The Sea is My Brother: The Lost Novel*, based on a manuscript Kerouac's brother-in-law discovered, slumbered for 70 years.

DECEMBER 2011

Death of George Whitman, founder of Shakespeare And Company, English book store in the Latin Quarters, which once welcomed Ginsberg, Burroughs and Corso among others, and continues to be a haven for book lovers passing through Paris.

2012

The screen adaptation of *On the Road* is finally available, shot by Walter Salles in 2010 and 2011, based on the screenplay by José Rivera. Sam Riley plays Sal Paradise and Garrett Hedlund takes the role of Dean Moriarty.

BY ETIENNE ROUILLON | TRANSLATED BY CAROL SHYMAN | ARTWORK BY SARAH KAHN

PACIFIC OCEAN

CANADA

DESOLATION PEAK

DENVER

SAN FRANCISCO

MATTERHORN PEAK

BIG SUR

YOSEMITE PARK

PHOENIX

UNITE

LOS ANGELES

MEXI

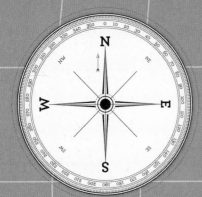

HIT THE ROAD

THE MAN

Jack Kerouac hit the road at 25, during the summer of 1947 and three more times in 1949 and 1950; the result was *On the Road*. After writing the book, he never stopped traveling, from Big Sur, California to Tangier, Morocco, including a stop in Lanmeur, France in search of his Brittany roots.

THE BOOK

On the Road scrambles Kerouac's real travels with the itineraries of his literary avatar, Sal Paradise. From east to west, his intended itinerary was constantly shaken up by happenstance meetings and lack of funds. Represented on this map are only the jaunts of the first road trip and not the subsequent trips mentioned in the novel.

THE FILM

Searching for the right locations for the screen adaptation of Kerouac's book, Walter Salles and his crew set out globetrotting: of course around the United States, from Louisiana to New Mexico passing through Arkansas, but also Canada, Mexico and even the snowy regions of Patagonia in Argentina.

(note: the routes marked on this map do not follow the chronology of the events told, but are simply indicative.)

A PHOTOGRAPH OF JACK'S PASSPORT, ISSUED ON AUGUST 20, 1942

NAME **KEROUAC**

FIRST NAME **JEAN-LOUIS**   NICKNAME **JACK**

THE MAN

BORN **MARCH 12 1922**   ORIGIN **LOWELL**

DESTINATIONS **NEW YORK-LOWELL** | **COLUMBIA**

UNIVERSITY-GREENWICH VILLAGE | **HARLEM**

-NEW ORLEANS | **GROSSE POINTE-DENVER**

SAN FRANCISCO-MEXICO CITY | **MATTERHORN**

PEAK-DESOLATION PEAK | **TANGIER-BIG SUR**

LANMEUR-LOWELL

NEW YORK CITY FROM AN EAST RIVER PIER ON JUNE 6, 1941

THE MAN
JACK KEROUAC

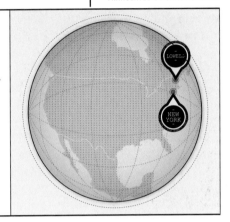

LOWELL

NEW YORK

FROM

NEW YORK

TO

LOWELL

BY JULIETTE REITZER | TRANSLATED BY CAROL SHYMAN

ON THE ROAD WITH KEROUAC

DELVING INTO JACK KEROUAC'S PERSONAL ARCHIVES IN THE BERG COLLECTION AT THE NEW YORK PUBLIC LIBRARY, WE RETRACED THE TRAVELS THEY CHRONICLED AND PERHAPS FORETOLD, BACK IN TIME TO THE WRITER'S CHILD-HOOD IN LOWELL, MASSACHUSETTS.

he first lead we investigated was Kerouac's personal archives, kept in the Berg Collection of English and American literature at the New York Public Library. Hard to know if real treasures were to be found or if they even existed. The brief descriptions of the documents in the online catalogue told us little. But Isaac Gewirtz, the Berg Collection's head librarian, assured us we would be welcome to see the archive at the library itself. Authorization to reproduce any of the material could be requested from a gentleman named John Sampas, executor of Kerouac's estate. When we contacted him, he responded, *"We can discuss this if you come see me in Lowell."* Lowell, Massachusetts? Kerouac's hometown and place where he was buried? This was an invitation not to be refused.

WITHSTANDING TIME

Handle with care. Sitting at an enormous wooden table, I nervously glance to my right where my neighbor is carefully going through a Keats manuscript. Others are religiously bent over thick volumes. The silence is broken only by whispers. Although I'm not a die-hard Kerouac fan, this was still a solemn moment. The librarian is about to bring me the first set of archives. I am about to page through Kerouac's personal meditations, maps, visions, sketches, poems, dreams, and prayers: Beat Generation roots. It's a humbling prospect.

The skyscrapers on 5th Avenue tower over the library, an imposing late 19th-century edifice covering two city blocks of ground. I crossed several immense reading rooms and climbed monumental staircases, beneath the stony gaze of busts, to reach the small wooden door of Room 320, where the Berg Collection is kept. Here one finds the Jack Kerouac archives, but also those of Byron, Woolf, and Nabokov. *"Kerouac did spend a lot of his time in or around New York, so when the papers became available in 2001, we decided it would be appropriate to have them at the New York Public Library,"* explained Isaac Gewirtz. He would not disclose the price the library paid (but in 2001, Christie's

---

4 NUMBER OF CROSS-COUNTRY TRIPS KEROUAC MADE

3 NUMBER OF WOMEN KEROUAC MARRIED

8500 MILES
DISTANCE COVERED DURING KEROUAC'S TRAVELS THAT INSPIRED *ON THE ROAD*

100 WORDS / MINUTE
THE SPEED AT WHICH HE TYPED THE ORIGINAL SCROLL VERSION

sold the original scroll version of *On the Road* to Indianapolis Colts owner Jim Irsay for 2.43 million dollars). Gewirtz added, "*If you ask me to estimate the number of Kerouac documents contained in this collection, I'd say a hundred thousand.*" One by one, I laid out the documents on the green felt table. Letters from Allen Ginsberg and Carolyn Cassady, diaries, poems, manuscripts, notebooks... Many date back to the period when he wrote *On the Road*, and it was amazing to see the proof that each character in the books and each adventure had really existed. But finding oneself at the point where a novelist's life and fiction intersect is troubling. There is a huge temptation to look for the tiniest details in writing from Kerouac's adolescence foreshadowing his future genius. "*Kerouac was almost incapable of writing a casual, routine letter. In every letter he wrote, he is always wrestling with big questions, he is always talking about himself or the persons he writes to, and what they really are. And what his work is, and how it's going, his relationships...*" confirmed Isaac Gewirtz.

TEMPORARY CLASSIFICATION

In my hands, an old brown leather notebook, decorated with art nouveau flourishes. Kerouac, aged thirteen, has jotted down the litany of schoolboy days, with their bowling matches and snowball fights with his friend Bill. On the page marked March 12th, his birthday, there's a note in a bolder, more manly hand, "*Now I am twenty-two years old. I don't bowl no more... Bill was at Bataan. He didn't run from that snow fight.*" Many of the documents bear Kerouac's later annotations and second thoughts, although sometimes he simply indicates a date or detail about the context. If he received an unsigned postcard, he would scribble in the name of the sender for future reference. He organized his life in chapters, like a novel, and he himself classified about 30% of his archives, according to a precise alphanumeric system. Isaac Gewirtz shared his fascination with me: "*Every writer's archive is really that, you can read their archives as a key to the work itself. From a very early age, he really had a complete saga in his mind.*" So which period had Kerouac catalogued first? His own inventory of his papers would give us a clue to his values. And I discover he skipped over *The Town and the City* (1950) and his first writings, concentrating on everything associated with *On the Road*: preparatory notes, drawings, rewrites, variants. Proof that the second book mattered to him far more than all the others. As the portraits of the man and the writer begin to take shape, I prepare myself for the deeper plunge into Kerouac's intimacy. I'll be in his hometown tomorrow.

BACK TO THE ROOTS

At the back of a crowded restaurant, a neon sign over the kitchen reads, "*Jack lived here.*" The sight of the bar reminds me of a series of photos I saw at the New York Public Library, of an aging Kerouac daydreaming in front of an empty glass, his elbow on the counter. I'm facing a plate of lobster ravioli (a local specialty) and an elegant octogenarian with a piercing gaze. He listens patiently as I explain the reason for my visit. John Sampas is Jack Kerouac's brother-in-law and the executor of his estate (see the box p. 26). After a grueling five-hour bus journey from New York to Boston, followed by a two-hour train ride, I have finally arrived in the typical small American industrial town of Lowell, Massachusetts, on the banks of the Merrimack River. Tall red-brick smokestacks, vestiges of immense textile mills, poke up from between the Victorian houses originally built for the factory workers. Jack and his family had lived in thirteen of them, and John took me to visit a few the next day, including his birthplace. We also saw the elementary school and the local library where he wore out his pants on the benches. Night had fallen and the temperatures were mild for December. Sampas wanted to show me a couple more things before dropping me off at my hotel. With his old dog Henri in the back seat, we drive over to John's.

It's a sweet little frame house, where we are greeted by a chorus of meows in the front yard. Kerouac, who loved cats, would certainly have stopped to rub their chins and make them purr. But we are following the dog Henri, who pays absolutely no attention to them and is much more interested in making a rush for his hearthrug in the warmth of the dining room. Sampas gestures toward a chair at the glass table in the living room, inviting me to sit down for a chat. "*I bet you've never seen these,*" he begins, as an introduction to the dozen cardboard folders filled with photos he lays out. Visions of Jack at all ages, but also his family,

From "Terry" the Mexican Girl in ROAD
(Bea Franco)

Nov. 18, 1947
Selma, Calif.

Dearest Jackie:

I was sure glad to get your, letter, after so long. Its good to know that you arrived home okey, I was hoping you would. Jackie I've written more, often, than you have.

I go to the Post Office, just about every, day, and no "letter" from you—is all I get.

Jackie, I didn't stay in L.A. at all, I come right back to Selma, after I brought Patsy, and I haven't left this little town since.

Jackie, Im sorry to say that I haven't been working too steady, you see little Al. was sick I had him in the hospital here in Selma for two nights, he had a touch of nemonia, he snaped out of it right away though, they gave him penicillian shots, that's what cured him so soon. I was so worried, I sat by his bed side for two nights, The Doctor told me I should stay there—

A LETTER FROM BEA FRANCO TO JACK. KEROUAC ADDED IN RED: *"FROM "TERRY" THE MEXICAN GIRL IN* (ON THE) *ROAD"*

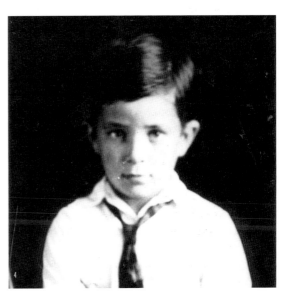

JACK KEROUAC SCORING TOUCHDOWN FOR LOWELL AGAINST LAWRENCE HIGH SCHOOL IN 1939. THIS PHOTOGRAPH WAS DEVELOPED IN REVERSE

JACK AGED 14

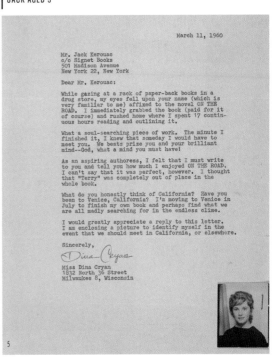

JACK AGED 5

March 11, 1960

Mr. Jack Kerouac
c/o Signet Books
501 Madison Avenue
New York 22, New York

Dear Mr. Kerouac:

While gazing at a rack of paper-back books in a drug store, my eyes fell upon your name (which is very familiar to me) affixed to the novel ON THE ROAD. I immediately grabbed the book (paid for it of course) and rushed home where I spent 17 continuous hours reading and outlining it.

What a soul-searching piece of work. The minute I finished it, I knew that someday I would have to meet you. We beats prize you and your brilliant mind--God, what a mind you must have!

As an aspiring authoress, I felt that I must write to you and tell you how much I enjoyed ON THE ROAD. I can't say that it was perfect, however. I thought that "Terry" was completely out of place in the whole book.

What do you honestly think of California? Have you been to Venice, California? I'm moving to Venice in July to finish my own book and perhaps find what we are all madly searching for in the endless clime.

I would greatly appreciate a reply to this letter. I am enclosing a picture to identify myself in the event that we should meet in California, or elsewhere.

Sincerely,

Dina Cryan
Miss Dina Cryan
1832 North 36 Street
Milwaukee 8, Wisconsin

A LETTER FROM A FAN. DINA CRYAN EXPRESSES HER ADMIRATION FOR *ON THE ROAD*, BUT ADDS: "I CAN'T SAY THE BOOK IS PERFECT. I THINK (THE CHARACTER OF) TERRY HAS NO PLACE HERE."

THE SAMPAS FAMILY, IN LIFE AND IN DEATH

Jack Kerouac met Sebastian Sampas at Bartlett Junior High School, in his home-town of Lowell, Massachusetts. Jack was an aspiring writer and Sebastian was interested in acting. Very quickly the two adolescents became inseparable, sharing their love for the theater, literature and authors such as Thomas Wolfe, William Saroyan and Lord Byron. Later separated by schools they attended and then by World War II, they wrote to each other regularly until December of 1943. *"There will always be the two of us,"* wrote Sebastian in 1940, four years before he was killed on the Italian front at the age of 21. *"You romantic Sampas"*, wrote Jack in a letter addressed to Stella, Sebastian's older sister who would become Jack's third and last wife. She died in 1990, and it was John, the youngest of the Sampas family offspring of 10 who would inherit Jack's legacy. Kerouac is buried in Lowell Cemetery next to Stella, and alongside Sebastian.

SEBASTIAN SAMPAS IN 1939

STELLA AND SEBASTIAN SAMPAS IN THE YARD OF THE FAMILY HOME IN LOWELL IN 1943

JOHN SAMPAS AT HOME IN LOWELL, DECEMBER 2011

THE *SUN* HEADQUARTERS IN LOWELL. JACK USED TO WORK HERE

JOHNNY DEPP IN FRONT OF THE KEROUAC MONUMENT IN LOWELL, 1991

ONE OF THE HOUSES WHERE JACK GREW UP IN LOWELL

ADMINISTRATING THE ARCHIVES IS A DAUNTING TASK – THE WRITER HAS MYTHICAL STATUS.

feel a bit light-headed. Recalling the alcoholism of his later years – photos show a bloated, sickly wreck of a man with a profound sadness in his eyes – I wonder if his writerly detachment from life and its experiences did not bring on his early death.

HISTORICAL HERITAGE

When he died in 1969, Kerouac willed his archives to his mother, who transferred them to Stella Sampas, Kerouac's last wife. Stella passed away in 1990, and her brothers and sisters inherited the cumbersome treasure. They elected the youngest, John Sampas, to be the administrator. It is a daunting task, John admits the following morning, driving to Kerouac's grave. He has to order a new tombstone and is having trouble choosing the design. Whatever he picks, he knows that someone in the pack of Kerouac-maniacs will protest: his brother-in-law is a legend, after all. Before the New York Public Library bought the archives, in fact, fans used to show up at Sampas's house, hoping to purchase memorabilia. In 1995, Johnny Depp had paid a visit, leaving with one of Jack's coats. I treated myself to a Jack Kerouac T-shirt, found in a Lowell souvenir shop. But I was warmed by the feeling I'd traveled a bit of the road that was so important to Jack Kerouac. ✸

his parents, his sister Nin and brother Gerard, the one who died when Jack was only four years old... All bear descriptions carefully inked in by Kerouac himself, proof of the importance the vagabond attributed to his roots, to his childhood home. I realize my English vocabulary is wearing thin as I repeat the words *"amazing"* and *"wonderful"* like a mantra. But the photos really do fill me with amazement and wonder. I'm especially happy to find the snapshot of Bea Franco, renamed Terry in *On the Road*. She is *"the cutest little Mexican girl in slacks"* Kerouac lived with briefly in Arcadia, California. I'd become

especially fond of her after reading the few letters she'd written to Jack, in the papers at the library. *On the Road* doesn't tell the whole story. The lovers did intend to meet up in New York and Bea's letters were full of hope, up to the last one, when she realized she would never see him again. In the picture, Bea is posing with her toddler son Albert. On the back, she wrote, *"To Jackie with love."* Underneath, Kerouac scribbled the laconic notation *"Terry"* in On the Road." Once again I am struck by the way he used his private life as raw material for his literary work. Seeing the parallels between reality and Kerouac's portrayals of it in his novels makes me

OPEN THE DOOR, I WANT SOME DOUGH! ⟶ SCREAMED A DRUNKEN KEROUAC STANDING AT THE DOORSTEP OF GALLIMARD PUBLISHING COMPANY

15 YEARS OLD THE AGE OF LUANNE WHEN SHE MARRIED NEAL CASSADY.

JACK THE FOOTBALL CHAMPION, HERE AT LOWELL HIGH SCHOOL IN 1938

© JOHN SAMPAS

FROM

COLUMBIA

TO

THE VILLAGE

BY QUENTIN GROSSET | | TRANSLATED BY CAROL SHYMAN

BEATMAN BEGINS

JACK KEROUAC ON CAMPUS AT COLUMBIA, OR LEARNING TO SPLIT FROM THE MAINSTREAM. HIS EXPERIENCES AS A YOUNG WRITER - STARTING AS A TOUCH-DOWN CHAMPION, THEN ADDICTED TO BENZEDRINE* - LED HIM TO MEET AND FORM A GROUP KNOWN AS THE BEAT GENERATION. FROM THE UPTOWN TO THE DOWNTOWN CROWD, THIS GROUP OF STUDENTS IN THE CLASS PHOTO WENT FROM VANGUARD TO OUTCAST.

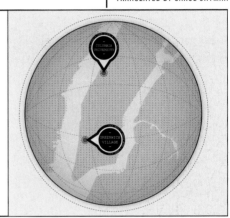

ife seemed pleasant on campus at Columbia University at the beginning of the 1939-1940 school year. Some students flirt on the grass, the hazing tribulations slowly begin, and the future financial tycoons step out of black limousines carrying enormous lunchboxes. Under the cheerleaders lustful gaze, the young Jack Kerouac strides onto the football field in tight-fit Levis sporting the ambition of a champion. An ace at marking touchdowns at Lowell High School, the athlete had just entered college preparatory school at Horace Mann in an attempt to improve his score and go on to a university. Against his mother's wishes, he snubbed the vaunting football players by refusing to wear the Phi Gamma Delta blue colors, and by preferring the company of puny acne-faced scoundrels.

A CLEAN-CUT, WELL-GROOMED SORT OF GUY

"*Guys, let me wring his neck! I'll show him what he's worth! Bam!*" At the beginning of the season, Jack took the tough guy approach with his coach, out training every day, running up and down steps shaping his calves, and was so effective that he soon became the number one player, donning the burgundy and white football shirt. But Jack the athlete was also a brilliant student, praised by all his professors.

AT NIGHT, THE ELIGIBLE BACHELOR UNCOVERED HIS VICIOUS SIDE, EYEING PROSTITUTES.

This was necessary as he knew he was in competition with offspring from the richest families in New York, and yearned to join their ranks, to wear grey flannel suits, carry a briefcase, and grease back his hair. But hidden under the appearances of an eligible bachelor, he was in search of something new and different. At night, the eligible bachelor would uncover his vicious side, stalking the streets of 42nd Street, eyeing prostitutes. Hungry for new adventures, Kerouac recounted his gay antics to his friend Sebastian Sampas, a dramatic arts student who began to worry about him. While Jack was hitch-hiking between Lowell and New York dressed in a Navy uniform, a guy stopped and asked him if he wanted a blow job. "*Why not*," replied Jack.

After a year of football, Jack enrolled in Columbia University and soon found himself swamped between 16 hours of training, having to read *The Iliad* and *The Odyssey*, plus a job washing dishes to pay for meals. Studying wasn't all it was made out to be. As fate would have it, he fractured his tibia, which meant he would not play for the rest of the season. He never found the champion football player in himself again; the coach found him too slow and he sat on the sidelines most of the time. Having given up hope,

KEROUAC WAS COMPLETELY CRAZY ABOUT THEM | A SLAP THE LAST MEMORY KEROUAC HAD OF HIS BROTHER GERARD, WHO DIED IN CHILDHOOD | AT 9 JACK BEGAN LEARNING ENGLISH |

HTED IN 1984, THE FRENCH MINISTRY OF CULTURE GAVE BURROUGHS THE ORDER OF COMMANDEUR DE L'ORDRE DES ARTS ET DES LETTRES | KEROUAC DECIDED TO DO JUST LIKE PROUST BUT FAST |

he considered dropping out of university and took on various jobs. He began reading Thomas Wolfe, and his descriptions of American landscapes instilled in him the desire to see the country for himself. When graduation day arrived, Jack was not able to buy a white suit. Lying in the grass behind the gym, playing with a blade of grass in his mouth, he read Walt Whitman in total disregard for the ceremony and the flags. That night by candle light, he cut a gash in his finger, wrote *"The Blood of a Poet"* in ink on an index card then spread his finger on the word *"Blood"* to cover it.

BENZEDRINE AND MAYO SANDWICHES

New calling, new friends. In Greenwich Village, the historical bohemian quarters in NY since the start of the 20th century, Jack typed away all night on his typewriter and girlfriend Edie Parker had trouble sleeping. The group squatting Joan Vollmer's apartment in 1943-1944 were night-owls. That particular night, Kerouac's new friends went out on the town. Allen Ginsberg, the scrawny adolescent with Dumbo ears, and William S. Burroughs, who had come straight from the Midwest to let himself loose in the seedy parts of town, were shaking up the neighborhood: one challenging God to a duel, the other parading as a

KEROUAC BEGAN TO GO BALD, JOAN SUFFERED FROM PARANOIAC DELIRIUM, AND EDIE LOST HER TEETH.

transvestite enjoying passers-by's reactions. Meanwhile, Lucien Carr, a 19-year old student with green almond-shaped eyes and a red scarf around his neck, recited Rimbaud, and David Kammerer, his ex-gym teacher and forlorn lover, attempted to attract his attention by trying to hang Kit Kat, Joan's cat.

Fin de siècle decadence settled in when the group moved into an apartment on 115th Street. Everyone congregated on Joan's big bed to discuss the decline of the bourgeoisie, while Burroughs, who was seeing a shrink, entered the room with a plate full of razor blades screaming, *"I've something real nice in the way of delicacies my mother sent me this week, hmf, hmf, hmf!"* Vickie Russel, the latest addition to the clan, showed them how to remove the flap, soaked in Benzedrine, from the 98-cent inhalators so as to guarantee an 8 hour amphetamine high. They were not in the best of physical form: Kerouac had begun to go bald, Joan suffered from

paranoiac delirium and Edie lost her teeth from eating only mayo sandwiches. As for Ginsberg, he was kicked off Columbia's campus for being *"a bad element."* Burroughs, in cahoots with Joan, invited Herbert Huncke, a friend of friends from the underworld, into his girl-friend's apartment. He proceeded to ask his new friends to help him hide firearms (including the one used by the Mad Killer of Times Square), and it was at this point that Jack's dying father called his group of friends a bunch of drug-addicted hoodlums.

Jack regretted bumming around throughout the end of the war (he had signed on for a few months in the Navy earlier), but drifting away from the mainstream was not fruitless. One day, under the influence, he heard Huncke proclaim, *"Hey you guys, I'm beat`!"* Later Kerouac said, *"To me, it meant being poor - like sleeping in subways, like Huncke used to do - and yet being illuminated and having illuminated ideas about apocalypse and all that."* ◆

The uncredited quotes and anecdotes are taken from the books: *Jack Kerouac: Angelheaded Hipster* by Steve Turner (The Viking Press, 1996), *Off the Road* by Carolyn Cassady (Black Spring Press, 1990), *Memory Babe* by Gerald Nicosia (Grove Press, 1983), *Vanity of Duluoz: Une éducation aventureuse, 1935-1946* de Jack Kerouac (10/18, 1995). by Jack Kerouac (Peguin Books, 2012).

☆ **Report card** ☆

EXCELLENT STUDENT, A BIT OF A DAYDREAMER

"Experience is the best teacher and not the twisted views of others," wrote Kerouac in *On the Road*. Yet his report cards were far from disastrous. At the end of his preparatory school year at Horace Mann, his work was positively evaluated by his teachers, *"Jack is able to live in harmony with his body and his mind."* He performed impressively in English and French, the subjects where he made his highest grades. But he was no slouch at geometry, either. Chemistry was the only class he flunked, even though he was so bored in history

class that he preferred to dream about girlfriend Mary Carney. At Columbia, poet/writer/critic/professor Mark Van Doren's lectures on Shakespeare and Blake sparked his interest and delight. Kerouac also took Van Doren's advice about writing to heart. Gossips say Van Doren's attention to Kerouac made Norman Podhoretz (editor of *Commentary* magazine 1960-95 and considered a founding father by today's neo-conservatives) jealous. Later in life, Podhoretz would lash out at Kerouac and his clan in *Partisan Review*. Q. G.

JACK AND LUCIEN CARR ON CAMPUS AT COLUMBIA IN 1944

THELONIOUS MONK, HOWARD MCGHEE, ROY ELDRIDGE AND TEDDY HILL IN FRONT OF MINTON'S PLAYHOUSE IN NEW YORK, SEPTEMBER 1947

FROM HARLEM
TO NEW ORLEANS

BY YVES BUIN | TRANSLATED BY JENNIFER GAY

JAZZ POET

LONG BEFORE HE INFLUENCED GENERATIONS OF ROCK MUSICIANS WITH LITERARY ASPIRATIONS, JACK KEROUAC'S DEFINING EXPERIENCE CAME FROM JAZZ. THE AUTHOR APPLIED THE ORIGINAL PULSE – THE BEAT – TO LITERATURE AND THE MELODIC PHRASING OF THE BURGEONING BEBOP SCENE GAVE THE AUTHOR THE FOUNDATIONS OF HIS STYLE. AS DID THE MARGINAL LIFESTYLE THAT WENT HAND-IN-HAND WITH THE "*SONG OF THE NIGHT.*"

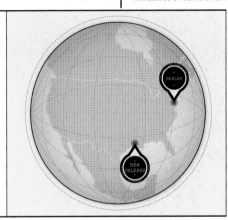

azz poet: that's how Jack Kerouac defined himself in the 1950s. What more is there to say, beyond the fact that the jazz component of his writing was clearly conveyed? In fact, the reference goes further. It calls for an identification with the life, behavior, and fate of a jazz musician. The jazzman - born into the oppressed black minority, a marginal in the music community - is pushed by his condition to the heights of non-conformity, as much by his attitude as by his art. Without necessarily being a damned soul, he is at odds with polite society. He is nocturnal, haunts the fiendish underground scenes where one finds drugs, sex, and prostitution, and produces music that, though sometimes popular, is often disarming. That is the image of the jazzman in the eyes of the middle class. It was bound to appeal to Jack Kerouac.

As a teen, he was in regular contact with the African-American arts via the radio programs he listened to in his native Lowell, Massachusetts. There were two distinct vectors: on the one hand, popular variety shows, where whites who borrowed from jazz excelled and where many hummable tunes, known as "*standards*," were played by the likes of Tommy Dorsey, and sung by a crooner who was just then making his name, Frank Sinatra; and on the other, the blues, especially the big bands led by Duke Ellington, Count Basie (with the famous tenor saxophonist Lester Young), Jimmie Lunceford, and Gene Krupa. Of all the tunes he heard and remembered, Kerouac chose *You Go to My Head* as his favorite song.

BEAT BOP

But the real shock came when Kerouac arrived in New York, in late 1939, at the age of 17. One knows that New York is the Big Apple. He had barely settled in as a Columbia University freshman when he began spending more time strolling the streets than going to class. Barriers were more fluid in the 40s, and Harlem was accessible: quite naturally, Kerouac went wandering there, eminently attuned to the complex and amplified hum of the city. And part of that hum was jazz. Among the jazz venues was Minton's Playhouse, on the ground floor of the Cecil Hotel in Harlem. There, the house band officiated: Thelonious Monk on piano, Nick Fenton on bass, Kenny Clarke on drums, and Charlie Christian -- the inventor of guitar's jazz style.

After hours, Minton's played host to musicians from the big bands who came to unwind in endless jam sessions after their gigs. Dizzy Gillespie and his trumpet were there as early as 1941, and Kerouac was too, since Dizzy cut an improvisation of *Exactly Like You* under the title *Kerouac*, thereby bringing Jack into the annals of bebop... It was at Minton's, with its impressive bar, that the first flashes of the bebop revolution were heard, with Kerouac as a privileged witness and listener.

THE BEAT AND THE TEMPO

The leader of those dazzling performances was alto saxophonist Charlie Parker, barely two years older

JACK EXULTING DURING A POETRY READING AT THE ARTIST'S STUDIO IN NEW YORK, FEBRUARY 15, 1959

than Kerouac. Parker was the absolute genius of jazz. He was "Bird," flying high above technical routine and limitations, whose meteoric and chaotic life was told by Clint Eastwood in his 1988 film *Bird*. It's difficult to communicate to an audience in 2012 what occured on those famous nights at Minton's between 1941 and 1944, and then detonated across the world after 1945 through records, the medium of Parker's achievement. Let's just remember that a new music, extraordinary for its time, was born. With phenomenal instinctive understanding, Kerouac immediately got it, while most critics and many musicians were completely thrown. As he listened to Parker, he reasserted what he'd sensed earlier with Lester Young

(to whom he devoted an admirable sketch in *Visions of Cody*): the poet as well as the novelist have a duty to write as if they were blowing into a sax, for prosody to develop like a long improvised and syncopated solo.

While bebop and the lifestyle of the boppers were a foothold for Kerouac, the author pursued his musical quest in parallel with the evolution of jazz itself. But in his relationship to bebop, let's not forget that an extraordinary, almost simultaneous, cultural conjunction was happening between the jazz musicians living in the "Dizzy-Bird sanctuary," a few blocks from Columbia, and the "regulars" of the West End, the bar where, as early as 1944, the core group of artists who would come to be known around 1950 as the Beat Generation met

up: Lucien Carr, Jack Kerouac, William S. Burroughs, Allen Ginsberg. These two movements, synchronous in a way that is rare in culture and in such a limited radius, were to set fire to America and much of the world.

COOL PHRASING À LA COOL

Kerouac, an indisputable initiate, remained faithful to jazz. However, he said little about it as he traveled through the south. Little mention of the Delta blues during his stays in New Orleans, though he liked to sing the blues (most of his poems that refer to the blues were later brought together in one volume, *Book of Blues*, published in 1995). On the other hand, just as he recognized bebop, he was won over by cool jazz – made famous by the 1949 sessions

98 CENTS | THE PRICE OF A BENZEDRINE INHALER, A FAVORED HIGH OF THE BEAT GENERATION | WHEREVER SHE LIVED, MÉMÈRE MADE SURE HER SON HAD A LITTLE QUIET CORNER FOR HIS WRITIN

| J. EDGAR HOOVER ⟶ FOR THE F.B.I. CHIEF, BEATNIKS WERE "ONE OF THE THE GREATEST THREATS TO AMERICAN SECURITY."

FOR KEROUAC, POETS AND NOVELISTS HAVE A DUTY TO WRITE AS IF THEY WERE BLOWING INTO A SAX.

led by Miles Davis, compiled as *Birth of the Cool* in 1957 – in which white musicians such as Lee Konitz and Gerry Mulligan played a dominant role. Kerouac was also one of the first to sing the praises of Stan Getz and John Coltrane. When he found himself in San Francisco with Neal Cassady, he scoured the bars and spent his nights listening to jazz radio programs that played the West Coast style, the counterpart of New York cool. Trumpeter Tony Fruscella – who later sank into oblivion, but was admired by Kerouac – also made a mark.

The fact remains that Charlie Parker was Kerouac's major and lasting inspiration. Well versed in both the structure and the emotional surge of Parker's music, he composed a series of choruses (two hundred and forty-two) in the summer of 1955 (a few months after Parker's death) imitating the phrasing of the alto sax. He shared with readers in his collection *Mexico City Blues* in 1959. The singular, intense undertaking had little future in cultural history. No doubt only Kerouac was able to wrestle with such a challenge, and no doubt it was a summit, an intensely close ecstasy between a writer and a musician of which there are few examples in history. With it, Kerouac probably took as far as possible the expression of what music could draw from him. In 1958 and 1959, following the enormous success of *On the Road*, he did several readings, less extreme perhaps, at the Village Vanguard, a Mecca of New York jazz, in the company of two cool school saxophonists: Al Cohn and Zoot Sims. Attesting to his openness to every style of jazz.

Kerouac didn't identify with any coterie, any literary genre. He suffered from being given the title of *"Beatnik pope."* According to his biographer Ann Charters, he confided to Allen Ginsberg that: *"he identified more with musical geniuses like Bud Powell, Charlie Parker, Billie Holiday, Lester Young, Gerry Mulligan and Thelonius Monk than he did with any established literary scene, and of all the books he ever wrote,* Mexico City Blues *is most directly related to jazz... His own method of spontaneous composition was meant to do the same thing with words that he heard bop musicians doing with their instruments."* ●

Reading corner

FOREIGN LITERATURE

Kerouac's other great love, in addition to jazz, was literature: American (see p. 66), but also and above all European, which he discovered at a young age. First the French writers: Rimbaud, the extraordinary revelation from his time at Columbia; the surrealists and automatic writing, devoured with Ginsberg and Burroughs; Jean Genet; Céline, for his language, realism, humor, articulated and forceful phrasing; Balzac; and finally Proust (photo above), for his work on memory and childhood. Kerouac would build his work as his own *Remembrance* (see p. 54). Then there was his Russian passion. First a foretaste at Columbia, when he first saw Jean Renoir's *The Lower Depths*, based on a play by Gorky. Later, he read Tolstoy and, above all, Dostoyevsky, a real model for him. And finally, his hidden passion, William Blake, the author of the famous words: *"If the doors of perception were cleansed everything would appear to man as it is, infinite."* Vision, purity, infinity: the Buddhist Kerouac of *The Scripture of the Golden Eternity*. **G.M.**

« A FAIRGROUND RIDE » WHAT A NEW YORK TIMES CRITIC SAID ABOUT *ON THE ROAD* | ALLEN GINSBERG ENDED UP IN AN OBSCENITY TRIAL AFTER PUBLISHING *HOWL*

MÈRE THREATENED TO GO TO THE FBI TO REPORT ALLEN GINSBERG'S HOMOSEXUALITY TO KEEP HIM AWAY FROM JACK | SGT PEPPER WILLIAM BURROUGHS APPEARS ON THE BEATLES' ALBUM COVER

FROM GROSSE POINTE
TO DENVER

BY CLÉMENTINE GALLOT | TRANSLATED BY JENNIFER GAY

HIGHER INTOXICATION

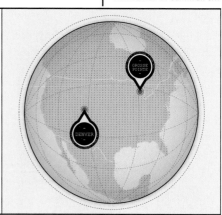

DURING A BREAK BETWEEN WILD TIMES IN NEW YORK, THE BUDDING WRITER SETTLED DOWN FOR A MOMENT BEFORE RETURNING TO HIS FIRST LOVES, THROWING HIMSELF INTO A NARCOTIC, HEADLONG RACE WEST. AN ART OF THE BIVOUAC THAT CONTINUOUSLY REDEFINED JACK KEROUAC'S CONFLICTUAL RELATIONSHIP TO CONVENTION.

n 1944, Kerouac, a one-woman man – his mother's – married a friend from Columbia, Edie Parker. An improvised union that above all allowed the bridegroom to get out of jail free (see sidebar), placing their commitment to each other under risky auspices. Kerouac followed his new wife to her home town, Detroit, expecting they would soon ship out for bohemian Paris. He cautiously took on the appearance of a steady middle class husband and slaved away at the Fruehauf Trailer Company. Grosse Pointe is a wealthy Detroit suburb with more than one country club; as a slovenly young writer, Kerouac felt understandably uncomfortable there, and started to wither: in his opinion, the narrow-minded town lacked *"tragedy."* So the couple returned to New York, where Kerouac ended up squatting alternately with Ginsberg and Burroughs. One evening, coming down off Benzedrine, he sent Edie away, and she immediately asked for a divorce.

This brief stage in his life exemplifies the tormented relationship with convention that pursued Kerouac his whole life. He adopted the ephemeral illusion of traditional married life, but put up with such a middle class way of life for only two months. Just as the years that bracketed the interlude were devoted to various literary and drug-related experiments, we can see this attempt in normalization as another form of experimentation.

GO WEST

In 1947, Kerouac hitchhiked across the country, taking a detour through Denver, Neal Cassady's hometown and headquarters. A den of iniquity and initiation, the capital of Colorado stood, in the beat ethos, for a larger-than-life authenticity. If Kerouac's anchorage point remained Queens, *"Mémère's"* lair, the writer endlessly turned toward Denver, where the grass seemed greener. He wrote the first chapter of

IN GROSSE POINTE, KEROUAC PUT UP WITH SUCH A MIDDLE CLASS WAY OF LIFE FOR ONLY TWO MONTHS.

On the Road there in 1949, the myth of the West providing his fictional material. The little time he spent there, often alone, was used to piece together the fantasy of an underground scene. In vain. Sal Paradise, distraught, would murmur: *"Down in Denver, all I did was die."*

The balancing act between the security of Grosse Pointe and the escape valve of Denver testifies to

GAS OVEN — LUCIEN CARR ATTEMPTED SUICIDE BY STICKING HIS HEAD INSIDE | GAP → THE BRAND BROUGHT BACK THE "BEATS" IN AN AD CAMPAIGN SELLING PANTS IN 199

PISTOL — BURROUGHS ALWAYS CARRIED ONE, EVEN TO BED | ACID — ALLEN GINSBERG TRIED IT AT THE MENTAL RESEARCH INSTITUTE IN PALO ALTO

IN ONE LAST EFFORT TO CONFORM, KEROUAC EVEN JOINED THE NAVY.

a deep-seated identity crisis: for his biographer and friend Ann Charters, *"Jack's desperate flights back and forth across the country during the next six years only mirrored his own confusion."* An existence at odds with society, on the margins, young Kerouac's escapades express his visceral refusal to bend to the values of the American dream, his ultimate foil. A point of view that calls for nuance, according to his ex-wife, the novelist Joyce Johnson: *"Jack was torn between contradictory aspirations: bohemia on one side, traditions on the other, mostly because of his Canadian background."* His ancestry, marking him from birth with outsider status, may have made access to upward social mobility more desirable to him.

In one last effort to conform, Kerouac even aspired to a military life: archives released in 2005 revealed that he joined the Navy in 1943. Unable to tolerate the strict imposed discipline, he was sent to a psychiatric unit and declared *"unfit for service."* Let's not forget that in his first major work, the novel about his youth, *The Town and the City*, the aspirations of the main character seem to embrace the ideals of the American dream. So *On the Road* isn't necessarily the anti-establishment manifesto we'd like it to be, but an ode to an idealized America incarnated by a symbol, Dean Moriarty.

Torn between opposite directions, Kerouac was disappointed by the hippies. The outsider, he was weary of trying to reconcile traditionalism with wandering and getting wasted. Meanwhile, the Beat group carried on, creating its own tempo and its own value system, redefining another American way of life. ✹

© THE U.S. NATIONAL ARCHIVES

JACK IN 1943, IN THE NAVY

CONJUGAL BOND

Wanted: Kerouac. Did all of the Beats have to do time? Car thief and bender enthusiast Neal Cassady grew up behind bars; Gregory Corso had been rotting in prison for two years when he started writing; well before the *Howl* obscenity trial, Ginsberg's unsavory companions had already gotten him involved in receiving stolen goods; Burroughs, fleeing marijuana charges, ended up in a Mexican jail for the accidental murder of his wife. Young thugs, always getting into fights, the Beats rubbed shoulders with serious crime. And their school of hard knocks had its victims: David Kammerer and Lucien Carr, New York friends of Kerouac, came out on the losing end in a dangerous ballet. Constantly rejected as a lover by Carr, Kammerer pursued him fervently. In August 1944, during an altercation, Carr stabbed him in self-defense, then tossed his body into the Hudson. Kerouac listened to his confession, and helped him get rid of the weapon, which earned him an arrest as a material witness. His only escape, marrying his girlfriend Edie Parker so her parents would post his bond. Witness to the union: a detective. **C.G.**

ANMEUR SMALL MARKET TOWN IN BRITTANY, HOST TO THE KEROUAC FESTIVAL | BEATLES ⟶ THE BAND'S NAME IS A WORD PLAY BETWEEN « BEAT » AND « BEETLES »

BECAUSE OF THE SUCCESS OF *ON THE ROAD*, MÉMÈRE HAD TO BARRICADE THEIR HOUSE ON LONG ISLAND TO KEEP THE FANS AT BAY

THE MAN
JACK KEROUAC

FROM SAN FRANCISCO
TO MEXICO CITY

BY LAURA PERTUY | TRANSLATED BY JENNIFER GAY

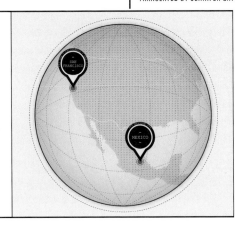

DUE SOUTH

A BEAT REUNION ON FOREIGN SOIL, THE EXPEDITION TO MEXICO IN 1956 MARKED A DESIRE TO LOOK ELSEWHERE FOR THE ESSENCE OF THE MOVEMENT AND TO RENEW A FAITH CORRUPTED BY THE PROGRESS OF CONSUMERISM. ALLEN GINSBERG LEFT THE UNITED STATES TO CHEERS FROM THE CROWD WHILE JACK KEROUAC WAS ABOUT TO ENCOUNTER RESOUNDING SUCCESS WITH *ON THE ROAD*, PUBLISHED UPON HIS RETURN. BUT THE GROUP'S MOST GLORIOUS PERIOD WOULD—INSIDIOUSLY—PRIME ITS DISMANTLING.

From the walls of the City Lights Bookstore oozed the words of an unsettling realization: America's successes were repudiating the beat principles. City Lights was where Ginsberg, Kerouac, and the crowd met up with publisher Lawrence Ferlinghetti before making boozy stops at the Vesuvio Café, whose very façade illustrated the enthusiasms of the little beat troop, sometimes surrealist, sometimes colored by an acrimonious reality. On October 7, 1955, Ginsberg hooted his famous *Howl* at the Six Gallery cooperative while Kerouac collected change to knead his alcoholic prosody. And all of a sudden San Francisco was detonating, launching its eminent Renaissance. In the fall of 1956, that effervescence led Kerouac, and then Ginsberg and Gregory Corso, back onto the roads. Well-versed in the art of hitching, the latter two visited Henry Miller on the way. Anaïs Nin welcomed them in L.A., where they poeticized, naked, at a literary gathering.

WHILE GINSBERG AND CORSO GALLIVANTED AROUND THE ANCIENT AZTEC CITY WITH BULIMIC ENTHUSIASM, KEROUAC APPLIED HIMSELF TO UNDERSTANDING MEXICAN SOCIETY FROM THE INSIDE.

CONQUISTADORES

In Mexico City, Ginsberg and Corso met up with Kerouac at Orizaba 210 in an apartment crammed with books, empty bottles, and old trinkets. This is where he composed *Mexico City Blues* under the influence of Bill Garver, the former Times Square pickpocket and acquaintance of William Burroughs. While Ginsberg and Corso, joined by the Orlovsky brothers (Peter and Lafcadio), were gallivanting around the ancient Aztec city with bulimic enthusiasm, ecstatic at the recognition of their new movement, Kerouac applied himself to understanding Mexican society from the inside, endlessly mystifying it to feed his writing. His long novella *Tristessa*, a tale of impossible love with a Mexican heroin addict, wails of misery with splendid accuracy. The writer rediscovered the religious hunger of his youth and likened his heroine to a Madonna and then to an Indian mystic, pointing to a questioning of faith he was to continue exploring relentlessly.

ECSTASY AND BEATIFICATION

Won over by a sentiment of "non-interference," the Beats interacted with the Mexican population on a new

"MEXICO CITY BLUES", PINTS OF PERCEPTION

Kerouac wrote the two hundred and forty-two choruses (poems with musical significance) of *Mexico City Blues* in two weeks, during his third stay in Mexico City, in August 1955. Drinking with his buddy Bill Garver, a morphine addict worn down by a life of excess, he imbibed Garver's strange ramblings, disconnected and loaded with references, before concentrating his prose in short poems. Sometimes lucid, sometimes sloshed, his writing sidesteps formalism to transcribe the dehydrated hallucinations as faithfully as possible. The lines shake their jazzy beat and paint a portrait of Mexico as arid as it is luminous; the typography articulates a changing rhythm, modeled on Kerouac's encounters with truth through meditation. The effervescence of the beat movement can be heard here and there in the roar of the dynamo so dear to Ginsberg, and be sipped in the ebb of flickering lucidity. We gradually forsake the hope of possible recognition for Kerouac in the United States to taste his ecstatic incantations. An amiably boorish liqueur. **L.P.**

BOB DONLIN, NEAL CASSADY, ALLEN GINSBERG, ROBERT LAVIGNE AND LAWRENCE FERLINGHETTI IN FRONT OF THE CITY LIGHTS BOOKSTORE IN SAN FRANCISCO, 1956

footing. Music, drugs, love, and contemplation were just so many feasts nourishing their imagination and then their work. The relationship to nature and to desertic expanses, blazing with spirituality, gave shape to the movement. In *On the Road*, Sal Paradise created an existence as a fellah for himself, one of those poor farmers whose tattered clothes symbolized their relationship, at once fervent and inescapable, to work. *"They thought I was a Mexican, of course; and in a way I am."* Kerouac allied dust, sweat, and simplicity to the beat spirit, far from the American straight and narrow: *"It's only in Mexico, in the sweetness and innocence, birth and death seem at all worthwhile."* (*Desolation Angels*). As for Burroughs, he hit the South American roads in search of an hallucinogenic drug (see *The Yage Letters*) after accidentally killing his wife, Joan Vollmer. *Queer* and *Naked Lunch* both poured forth from his guilt and despair.

OF ROOTS AND WINGS

The year 1956 ended on a high note: Viking Press finally accepted to publish *On the Road*. In 1957 Kerouac returned to American soil. In May, Ferlinghetti was arrested on obscenity charges related to the publication of Ginsberg's work. The success of *Howl* was only more spectacular and Kerouac's began to pulse: in September he suddenly became the *"incarnation of the Beat Generation."* Nevertheless, the joy was short-lived as the members of the movement headed for divergent literary and spiritual territories. Mexico hosted Kerouac once again in 1961, after the death of Bill Garver. He wrote the second part of *Desolation Angels* there, a long tirade on solitude and melancholy inspired by his stateless condition: *"I'm not American, nor West European, somehow I feel like an Indian, a North American Exile in North America."* (*Selected Letters*). ❀

FACE OF BUDDHA, A DRAWING BY JACK KEROUAC, 1958

THE MAN
JACK KEROUAC

FROM

MATTERHORN PEAK
TO
DESOLATION PEAK

BY GLADYS MARIVAT | TRANSLATED BY JENNIFER GAY

ON CLOUD NINE

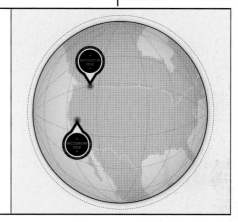

GARY SNYDER, POET, PARK RANGER AND SPECIALIST IN ASIAN CULTURES INTRODUCED JACK KEROUAC TO ZEN AND THE WILDERNESS OF SOLITARY LIFE IN THE MOUNTAINS. HE EXPERIENCED HIS LIMITS, AS MAGICAL AS IT WAS DESTRUCTIVE, AT MATTERHORN PEAK AND DESOLATION PEAK, AS RECOUNTED IN *THE DHARMA BUMS* AND *DESOLATION ANGELS*.

t was Jack Kerouac's lifelong dream. In 1949, in Denver, he looked at the mountains in the west and, according to Allen Ginsberg, said that he would buy a horse for 30 dollars, an old saddle, an army sleeping bag (...) and a gun, and that he would go to live in the mountains forever. So, meeting Gary Snyder, in September 1955 in San Francisco, was a revelation. The man who would become Japhy Ryder in *The Dharma Bums*, looked to him like the *"a great new hero of American culture."* Kerouac, stayed up every night reading *The Diamond Sutra*, one of Buddhism's major texts. He was attracted to the scholar's intelligence, the simplicity of his cabin, the refinement with which he spoke of tea˚, translated, drank, and made love in open relationships inspired by Tibetan Yab-yum. As for Snyder, he envied the writer who spoke the language of America's workers, the language of lumberjacks and railroad workers. The two writers soon became inseparable.

WHAT IS HAPPINESS?

From the age of 19, Gary Snyder had worked for the Forest Service in the mountains of the Northwest. Kerouac confided to him his desire for life in the wild. By way of training, Snyder suggested ascending Matterhorn Peak, in Yosemite. He was the lead climber and thinker. As they hiked, he played the part of the scout, leaping easily from stone to stone, and exchanging spontaneously invented haikus with Kerouac. They were utterly alone, surrounded by towering peaks. *"This is the beginning and the end of the world right here."* The blue, pink, purple and then starry sky exploded in their eyes.

Kerouac soaked up the Void, the "Golden Eternity." Up there, he went in search of answers. He felt rapturous, hopeful, and overwhelmed with devotion; full of wonder at the sight of himself and Snyder, two sincere young men meditating and praying for the world. A witness to Snyder's extraordinary happiness, Kerouac decided to *"begin a new life." "All over the West, and the mountains in the East, and the desert, I'll tramp with a rucksack and make it the pure way."* Was the end of the expedition premonitory? Gary Snyder climbed Matterhorn Peak alone, *"letting out his triumphant mountain conquering Buddha*

KEROUAC CONFIDED TO SNYDER HIS DESIRE FOR LIFE IN THE WILD. BY WAY OF TRAINING, SNYDER SUGGESTED ASCENDING MATTERHORN PEAK.

JOCKEY. | FOOTBALL PLAYER OR RUNNER, THOSE WERE KEROUAC'S CAREER CHOICES AGED 12 | BURROUGHS SPENT 13 DAYS IN PRISON FOR MURDERING HIS WIFE

4 PACKS | KEROUAC'S LAST JOURNAL ENTRY STATED HIS INTENTION TO GO OUT AND BUY SOME BEER | WILLIAM S. BURROUGHS LOVED SNAKES

GARY SNYDER, PETER ORLOVSKY AND ALLEN GINSBERG IN THE INDIAN MOUNTAINS IN FEBRUARY 1962

Mountain Smashing song of joy." Lying in the grass, Kerouac had a hunch about his limits and declared that he would never return. His next ascent would also be a fall.

NOTHING HAD PREPARED KEROUAC FOR THE EXTREME SOLITUDE AT DESOLATION PEAK.

HEADING BACK

In San Francisco, Kerouac bought *"a regular kitchen and bedroom right on my back"* He saw himself as a placid saint. Encouraged by Snyder, he applied to be a forest ranger the following summer in North Cascades National Park. He went off to spend the winter with his mother, in North Carolina, and there he received the good news: the Park Service had assigned him to Desolation Peak. By March, he was back with Gary Snyder in his cabin near Mill Valley, California. They meditated during the week. At weekends, the house was open to all and one party would lead to another. In May, Snyder left for a monastery in Japan.

The moderate isolation suited Kerouac perfectly. But nothing had prepared him for the extreme solitude awaiting him at the aptly named Desolation Peak. When he headed off in July 1956, he had no idea he would go sixty-three days without seeing another soul. Even Thoreau hadn't experienced that at Walden. At first, it was wonderful. In love with the rivers, Kerouac was captivated by the Skagit. Despite a difficult journey, he felt strongly that he was walking in Snyder's steps, and his body trembled when he saw the dual peaks of Hozomeen Mountain.

LOST IN DESOLATION

Beyond this, it is impossible to know what Kerouac went through, alone up there in his lookout, surrounded by thousands of miles of forests and lakes. There's the version in *The Dharma Bums,* rather light and optimistic, written in the effervescence of *On the Road*'s success. Kerouac missed his friends, to the point where he ended up finding his lookout sordid, but *The Dharma Bums* ends with a vision of Snyder as an old Chinese hermit and Kerouac thanking the mountain for all it taught him.

And then there is the dark counterpart, *Desolation Angels,* written in large part during his stay on Desolation Peak: *"I'd thought (...) hitch hiking up there to the Skagit Valley (...)*

THE DESOLATION PEAK OBSERVATORY, WITH A VIEW OF MOUNT HOZOMEEN, WHERE KEROUAC SPENT 63 DAYS ALONE IN THE SUMMER OF 1956

HE WROTE LONG LETTERS, MADE A LIST OF THINGS TO DO IN HIS NEW LIFE. "HAVE FUN" IS AT THE TOP OF THE PAGE.

'When I get to the top of Desolation Peak and everybody leaves on mules and I'm alone I will come face to face with God or Tathagata and find out once and for all what is the meaning of all this existence (...)' *but instead I'd come face to face with myself, no liquor, no drugs, no chance of faking it..."*

In his edifying essay, *Poets on the Peaks*, unfortunately out of print, the photographer and journalist John Suiter, relying on Kerouac's journal, recounts his fear that Hozomeen Mountain would devour him. And then there was the day that the lack of tobacco drove him crazy. Kerouac took a boat, bought some smokes, and headed back to his lookout, terrified by the mountains that were closing in on him. He still had five weeks left. He wrote long letters to a lover he'd met in Mexico, made a list of things to do in his new life. At the top of the page one can read *"Have fun."* He dreamt of drugs and alcohol. He started work on a transliteration of *The Diamond Sutra*. On August 26th, Kerouac heard a message on the radio system connecting all the forest guards. He howled with joy. The season was over.

The uncredited quotes are taken from *Desolation angels* and *The Dharma bums* by Jack Kerouac

Sacred text

KEROUAC & THE GOLDEN ETERNITY

In the spring of 1956, Kerouac was living in Mill Valley like a Bodhisattva – a spiritual being filled with compassion and freed of constraints. Encouraged by Snyder to write his own sutra (book of philosophy), in May of that year he wrote one of his most important and least known works. Made up of sixty-six prose poems of several lines each, *The Scripture of the Golden Eternity* is the summit of the author's quest for Buddhist illumination and revelation, moments in which the order and harmony of the universe, the meaning of emptiness and wholeness, the unity of the One appeared to him. We come away with these sublime lines: *"When you've understood this scripture, throw it away. If you can't understand this scripture, throw it away. I insist on your freedom."* Another important text that brings together the comments and annotations he made between 1953 and 1956, *Some of the Dharma*, was published only in 1997. It took a new generation of suits to see the interest in Jack the boddhisatva. G.M.

STELLA WAS KEROUAC'S LAST WIFE AND HAD THE SOLE TASK OF CARING FOR MÉMÈRE UNTIL SHE DIED

KEROUAC HAD A GRUDGE AGAINST NORMAN MAILER FOR HAVING DISCUSSED THE DEATH OF GOD

WILLIAM S. BURROUGHS WAS INTRODUCED TO OPIUM BY THE HOUSEKEEPER

MILLION DOLLARS, THE PRICE OBTAINED FOR THE *ON THE ROAD* ORIGINAL SCROLL

THE BIG SUR COAST IN CALIFORNIA (HERE IN 1952) WILL BE JACK'S LAST DESTINATION OUT WEST.

FROM TANGIER
TO BIG SUR

BY LAURA TUILLIER | TRANSLATED BY JENNIFER GAY

QUICKSAND

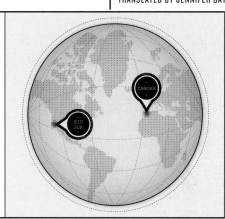

KEROUAC'S LAST JOURNEYS WERE EXILES IN THE WILDERNESS. JUST AS HE WAS FINALLY ACHIEVING RECOGNITION, AFTER THE PUBLICATION OF *ON THE ROAD* (1957), THE STAR WRITER OF THE BEAT GENERATION WAS SINKING INTO DEPRESSION AND ALCOHOLISM. FROM MOROCCO TO CALIFORNIA, KEROUAC WAS GETTING BOGGED DOWN, HIT AND SUNK.

Tangier, late winter 1956-57, a room in the el-Muniria Hotel in the seamy Petit Socco neighborhood. Jack Kerouac is typing, as fast as he can, the hallucinatory lines of *Naked Lunch*, as dictated by William S. Burroughs. On the menu: sexual violence, desperate fury, scatology, decaying fantasies mingling possessed creatures and faithless, lawless beatniks. The transcription sessions left Kerouac exhausted, plagued by hellish night-mares. While on the other side of the Atlantic *On the Road* was finally going to press, its author was beginning to founder. He was thirty-four years old, with a decade of knocking about America behind him, from which he emerged battered, disillusioned, and profoundly alcoholic.

For his first trip away from the American continent, Kerouac (soon joined by Allen Ginsberg and Peter Orlovsky) hoped to find the lascivious, easy life Burroughs had described in his letters. Instead, he found himself afraid of an unknown city that felt dangerous to him, and the local hashish and opium didn't go down well. Suffering from his first episode of paranoia, he even thought he'd been poisoned with arsenic. The South made him sick.

SAD SUMMIT

After quick stops in Paris and London, Kerouac returned to New York, in a hurry to see his mother, "Mémère," with whom he would spend his last days, aspiring to a provincial, seden-tary and orderly life. A fervent Catholic, Mémère had always viewed her son's wanderings with ambivalence, fearing depravation even as she hoped for glory. *On the Road* was published in September 1957, and Kerouac was crowned "King of the Beats." The critical reception was mitigated yet the book raced to the top of the bestseller lists and stayed there for five consecu-tive weeks. Above all, Kerouac became the hero of the "beatniks," those young people lampooned by editorialist Herb Caen. However Kerouac didn't identify with the new generation which was quickly becoming a fad: one dressed like a beatnik and partied like a beatnik during the frivolous hiatus between the

AFTER A DECADE OF KNOCKING ABOUT AMERICA, KEROUAC IS BATTERED, DISILLUSIONED AND ALCOHOLIC.

Beat Generation of the early 1950s and the pacifist Flower Power of the late 1960s.

Between the gestation and the publication of *On the Road*, Kerouac had aged, and a certain scorn had sett-led in: while Dean Moriarty was well and truly a beat hero, Sal Paradise was only an observer in the background, fascinated by Moriarty's lifestyle, but he never really joined in. *"I'm the King of the Beats, but I am not a beatnik,"* he confided to the press. His fans saw things differently, crowding around his house on Long Island and frightening Mémère, who had to barricade herself inside for weeks.

Having reached the summit, the author had a premonition of his fall, symbolized by the failed reunion with Neal Cassady as Kerouac held a copy of *On the Road* in his hands for the first time: *"When Cody said goodbye to all of us that day he for the first time in our lives failed to look me a goodbye in the eye (...) I knew something was bound to be wrong and it turned out very wrong."* (*Desolation Angels*).

LAST TRIP WEST

When Kerouac reached Big Sur in the summer of 1960, at night and in a taxi (!), the first thing he saw was a crashed car. Kerouac's last destination in the West, Big Sur, was meant to be an opportunity for solitude, calm, and sobriety. In a cabin perched above the monumental cliffs of the Californian coast, the writer spent two weeks alone before giving in: he invited his old drinking buddies (Neal Cassady, the San Franciscans, Lawrence Ferlinghetti, Philip Whalen...)

to Big Sur and let his body go numb and his mind cloud with alcohol. Far from the light-footed joy of *On the Road*, Kerouac's last major work, *Big Sur*, is a deeply anguished account of a journey through the stagnant waters of decay, transcribed with sadness and lucidity. Kerouac recounts how he met a kid who

KEROUAC FOUND REFUGE IN CATHOLICISM, CONSERVATISM AND PATRIOTISM.

started following him, eager to know how the beat legend lived: *"The poor kid actually believes there's something noble and idealistic and kind about all this beat stuff"* He didn't believe it anymore himself, and left the west coast for the last time, to bury himself in his mother's bosom.

BACKTRACK

Following Big Sur, Kerouac never hitchhiked again. Isolated in Northport, New York with Mémère, he lost touch

with the other members of the Beat Generation. Mémère had even threatened to denounce Allen Ginsberg's homosexuality to the FBI if he didn't keep away from her son. Disappointed by the beatniks, disgusted by the excesses that drove him to alcoholism, Kerouac found refuge in Catholicism (a big crucifix hung above the last bed he slept in), conservatism, and patriotism (he insisted he was ready to serve in Vietnam). While he had stopped writing any further major works, the inspired *Visions of Cody* and *Visions of Gerard*, written in the 1950s, were published in the 1960s, thanks to the success of *On the Road*. Back in Lowell, he married his childhood friend Stella Sampas, the perfect wife to look after him and Mémère who was weakened by a stroke. He settled with them in well-to-do St. Petersburg, a cushy town in Florida and twilight home for average Americans. That's where he learned of Cassady's death in February 1968, a mysterious incident on a train embankment in Mexico. The Beats were finished, and with them Kerouac, whose last piece of writing, the bitter *After Me, the Deluge*, accused the young of highjacking his inspiration. But the momentum he'd created was already unstoppable. ✸

★ **Drunk culture** ★

FROM TARMAC TO TAVERN

"His last years must have been tough, nobody was paying him attention, he was just a conservative and an old drunk," according to Hettie Jones, beat author and now a quiet East Village grandmother. Jean-Jacques Lebel, who worked at Gallimard, remembers Kerouac's visit to France in 1965, and the unforgettable nights when, completely drunk, he would bang on the doors at Gallimard screaming *"Open up! I want some dough!"* Amazingly, for Kerouac, alcoholism went hand in hand with rigid political positions, which he tried to clarify

in *After Me, the Deluge*, his last work, published posthumously by the *Chicago Tribune*. Private property, religion, and capitalism, Kerouac proclaimed his faith in the American way of life. Isolated from his former companions of the road (Ginsberg, Snyder, Whalen) who saw the major liberation struggles of the 1970s coming, Kerouac opted to retire to Republican Florida, with baseball on TV and quickly-drained six-packs. One couldn't imagine a more sedentary life. **L.T.**

JACK IN THE AUTUMN OF 1964, DURING HIS LAST VISIT TO ALLEN GINSBERG IN NEW YORK

FROM LANMEUR TO LOWELL

BY ARNAUD CONTRERAS | | TRANSLATED BY AUDREY CONCANNON

MY ARMORICAN UNCLE

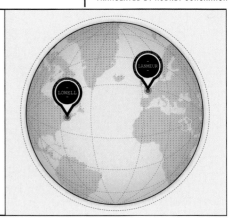

WHAT IF IT WAS IN FRANCE THAT KEROUAC UNDERTOOK HIS REAL JOURNEY OF INITIATION? OBSESSED BY HIS ORIGINS, THE "AMERICAN BRETON" ARRIVED IN PARIS IN 1965, AND IN ELOQUENT MIMICRY, HEADED WEST TO THE LAND OF BRITTANY. THERE, HE ATTEMPTED TO RESOLVE HIS QUEST FOR IDENTITY BUT ONLY MANAGED TO LAUNCH A GENEALOGICAL INVESTIGATION THAT ENDED UP OUTLIVING HIM, TAKING NEARLY THIRTY-FIVE YEARS TO DISCLOSE ITS MYSTERIES.

ack Kerouac finally arrived in Brest in 1965 after a week of wandering, a few hours by train and years of fantasies. This journey provided material for *Satori in Paris,* in which the main character Duluoz searches for his origins, the hypothetical trace of an aristocratic Breton ancestor. Forty-six years on, the retired bookseller and publisher, Pierre le Bris, a key figure of the Ouest's literary scene, leafs through the pages of his guestbook. *"Quefféléc, Blondin, Robbe-Grillet... they all used to come here!"*. He pauses at a yellowed page. *"There!"* He hands me the precious book. It contains these words in childish handwriting, *"Jean-Louis Le Bris de Keroack."* A few inches below, a firm signature, *"Jack Kerouac"*: two identities.

Born march 12th, 1922 to Quebecer parents originally from Brittany, the child was baptized "Jean-Louis Kerouac". The family lived in the Franco-Canadian community in Lowell, Massachusetts.

Joual* (a French dialect spoken in Quebec and Montreal among the working classes) crossed with some Breton expressions, was the language spoken at home. Jean-Louis's father regularly reminded his son of his origins, *"Ti-Jean, remember you're Breton."*

THE IDEA THAT HE COULD BE DESCENDED FROM A "KNIGHT" OR "PRINCE OF BRITTANY" AMUSED KEROUAC, HE SIGNED SOME OF HIS LETTERS AS SUCH.

WON OVER BY BRITTANY.

"Ti-Jean" didn't learn English until the age of 9, when he attended an American school. Unlike his classmates, he didn't master the language until he was 12. Some of his biographers consider this a key factor in explaining Jack's shyness and his solitary character, even his taste for isolation.

On a recent trip to Lowell, Roger Brunelle, one of the founders of the *Lowell Celebrates Kerouac Festival!* tells me that he thinks this is where the automatic writing comes from, that he constructed a poetic language in his head arising from hesitations between

French, joual, Breton and English that merged in the automatic writing. Books by the great French authors have always been shared in the Franco-Canadian community. Kerouac, like all the children, must have read Flaubert or Balzac. Brunelle's grandmother has a small theatre troupe there and Zola (*Nana, L'Assommoir*) was the most popular author in a working class city

PIERRE LE BRIS, «ULYSSE» IN *SATORI IN PARIS*, HOLDING THE GUEST BOOK JACK SIGNED DURING HIS VISIT TO BREST IN 1965

WHO WANTS TO REMEMBER JACK KEROUAC?

The small town of Lanmeur in the Finistère has been organizing the Jack Kerouac Festival for the past two years. Genealogists and fans all seem to agree on the fact that the name Kerouac comes from Kervoac, a hamlet on the edge of the village that is pronounced "Kerouac." The ancestor, Urbain-François Le Bihan, is said to have owned a few acres there and – by means of *"savonette à vilains"* (literally "soaping clean his family tree"), according to the colorful local expression – added "de Kervoach" to his name in an act of self-ennoblement. According to the festival organizer, Valérie Derrien-Remeur, Kerouac's personality is the source of some lively debate in the village, as well as around Brittany. She confides to me that, *"it wasn't easy to convince the officials":* What could Kerouac do for Brittany? Wouldn't it encourage the cliché of associating alcoholism with Brittany? Philippe Chain, who hails from Lanmeur and is president of the Paris-Brittany network, has no such qualms. He considers Kerouac a tremendous asset towards nurturing cultural and economic links between this Celtic desert and Silicon Valley. In his view, they should "capitalize" on this connection with the writer. Across the Atlantic in Lowell, the same issues have arisen. When I meet the local newspaper chief, he tells me, smiling ironically, *"We've recruited him and fired him, ha-ha, poetic, isn't it?"* Even in his hometown, apart from a few enthusiasts, for now, no one seems specially inclined to remember Kerouac, dharma bum and tiresome neighbor. **A.C.**

© ARNAUD CONTRERAS

VILLAGE SIGN FOR KERVOAC, OUTSIDE LANMEUR

KEROUAC HELD THE DREAM OF GOING TO HUELGOAT, UNAWARE THAT HIS FAMILY'S ORIGINS WERE THERE. HE TRIED TO GAIN A BETTER UNDERSTANDING OF BRETON CULTURE AND MAINTAINED A RICH CORRESPONDENCE ON THE SUBJECT.

like this... Kerouac also read Proust, the surrealists, poetry and prose in French. Over the years and as his books were published, the search for and reference to his origins occurred with greater frequency. The idea that he could be descended from a *"knight"* or a *"prince of Brittany"* amused Kerouac to the point of even signing his letters as such.

Pierre Le Bris, the wise bookseller from Brest, renamed "Ulysse" in *Satori in Paris*, says, *"whenever he came to my home, he used to talk to me almost entirely about his last name. I told him that I did not see any connection with my own Lebris family tree. All my ancestors were country bumpkins and peasants. Kerouac sounds Breton, but not completely Breton as there are Kerouasks and Keroual, but I've rarely come across Kerouac... although there is a Kerouac in the Morbihan. The Americans and Canadians are obsessed by their origins and once they find a Breton in their family history, they are immediately convinced of a noble lineage."*

Finally in 1999, Patricia Dagier, a freelance genealogist in Quimper, identified Jack's ancestor, in collaboration with the Kirouac Families Association: the unknown Britton is named Urbain-François Le Bihan, a landowner at Kervoac, near the village of Lanmeur, the son of a notary from Huelgoat who, fleeing legal problems in his parish, set sail for New France in the 1720s. For reasons no one can explain, he repeatedly changed his name, signing various documents "Alexandre de Kervoach," "Alexandre Le Breton," or Maurice-Louis Le Bris de Kervoach." The last pseudonym misled generations of Keroacks and Kirouacs, not to mention Jack, all looking for a Le Bris.

FROM ONE WEST TO ANOTHER

In *Satori in Paris*, Jack Kerouac mentions that he is the first to return to the land of his forebears. But Patricia Dagier asserts that he says this because *"he wants to be the first to hit the jackpot, as in addition to seeking a noble ancestor, he believes that there is a great legacy in store! She continues to say that he was well aware of the many more or less distant cousins who had set sail for Brittany seeking their origins and inheritance. None of them could find their origins in the registries as they were all convinced that they descended from nobility. They believed that they were related to the Keroüartz family, who own a lovely chateau in Lannilis. The Kerouacs regularly turned up at the family castle claiming their rightful inheritance."*

Standing in front of the monument dedicated to Jack Kerouac in the center of Lowell, Roger Brunelle looks up at the sky. *"If he believed himself noble, he would never have been called Jack. That first name bound him to the American working class into which he was born. Why is it that in virtually every photo he's wearing a laborer's shirt? Why did he admit that he was uncomfortable in highbrow circles with Ginsberg and other New Yorkers? American, Breton, French, yes. But aristocrat... pure invention!"*

I didn't find any evidence either of a search for a legacy in Kerouac's writings. However, several people in Huelgoat told me about the fine friendship Jack maintained in the last years of his life with a young man from the area called Youenn Gwernig who immigrated to New York. Youenn came into contact with Kerouac through the literary magazine *Evergreen*. *"The first time he arrived in front of Kerouac's house, Youenn shouted out 'Cadoudal', the agreed password so as to avoid unwelcome visitors. 'You're tall,' Kerouac flung at him before welcoming him with a whiskey."* The two friends held the dream of going to Huelgoat together; unaware that Kerouac's origins were there. Kerouac tried to gain a better understanding of Breton culture and maintained a rich correspondence on the subject.

In Lowell's cemetery in Massachusetts, there is no Jack Kerouac. But between two miniature bottles of whiskey, a bottle of beer in a brown paper bag and a few cigarettes, a stone slab clearly shows the location of the grave of a certain "'Ti Jean' John L. Kerouac." A third identity for Jean-Louis Kerouac. ❋

THE ORIGINAL SCROLL OF *ON THE ROAD*, WRITTEN IN 3 WEEKS ON A ROLL OF PRINTER'S PAPER 118 FEET LONG, IT SOLD FOR 2.43 MILLIONS DOLLARS IN 2001 AT CHRISTIE'S

ORIGINAL TITLE ON THE ROAD

PUBLICATION DATE

PUBLISHER VIKING PRESS | 1957

THE BOOK

GENRE NOVEL | ORIGIN UNITED STATES

CHARACTERS SAL PARADISE | DEAN MORIARTY

OLD BULL LEE | CARLO MARX | MARYLOU

ED & GALATEA DUNKEL | CAMILLE | REMI

BONCOEUR | ROLAND MAJOR | CHAD KING

TOM SAYBROOK | DAMION

ON THE ROAD'S COILED SPRING

IN SEARCH OF PAST HIGHWAYS

BY ISAURE PISANI-FERRY
TRANSLATED BY ANITA CONRADE

★

BEGUN IN 1948, *ON THE ROAD* WENT THROUGH SO MANY REWRITES IT BECAME A QUEST FOR IDENTITY OF PROUSTIAN DIMENSIONS. KEROUAC CITED THE FRENCHMAN AS AN EXAMPLE: *"I READ ALL OF* REMEMBRANCE OF THINGS PAST, *BY MARCEL PROUST, AND I DECIDED TO DO EXACTLY WHAT HE DID, ONLY FAST."* CHRONICLE OF A TORMENTED NINE-YEAR PREGNANCY...

★

How long did it take you to write On the Road? TV talk-show host Steve Allen asks Jack Kerouac in 1959. *"Three weeks,"* Kerouac replies. *"That's amazing,"* Allen marvels. *"How long were you on the road itself?"* Kerouac thinks. *"Seven years."* The studio audience murmurs in admiration. Allen continues: *"I've heard that you write so fast that you prefer not to use regular typing paper, but instead you use one big, long roll of paper. Is that true?"* Kerouac nods. But the truth is that Kerouac started *On the Road* in the summer of 1948, not in 1951, as he later claimed, and did not finish it until 1957.

Returning from his first transcontinental road trip in August 1948, he wrote in his diary, on the 23rd: *"I have another novel in mind,* On the Road, *which I keep thinking about, about two guys hitch-hiking to California in search of something they don't really find, and losing themselves on the road, and coming all the way back hopeful of something else."* He did not realize he would sweat bullets for years, seeking the most accurate expression of his experience.

BYWAYS AND DETOURS

On the Road was Kerouac's second novel. The first, *The Town and the City*, was strongly influenced by his heroes, Mark Twain, Thomas Wolfe, and Walt Whitman, authors who celebrate America's vastness and splendor. Kerouac began the new novel hoping to find a revolutionary way of writing. But his notebooks still strove to attain the lyricism of his elders: *"a riding of the tide down the eternal waterbed, a contributing to brown, dark, watery foams; a voyaging past endless lands & trees & immortal levees."*

He rummaged about restlessly for a narrative structure. For months on

> For months on end Kerouac accumulated protoversions of *On the Road.*

end, he accumulated protoversions of *On the Road*, some of them one page long, others hundreds. He wrote sometimes in the first person, sometimes the third. He hesitated between travel companions: Warren Beauchamps (Lucien Carr), Dean Pomeray (Neal Cassady); solo. In other words, he rode off in all directions, and after several months of torment, ran dry. So when Neal Cassady, Lu Anne, and Al Hinkle offered to take him on the road again, he immediately accepted.

In February 1949, he was back on the East Coast, writing *On the Road*. He figured he'd have it finished in a matter of months. His trip had convinced him that what he wanted to say about America, the reality, the friendships, the serendipity, required the present immediate tense. He wanted to write a

I first met met Neal not long after my father died...I had just gotten over a serious illness that I won't bother to talk about except that it really had something to do with my father's death and my awful feeling that everything was dead. With the coming of Neal there really began for me that part of my life that you could call my life on the road. Prior to that I'd always dreamed of going west, seeing the country, always vaguely planning and never specifically taking off and so on. Neal is the perfect guy for the road because he actually was born on the road, when his parents were passing through Salt Lake City in 1926, in a jaloppy, on their way to Los Angeles. First reports of Neal came to me through Hal Chase, who'd shown me a few letters from him written in a Colorado reform school. I was tremendously interested in these letters because they so naively and sweetly asked for Hal to teach him all about Nietzsche and all the wonderful intellectual things that Hal was so justly famous for. At one point Allen and I talked about these letters and wondered if we would ever meet the strange Neal Cassady. This is all far back, when Neal wasnot the way he is today, when he was a young jailkid shrouded in mystery. Then news came that Neal was out of school and was coming to New York for the first time; also there was talk he had just married a 16 year old girl called Louanne. One day I was hanging around the Columbia campus and Hal and Ed White told me Neal had just arrived and was living in a guy called Bob Malkin's coldwater pad in East Harlem, the Spanish Harlem. Neal had arrived the night before, the first time in NY, with his beautiful little sharp chick Louanne; they got off the Greyhound bus at 50 St. and cut around the corner looking for a place to eat and went right in Hector's, and since then Hector's cafeteria has always been a big symbol of NY for Neal. They spent money on beautiful big glazed cakes and creampuffs. All this time Neal was telling Louanne things like this, "Now darling here we are in Ny and and although I haven't quite told you everything that I was thinking about when we crossed Missouri and especially at the point when we passed the Booneville reformatory which reminded me of my jail problem it is absolutely necessary now to postpone all those leftover things concerning our personal lovethings and at once begin thinking of specific worklife plans..." and so on in the way that he had in his early days. I went to the coldwater flat with the boys and Neal came to the door in his shorts. Louanne was jumping off quickly from the bed; apparently he was fucking with her. He always was doing so. This other guy who owned the place Bob Malkin was there but Neal had apparently dispatched him to the kitchen, probably to make coffee while he proceeded with his loveproblems....for to him sex was the one and only holy and important thing in life, although he had to sweat and curse to make a living,and so on. My first impression of Neal was of a young Gene Autry—trim, thin-hipped, blue eyes, with a real Oklahoma accent. In fact he'd just been working on a ranch, Ed Uhl's in Sterling Colo. before marrying L. and coming East. Louanne was a pretty, sweet little thing, but awfully dumb and capable of doing horrible things, as she proved a while later. I only mention this first meeting of Neal because of what he did. That night we all drank beer and I got drunk and blah-blahed somewhat, slept on the other couch, and in the morning, while we sat around dumbly smoking butts from ashtrays in the gray light of a gloomy day, Neal got up nervously, paced around thinking, and decided the thing to do was Louanne making breakfast and sweeping the floor. Then I went away. This was all I knew of Neal at the outset. During the following week however he confided in Hal Chase that he absolutely had to learn how to write from him; Hal said I was a writer and he should come to me for advice. Meanwhile Neal had gotten a job in a parking lot, had a fight with Louanne in their Hoboken apartment God knows why they went there and she was so mad and so vindictive down deep that she reported him to the police, some false trumped up hysterical crazy charge, and Neal had to lam from Hoboken. So he had no place to live. Neal came right out to Ozone Park where I was living with my mother, and one night while I was working on my book or my painting or whatever you want to call it there was a knock on the door and there was Neal, bowing, shuffling obsequiously in the dark of the hall, and saying "Hel-lo, you remember me, Neal Cassady? I've come to ask you to show me how to write." "And where's Louanne?" I asked, and Neal said she'd appa-

THE FIRST LINES OF THE ORIGINAL SCROLL OF *ON THE ROAD*, TYPED BY KEROUAC IN 1951

1

I first met Dean not long after ~~my father died and I thought~~ *my father died and I thought everything was dead.*

~~[struck out lines]~~

My knowledge of the beat generation and the road began. Before
that I'd always dreamed of going west, seeing
the country, always ~~vaguely~~ planning and never taking off. ¶ ~~Dean was~~
~~actually born on the road~~ ~~[struck out]~~

First reports of Dean came to me through Chad King, *who showed*
~~who showed~~ me a few
letters from him written in a Wyoming reform school. I was ~~tremendously~~ *amazed by*
~~interested in~~ these letters because they ~~[naively]~~ naïvely and sweetly asked
for Chad to teach him all about Nietzsche and all the ~~wonderful~~ intellectual things that ~~[struck out]~~ *we all admired Chad for knowing.* At one
point *Justin* ~~Allen~~ Moriarty and I talked about the letters and wondered if
we would ever meet the strange Dean *Pomeray.* ~~Pomeray.~~ This is all far back, when
~~[struck out]~~ *Dean* was a young jailkid shrouded
in mystery. Then news came that ~~the kid~~ *he* was out of reform school and was
coming to New York for the first time; also there was talk that he had
just married a sixteen year old girl called Marylou.

One day I was hanging around the campus and Chad ~~and Tim Gray~~ told
me Dean had just arrived and was living in a coldwater pad in *Espan*
~~East~~
Harlem, ~~the Spanish Harlem.~~ Dean had arrived the night before, his first
hour in New York, with his beautiful little sharp chick Marylou; ~~they~~ *they*
got off the Greyhound bus at 50th street and cut around the corner looking
for a place to eat and went right in Hector's *Cafeteria* and since then Hector's
~~cafeteria~~ has always been a big glowing symbol of New York for Dean.
They spent money on beautiful big glazed cakes and creampuffs ~~that~~ *that* you
never get in western cafeterias. All this time Dean was telling Marylou things like this:¶"Now darling here we are in New York and although
I haven't quite told you everything that I was thinking about when we
crossed Missouri and specially at the point when we passed the Booneville
reformatory(which reminded me of my jail problem)it is absolutely necessary now to postpone all ~~those leftover things~~ concerning our personal
lovethings and at once begin thinking of specific worklife plans..." and

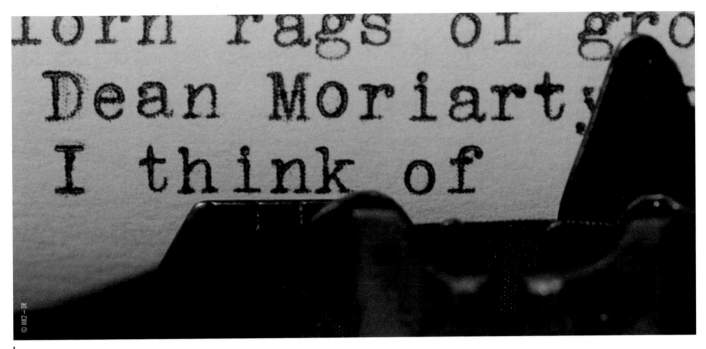

| A CLIP FROM THE MOVIE *ON THE ROAD* BY WALTER SALLES

novel about his generation, "*a study of the young people of this age who 'refuse to work,' as it were, and who roam the country half on the verge of crime, half on the verge of hoboism.*" (November 1949 entry in his notebook *Night Notes and Diagrams for On the Road*.)

He had succeeded in defining the Beat Generation as his subject, but he was still casting around for the right way to tell the story. He hesitated between a Dostoyevskian approach, where each character symbolizes a value or passion, and a more realistic bent. The style was especially crucial. One of his New York friends, John Clellon Holmes, tells how awestruck he was by the writing in the drafts of *On the Road*: "*long, intricate, Melvillean sentences that unwound*

> "I've never had a language of my own. Spoke French patois until I was 6, and after that the great forms of expression of the poet, the philosopher, the prophet."

adroitly through a dense maze of clauses; astonishing sentences that were obsessed with simultaneously depicting the crumb on the plate, the plate on the table, the table in the house, and the house in the world, but which (to him) always got stalled in the traffic jam of their own rhetoric." (Cited by Ann Charters.) Yet Kerouac doubted he possessed the same "*tragic fury*" or "*passionate intensity*" as the great writers. When he wrote, he felt "*wrapped in a shroud of words and arty designs. That's not life – not how one really feels. Not passion! (...) Great God, how much must I pirouette to get back to myself! Peste!*" (Quoted by Isaac Gewirtz.)

PROBLEMS WITH THE STARTER

A year after beginning *On the Road*, Kerouac was in the nitty-gritty of writing, when it becomes an existential issue of self-understanding and assertiveness. Language was the vortex of his personal identity storm, as he confessed in one of the *On the Road* manuscripts, written in Quebec-inflected French: "*I've never had a language of my own. Spoke French patois until I was six, and after that, the great forms and expressions of*

the poet, the philosopher, the prophet. And now all that is mixed up in my noggin..." One night in 1950, after a nightmare in which "*un ambassadeur du Bon Dieu*" ordered him to "*become French again,*" he tried to write *On the Road* in French. It begins, "*After the death of his father, Peter Martin found himself alone in the world; and after all what is a man going to do when his father is buried deep in the ground other than die himself in his heart and know that it won't be the last time before he dies finally in his poor mortal body, and, himself a father of children and sire of a family he will return to the original form of a piece of adventurous dust in this fatal ball of earth.*"(Kerouac's translation.) He soon gave up, but the return of his repressed identity prompted this diary entry: "*...after all the years since I was a child trying to become 'un Anglais' in Lowell from shame of being a Canuck; I never realized before I had undergone the same feelings any Jew, Greek, Negro or Italian feels in America*"(Note dated May 19, 1950 in the *Road Log*.)

Kerouac was also tormented by indecision about the identity of his narrator-alter egos, Ray Smith, Pictorial Review Jackson, Bruce

Smiley Moultrie, Chad Gavin, Freddie Boncœur, Peter Martin, or Sal Paradise. He continually changed the name, story, and background of the hero. But they all shared certain things: a feeling of loss, a quest.

BURNING OIL

From 1949 to 1950, Kerouac swung between intensive writing and wandering. He moved to Denver alone, hoping to finish his book there; went to live with Neal Cassady in San Francisco; had a fight with him, returned to New York, left for Denver again, made up with Neal, and spent two months in Mexico City with Burroughs, high as a kite 24 hours a day, returned definitively to New York in late 1950, married a young woman he'd just met, moved into her place, and got a job as a scribbler at 20th Century Fox. The whole time, he progressed with the novel as if in a labyrinth – getting lost.

In spring 1951, he was hospitalized for weeks with phlebitis. The day he was discharged, he told Holmes: *"You know what I'm going to do? I'm going to get me a roll of shelf-paper, feed it into the typewriter, and just write it down as fast as I can, exactly like it happened, all in a rush, the hell with these phony architectures – and worry about it later."* (Cited by Ann Charters.) Three weeks later, the novel that was an eternal recommencement was finished.

Thoughts of Neal Cassady were what got Kerouac out of his funk and rolling with *On the Road.* Hanging out with Neal, he saw the Roman candle, blazing through life with freedom and fury, and the sight helped him focus. He realized his best model was not Thomas Wolfe, but the extraordinary unknown Neal, and the story of *On the Road* is the story of their friendship. According to Allen Ginsberg, *"Jack finally discovered the kind of things he and Neal were talking about were the subject matter for what he wanted to*

write down." (Quoted by Ann Charters.)

Kerouac was dazzled by Neal's letter-writing style: powerful geysers, directly erupting experience, oblivious to literary effects. Their immediacy was what Kerouac had spent years searching for. Finally, the long rest imposed by the hospital stay enabled all the novelistic sediment he had accumulated to settle. When Jack got out in early April, he had a clear plan.

One morning, Kerouac took the huge roll of paper to Robert Giroux at Harcourt Brace. The scroll was a single paragraph, 120 feet long. *"Here's your novel!"* he cried. Giroux was taken aback: *"But Jack, how can you make corrections on a manuscript like that?"* In a rage, Kerouac refused to change a single comma, took his scroll, and vanished. (Quoted by Ann Charters.)

FINDING A PLACE TO PARK

Months and years went by. A new search had begun: now that Kerouac had found his identity as a writer, he needed a publisher. He submitted the typescript of *On the Road* 6 times, and got 6 rejection slips. He threw himself into writing other novels, but feelings of bitterness at being misunderstood were overwhelming him.

Finally, in 1955, he met Malcolm Cowley, an editorial consultant at Viking Press. Cowley was enthusiastic about *On the Road,* but asked Kerouac to make some changes. Otherwise, the book was not publishable. It had to be shortened, cleaned up so that the vocabulary conformed to decency laws, and the characters' identities had to be disguised, to avoid libel charges. A battle-weary Kerouac accepted. In fact, he attacked the book with a chain saw.

On the scroll, the book begins: *"I first met Neal not long after my father died… I had just gotten over a serious illness that I won't bother to talk about except that it had something to do with my father's death and my*

> Hanging out with Neal, he saw the Roman candle, blazing through life with freedom and fury, and the sight helped him focus.

awful feeling that everything was dead. With the coming of Neal there really began for me that part of my life that you could call my life on the road." In the corrected version, that became: *"I first met Dean not long after the death of my father and I thought that everything was dead. My knowledge of the Beat Generation and the road began."* Fortunately, he realized that he was killing his work and at the last minute, he returned to a more faithful version.

THE ROAD TO ACCEPTANCE

Mainly, he erased sex scenes and changed characters' names. For instance, in the scroll, when Jack turns up at Neal's, he reports that as Neal opened the door, *"Louanne was jumping off quickly from the bed; apparently he was fucking with her. He was always doing so."* Kerouac suggested a softer version to his publishers: *"Marylou was jumping off the couch, buttoning her blouse."* But even that was too strong for Viking Press, and the published version simply says: *"Marylou was jumping off the couch."*

On the Road was published on September 5, 1957, after a nine-year journey into the abyss. Recognition had come too late. That's what Kerouac was hinting at, when he glossed over the book's painful birth. As if to say *"Where were you squares on that April day when I finished the book? That's when we should have met."* ✸

ON THE ROAD

Reverting to a simpler style —

Further draft & beginning — Nov. 1949

ITINERARY & PLAN

PORTLAND · BUTTE · SALT LAKE · FRISCO · DENVER · CHI · DET. · N.Y. · WASH · FRESNO · L.A. · EL PASO · HOUSTON · N. ORLEANS

① New York Jail
② Times Square I
③ Road to New O'eans
④ New Orleans
⑤ Road to Frisco
⑥ Frisco (+ Valley)
⑦ Road to Butte
⑧ Butte
⑨ Road to Denver
⑩ Denver

⑪ Road to New York
⑫ Times Square Again

From May to May

CHARACTERS

Red Moultrie
Clem Lemke
Slim Jackson
Old Bull
Dean Pomeray
Marylou
Evelyn Johnson

Mrs. Moultrie
Elena
Old Moultrie
Laura Moultrie
Laurette

And Various Shades

LAST PAGE OF ONE OF KEROUAC'S NOTEBOOKS, TITLED *"NIGHT NOTES AND DIAGRAMS FOR* ON THE ROAD." NOVEMBER 1949

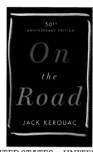

THE BOOK
ON THE ROAD

UNITED STATES ≫ UNITED STATES ≫ UNITED STATES ≫ UNITED STATES ≫ UNITED STATES ≫ UNITED STATES ≫ UNITED STATES ≫ UNITED STATES ≫ UNITED STATES ≫ UNITED STATE

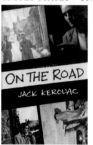
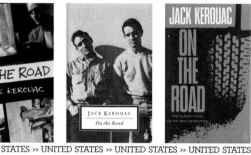

COVER

ON THE ROAD BY JACK KEROUAC

UNITED STATES ≫ UNITED STATES ≫ UNITED STATES ≫ UNITED STATES

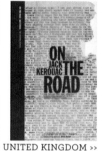

UNITED KINGDOM ≫ UNITED KINGDOM ≫ UNITED KINGDOM ≫ UNITED KINGDOM ≫ UNITED STATES ≫ UNITED STATES

UNITED KINGDOM ≫ UNITED KINGDOM ≫ NETHERLANDS

ITALY ≫ ITALY ≫ ITALY ≫ ITALY ≫ ITALY ≫ ITALY

FRANCE ≫ FRANCE ≫ FRANCE ≫ FRANCE ≫ FRANCE ≫ FRANCE

NETHERLANDS ≫ NETHERLANDS ≫ NETHERLANDS

SPAIN ≫ SPAIN ≫ SPAIN ≫ SPAIN ≫ SPAIN ≫ SPAIN

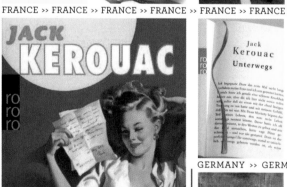

GERMANY ≫ GERMANY ≫ GERMANY ≫ GERMANY ≫ GERMANY ≫ GERMANY ≫ YUGOSLAVIA ≫ VIETNAM ≫ VIETN.

GERMANY ≫ GERMANY ≫ GERMANY ≫ UKRAINE ≫ UKRAINE ≫ UKRAINE ≫ UKRAINE ≫ TAIWAN ≫ TAIWAN ≫ SWEDEN ≫ SWEDEN ≫ SWEDEN ≫ SWEDEN ≫ SWEDEN

DR

TURKEY >> TURKEY >> TURKEY >> TURKEY >> TURKEY >> TURKEY >>   SLOVAKIA   SERBIA >> SERBIA   RUSSIA >> RUSSIA >> RUSSIE >> RUSSIA >> RUSSIA >> RUSSIA

PORTUGAL >> PORTUGAL >> PORTUGAL   ROMANIA >> ROMANIA >> ROMANIA   JAPAN >> JAPAN >> JAPAN >> JAPAN >> JAPAN

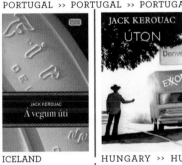

POLAND   NORWAY   PORTUGAL >> PORTUGAL >> PORTUGAL   LITHUANIA >> LITHUANIA >> LITHUANIA >> LITHUANIA >> LITHUANIA >>

ISRAEL   LEBANON   ICELAND   HUNGARY >> HUNGARY >> HUNGARY   CHINA >> CHINA >>

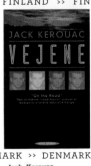

STORY

在路上
on the road

...you could call my life on the road. Prior to that I'd always dreamed of ...

GREECE   FINLAND >> FINLAND >> FINLAND   CHINA >> CHINA >> CHINA >> CHINA >> CHINA

DENMARK >> DENMARK >> DENMARK   CZECH REPUBLIC >> CZECH REPUBLIC >> CZECH REPUBLIC   CROATIA >> CROATIA

ARGENTINA >> ARGENTINA >> ARGENTINA   CZECH REPUBLIC >> CZECH REPUBLIC >>   BULGARIA >> BULGARIA >> BULGARIA   BRAZIL >> BRAZIL >> BRAZIL >> BRAZIL >> BRAZIL

"That's not WRITING, it's typing..."

TRUMAN CAPOTE
TALKING ABOUT
ON THE ROAD

AS REPORTED BY BRUCE COOK IN *THE BEAT GENERATION*
(SCRIBNER'S, 1971)

THE IMPACT OF
ON THE ROAD

ACCLAIM AND BLAME

BY GLADYS MARIVAT
TRANSLATED BY ANITA CONRADE

DRAWING RAVES OR RANTS FROM REVIEWERS, CELEBRATED YET OFTEN MISINTERPRETED BY THE PUBLIC, *ON THE ROAD* WAS FIRST AND FOREMOST AT THE ORIGIN OF A HUGE MISUNDERSTANDING. OVERTAKEN BY THE SOCIOLOGICAL SCOPE OF HIS NOVEL, KEROUAC FOUND HIMSELF CRUSHED BY THE MYTH HE HAD HELPED CREATE.

---

eptember 4, 1957: It's midnight, and Jack Kerouac and his girlfriend Joyce Glassman Johnson are taking a stroll in Manhattan. They have just gotten dressed after making love and are heading for the newsstand at 66th and Broadway in Manhattan to pick up the September 5th edition of the *New York Times*, hot off the press: they're eager to read Gilbert Millstein's review of *On the Road*. Joyce Johnson recalls that night in her famous 1983 essay *Minor Characters*: she says she felt her mind reeling as she read Millstein's first paragraph. They read the review under a streetlamp. When Jack had finished the article, he asked her, 'It's good, isn't

it?' 'Yes,' she said, '*very good.*'" Afterwards, as students would, they adjourned to a bar to reread it, over and over. Kerouac is not overly enthusiastic. Yet Millstein's review is a rave, full of high praise: "*An authentic work of art,*" Millstein wrote, "*a historic event.*" Overnight, Jack Kerouac, aged 35, had become a famous writer. Nevertheless he was already weary. He'd spent 6 years peddling *On the Road* to publishers.

CRITICAL MISJUDGMENT

The success of *Howl* by Allen Ginsberg – mythified by its 1957 obscenity trial in San Francisco, resulting in an acquittal – and the publication of excerpts from *On the Road* in the *Paris Review* had created a buzz of anticipation over the novel's publication. Yet the critics were far from unanimous in their approval. By the end of the year, Kerouac was the subject of vitriolic, hateful, mocking reviews. It is a delectable detail that the day Millstein wrote the review exalting *On the Road* in the *Times*, he was filling in for Orville Prescott, a notoriously conservative critic, then on vacation. Prescott hadn't even bothered to read the novel, and if he'd been at his desk, would have

undoubtedly execrated it.

By September 8th, another *New York Times* critic, David Dempsey, had taken issue with Millstein: "*Jack Kerouac has written an enormously readable and entertaining book but one reads it in the same mood that one might visit a sideshow - the freaks are fascinating although they are hardly part of our lives.*" The following year, in *Horizon* magazine, Robert Brustein published a fiery essay called "*The Cult of Unthink,*" associating Kerouac's neo-tramps Sal Paradise and Dean Moriarty with menacing motorcycle hoodlums, "*tribal followers of Marlon Brando and James Dean.*" In brief, most critics saw *On the Road* as a sweet fantasy, written for circus performers and other lunatic-fringe hipsters, devoid of true literary value.

In France, condescending critics popped the same bubble of anticipation. In September 1959, Ernest van den Haag wrote in *Les Temps Modernes* that the book's success was a mere flash in the publisher's pan, written to satisfy what he called "*beat hipsters,*" frighteningly idle youth, self-destructive and violent. He firmly believed that within a few years, *On the Road* would be considered devoid of any literary interest. He added, "*Kerouac has*

> # " He fondly congratulated me FOR THE BOOK I had finished, which was now accepted by the publishers

> " *On the Road*, Penguin Classics, 2002

nothing to say, and says it badly. But the most embarrassing part is that he's absolutely sincere. Could one be inspired by anything worse in such a case?" Kerouac liked to compare his writing to Marcel Proust's and he worshipped Thomas Wolfe, Fyodor Dostoyevsky, James Joyce, and Henry Miller. The critics had derailed.

A HERO DESPITE HIMSELF

Beyond the small world of the critics, the novel continued to make waves, conquering a large audience. By January 1958, *On the Road* had become required reading at two American universities. The following month, the book was reprinted three times. American youth immediately identified with Sal and Dean, the way they had with Jim Stark (James Dean) and Judy (Natalie Wood) in *Rebel Without a Cause* (1955). Kerouac was flooded with more fan mail than he could handle. In a 1971 interview with Daniel Odier, William Burroughs remarked: "*The literary importance of the Beatnik movement is perhaps not as obvious as its sociological importance... it really has transformed the world and populated the world with Beatniks.*" Had he needed to, he could have cited Ken Kesey leading a horde of Merry Pranksters

across the country in 1965, all aboard a bus driven by... Neal Cassady. As if Gary Snyder's prophecy, transcribed in *The Dharma Bums* by Jack Kerouac, had finally come true: "*Think of the millions of guys all over the world with rucksacks on their backs tramping around the back country and hitchhiking and bringing the word down to everybody.*" Would Kerouac be the "Beat Generation's Pope"? In *After me, the deluge*, an explosively violent rant published in the *Chicago Tribune* a month before he died, Kerouac attacked the "*leftists*" inspired by his heroes' rebellion. Now the public was guilty of misjudgment.

SAVAGE INNOCENCE

In the 70s and 80s, a few critics, like writer Gérard-Georges Lemaire, attempted to point out the complexity of Kerouac and his work. John Byrum's film *Heart Beat* was a huge flop, criticized for showing something other than the fantasy image of a free-spirited lad and his jolly group of followers. In the 1990 French edition of *Visions of Cody*, Yves Buin wrote a postface entitled "*Jack Kerouac and the Golden Eternity*," in which he insists on the profoundly religious nature of the writer's work. But the misunderstanding continued.

From very early on, Kerouac had faith in the vision that his work was valuable, and would become an American classic. In a 1952 letter to his friend John Clellon Holmes, he borrowed idioms from bebop to write: "*I am blowing such mad poetry and literature that I'll look back years later with amazement and chagrin that I can't do it anymore.*" He claimed that no one would understand for another 15 or 20 years, except for himself and Allen Ginsberg (maybe). In 1974, five years after the death of their friend, Allen Ginsberg and Anne Waldman founded the Jack Kerouac School of Disembodied Poetics at Naropa University, in Boulder, Colorado. Created by Chögyam Trungpa, a Buddhist monk and former Oxford professor, the university welcomes thousands of students to its creative writing program every year. They are asked to open wide their mind and consciousness in order to develop a contemplative approach to literature. As if, at last, they'd been invited to ride on Kerouac's true road, described in this 1952 letter to Holmes: "*I have begun to discover something beyond the novel and beyond the arbitrary confines of the story... into the realms of revealed picture... revealed whatever... revelated prose... wild form, man, wild form!*"

THE BRIDGE FROM CITY LIGHTS BOOKSTORE TO SHAKESPEARE AND COMPANY

In San Francisco, the alley alongside City Lights Bookstore on Columbus Avenue in North Beach is named after Jack Kerouac. Sal Paradise lives! City Lights is where former Czech dissident Václav Havel made his first stop on American soil, just after being released from jail and elected president. Lawrence Ferlinghetti, who founded the bookshop in 1953, was a poet himself, and the first who dared to publish Allen Ginsberg's sultry *Howl*. Hordes of tourists, nostalgic for the Beat Generation, now congregate at the shrine. But it's hard to imagine that this quiet, well-lit space once housed raucous readings where Cassady, Kerouac, Ginsberg, Corso and Burroughs caroused and drank until the wee hours… before adjourning to the Vesuvio Café next door. In the 1950s, Beat poets who regularly drove or hitched from the East Coast to the West could get their mail c/o City Lights Bookstore. When it opened, the shop was the only one in the country selling quality paperbacks, including the Pocket Poets Series Ferlinghetti brought out. Its affordable editions of Rexroth, Patchen, Levertov, and Bly were a delight to penniless young poetry lovers. A 1968 photograph shows a VW bus parked in front of the bookshop. Ferlinghetti would fill it with aspiring writers and drive them around the Bay Area. And if all the rooms upstairs from the bookstore were full, there were beds in the bus.

Shakespeare And Company, in Paris, is known for the same commitment and hospitality to aspiring writers. When the Paris authorities wanted to shut down the bookstore in 1961, the owner George Whitman appealed to the Minister of Culture, André Malraux. He wrote that, in his opinion, he was less a bookseller than someone practicing *"friendship through books."* Whitman, who died in December 2011, had opened the shop in 1951, two years before City Lights. He knew Ferlinghetti, having met him

GEORGE WHITMAN (FACING) WITH THE AMERICAN POET TED JOANS (ON THE RIGHT, WITH THE *BÉRET*) IN FRONT OF THE SHAKESPEARE & CO. LIBRARY IN PARIS.

in Paris shortly after the war. Together, they had dreamed of a bookstore where young writers could meet in a friendly environment. They chose different locations, but always maintained strong bonds. Whitman hosted legendary readings of *Howl* by Ginsberg and *Naked Lunch* by Burroughs, where the crowd filled the sidewalk all the way to the banks of the Seine. According to the anecdote, Burroughs picked up his last lover browsing at Shakespeare And Company; Kerouac undoubtedly spent time there, but left absolutely no trace. Like Ferlinghetti, Whitman published writings by Ginsberg: *Kansas City to St. Louis* is a long ballad about a journey, printed in the October 1967 issue of *Paris Magazine*, a literary magazine published sporadically by Shakespeare And Company.

Perhaps the best illustration of the fact the Beat Generation formed one big family, from the Left Bank of Paris to the Left Coast of the US, is the book *Fire Reading,* published in 1991 to pay for stock destroyed in a tragic blaze. Ferlinghetti contributed a text about the day he met George Whitman. He likens him to *"the ghost of Stephen Dedalus,"* hero of *Ulysses*, by James Joyce, lost among the stacks of books in his small room at the Hôtel de Suez. **GM**

ON THE ROAD AND THE TRADITION OF THE "GREAT AMERICAN NOVEL"

A NOVEL IN SPACE

BY GLADYS MARIVAT
TRANSLATED BY ANITA CONRADE

★

FINDING ONE'S PLACE AS AN INDIVIDUAL AND GRASPING THE ESSENCE OF THE UNITED STATES: WITH *ON THE ROAD*, KEROUAC RECONNECTS WITH THE TRADITION OF THE "GREAT AMERICAN NOVEL" FIRST SHOULDERED BY MARK TWAIN AND THOMAS WOLFE, AND THEIR SUCCESSORS WILLIAM T. VOLMANN, HUNTER S. THOMPSON, AND THOMAS PYNCHON.

★

ver since *The Adventures of Huckleberry Finn* by Mark Twain (1884) was crowned the first modern American novel, generations of young writers have racked their brains to write "The Great American Novel.." The form was first defined in 1868 by Civil War soldier, reporter, and novelist John William De Forest, writing in the magazine the *Nation*. Such a novel, he said, would be the picture of *"the ordinary emotions and manners of American existence."* It would declare its independence from the influence of English literature, and be written in a Yankee idiom capable of expressing the history of a new country. Because

Huck and Jim spoke the vernacular English of 50 million Americans, celebrating its spontaneity, because the book showed the true face of America's common man, without scorn for his lack of sophistication, Twain's novel was a radical departure. In the late 40s, when the young Kerouac set out on his journey his mind set on his writing, his ambition was *"to bust out from the European narrative into the Mood Chapters of an American poetic 'sprawl'."* A great admirer of the poet Walt Whitman (1819-1892), Jack Kerouac wanted, like Whitman, to invent *"a modern prose for America."* According to Whitman, the poet worthy of America would employ the native dialect of the United States to pen *"mighty and vital breezes, proportionate to our continent, with its powerful races of men, its tremendous historic events, its great oceans, its mountains and its illimitable prairies."*

"A STRANGER IN HIS OWN HOME"

Kerouac began his search for a new style, a language broad enough to encompass the American continent. Like Mark Twain and Thomas Wolfe before him, Kerouac was fired by the

> *"(Thomas Wolfe) opened my eyes to America as a subject in itself."*
> JACK KEROUAC

specifically American feeling of a restless identity. In 1941, after dropping out of Columbia University, he reread Thomas Wolfe's autobiographical narratives *Look Homeward, Angel* (1929) and *Of Time and the River* (1935). Both written in the Joycean *"stream of consciousness"* style, relating the adventures of a young American who travels to Europe, the novels seek to express *"the strange and bitter magic of life."* Kerouac later called Wolfe *"a torrent of American heaven and hell that opened my eyes to America as a subject in itself."* Indeed, Kerouac's first novel, *The Town and the City,* could be said to be entirely Wolfeian. Finding his own true voice and liberating himself from Wolfe's formality and classicism came when Kerouac met Neal Cassady. Cassady, born in Utah and raised in half-outlaw style, seemed

JACK AND JOYCE JOHNSON, AUTUMN 1957, IN FRONT OF THE KETTLE OF FISH BAR IN GREENWICH VILLAGE, NEW YORK

> ## "
> # IT WAS WESTERN,
> ## the west wind, an ode from the Plains,
> # SOMETHING NEW,
> ## long prophesied, long a-coming
>
> **"** *On the Road*, p. 24, Penguin Classics, 2002

to Kerouac to incarnate the myth of the West and the pioneers crossing the Great Plains, the Rockies, and the deserts to reach the Pacific.

Like many Americans of his generation, Kerouac was nostalgic for the pioneer myth of going ever westward, synonymous with *"health, open-mindedness, and an immemorial dream of freedom and joy,"* according to John Clellon Holmes. For the Beat Generation writers wandering was part of wondering. In his *Autobiography*, Lawrence Ferlinghetti, the Beat poet, publisher, and bookseller of San Francisco, explains that the most prevailing concern of a Beat writer was to explore the world and discover his identity, not to settle down. In *On the Road*, Sal Paradise wants to be *"reading the American landscape"* and *"the American night"* through the car window. But he is crushed by the vastness of the wide open spaces, especially in the Great Plains, in the

central American city of Des Moines and feels he will always be a outsider. In *Visions of Cody* (written between 1951 and 1952), Kerouac again expressed this vision of America, simultaneously cruel and tender, petty and immense. In fact, in an ultimate avowal of defeat, the book is dedicated *"To America, whatever that is."*

SELF RENEWAL

In 1949, in his *Journal*, Kerouac scribbled, *"I feel that I'm the only person in the world who doesn't know the feeling of calm irreverence - the only madman in the world therefore - the only broken fish. All the others are perfectly contented with pure life. I am not."* Travel, solitude in the wilderness at Big Sur, and adventure could then be envisaged as quests in themselves - not to discover one's identity, but to change it in the search. *"Renew yourself each day; do it again, and again, and forever again,"* wrote American philosopher

Henry David Thoreau from his retreat at Walden Pond. A century earlier, the French philosopher Rousseau admonished, *"Perish, or change."* For the writers who have submitted to the ordeal of self transformation - Kerouac, Thoreau, or Jim Harrison, in his novella *Legends of the Fall* (1979) – encountering Nature one-on-one is a powerful experience, the source of comfort and counsel. According to Kerouac, *"No one should go through life without once experiencing healthy, even bored solitude in the wilderness, finding himself depending solely on himself and thereby learning his true and hidden strength."*

HOBO LIT

Kerouac joined the great family of writers wandering the American countryside, from Thoreau to Vollmann, Jack London to Hunter S. Thompson. *"The mad people, the mad ones, the ones who were mad to live, mad to talk, mad to be saved,"* as Kerouac himself described them in *On the Road*. Jack London's *curriculum vitae* could have applied to them all: adventurer, writer, sailor, farmer, dreamer, wanderer and alcoholic. They were often considered literature's outlaws, scribbling wild poems or memoirs of Alaska that immortalized them.

From Whitman's *Song of the Open Road* to Cormac McCarthy's *The Road*, leaving home has played a central role in defining America's image of itself. Exploring the great country is a path to knowing oneself, to freedom from convention, conformism, convenience, and excessive comfort. As an outsider, the traveler is a keener observer, of himself and others. Sal Paradise, Kerouac's hero, strikes out in search of a beyond where he will find the answer to the great human question: *"how should one live?"* Kerouac would join his predecessors Thoreau and Twain as an influence on American writers pursuing distant horizons, hungry for transcendent visions, for *"rare pearls."*

LIKE A *HOBO*

Although Hunter S. Thompson never refers to them directly, the ghosts of Dean Moriarty and Sal Paradise haunt the duo experiencing *Fear and Loathing in Las Vegas*. Visions induced by LSD, ether, cocaine, whiskey, mescaline, and cannabis keep the narrative jumping. Spontaneity and the spoken word triumph: life and writing become one. Thompson, who coined the term *gonzo journalism* for his first-person tales, asserted in his

Jack London's *curriculum vitae* could have applied to them all: Adventurer, dreamer, writer, alcoholic.

> Leaving home has played a central role in defining America's image of itself. Exploring the great country is a path to knowing oneself, to freedom from convention, conformism, convenience, and excessive comfort.

biography by William McKeen: *"I almost never try to reconstruct a story... I like to get right in the middle of whatever I'm writing about - as personally involved as possible."* Kerouac might have said the same thing, as he furiously noted his conversations with Cassady, in a breathless effort to record life's profuse blossoming of impressions with spontaneous prose.

In 2008, when writer and journalist William T. Vollmann published *Riding Toward Everywhere*, based on his roamings across America, he could not help but be permanently attuned to *On the Road*. Just as the writings of Wolfe and Thoreau colored Kerouac's vision of America, Kerouac's tales of the *"dharma bums"* haunted Vollmann as he vagabonded by train, listening to the rustic clackety-clack. In the 1950s, Kerouac and the Beat writers took to the highway to flee the constraints of conformism. Half a century later, Vollmann vagabonds from Wyoming to Montana in search of the place of self-awareness, in reaction to the increasingly extremist and securitarian politics of America (he wrote the book in 2005, during George W. Bush's term). He says that riding a freight train is like *"being in a kernel of popping popcorn,"* and it saves his sanity. The questions *"Where am I?"* and *"Who am I?"* blur, forming one. Like Kerouac, Vollmann is eager to find *"the true West,"* despite his affection for the bodhisattva Hanshan – the Tang Dynasty poet whose name means *"Cold Mountain"* and whose

wisdom inspired Beat poet Gary Snyder, romping through *The Dharma Bums* as Japhy Ryder. Vollmann, like the author of *On the Road*, notes that he only loves the landscapes seen from the moving train, as if home, the place where one comes from, existed mainly and most perfectly in one's florid imagination. Like Hemingway's novella *Last Good Country*, which remained unfinished.

In one of the many letters Kerouac wrote to his friend Holmes in 1952, he enthused over his plans for his own "Great American Novel," *"an enormous Dostoyevskyan novel about all of us."* The undertaking was pursued by others, including Tom Robbins, David Foster Wallace with *Infinite Jest*, or Thomas Pynchon with *Mason & Dixon*. When the latter was published, *New Republic* literary critic James Wood accused Pynchon, who acknowledges his debt to Kerouac and the Beat Generation writers, of *"hysterical realism."* Wood nevertheless admits that today, any American author who tries to embrace the whole country – its excessive vitality, its cults of image and wealth – can tackle the job only with hyperbole and anger. He would undoubtedly have panned Kerouac's attempt, with its *"wild form, man, wild form."* ●

"THE ONLY WAR THAT MATTERS IS THE WAR AGAINST THE IMAGINATION"

DIANE DI PRIMA

EXTRACT FROM DIANE DI PRIMA'S POEM *RANT* (1985), IN *PIECES OF A SONG* (1990)

THE BEATS AND MINORITIES

DISSONANCE IN A MINOR KEY

BY CLÉMENTINE GALLOT
TRANSLATED BY ANITA CONRADE

★

IN ITS CELEBRATION OF THE HEALTHY, HANDSOME, FIT WHITE MALE, *ON THE ROAD* CONTAINED STRONG UNDERCURRENTS THAT SHIFTED THE FOUNDATIONS OF THE BEAT GENERATION IN AMBIVALENT DIRECTIONS. THE MOVEMENT THAT DARED NOT SAY ITS NAME AFFIRMED, IDEALIZED, INSTRUMENTALIZED, AND IGNORED MINORITIES. DOWN WITH THE AMBIGUITIES.

★

What if the hedonism of *On the Road* were just a decoy? Behind the seemingly apolitical screen of its frenetic quest for pleasure, the novel's ideology is a brew of American racial, sexual, and gender stereotypes. It vacillates between backwardness and being ahead of its time. The autobiographical ode to the white Adonis leaves very little space for homosexuals, women, Indians, blacks, and Hispanics. The Beats' relations with minorities demonstrate a plurality of attitudes. When Kerouac's novel was published, he was propelled into an artistic vanguard, where many figures who occupied borderline areas and subcultures were the forerunners of radical societal change. The entire spectrum of political tendencies existed within the movement, although Kerouac usually remained an observer. According to writer Barry Miles, Kerouac was a pro-McCarthy Republican who *"thought existentialism was a Communist plot."* But on good days, Kerouac professed detachment and non-involvement, writing, in 1963, *"Camus would have had us turn literature into mere propaganda... Myself, I'm only an ex-sailor, I have no politics, I don't even vote."* Meanwhile, William Burroughs was writing about systems of thought control, while Allen Ginsberg was involved in campaigns against nuclear weapons and, later, the Vietnam War. Both Burroughs and Ginsberg supported the early gay-rights movement.

UNCOMMITTED

In relation to the reigning de facto racial segregation, the young Beat authors were fairly free, gladly venturing into the *"Negro streets,"* seeking entertainment and kicks in jazz clubs that were supposed to be off-limits to whites. Black music, particularly bebop, is a founding theme of Beat

Racial injustice is rarely challenged in *On the Road*, a *"race blind"* novel.

writing, and essential to the quest for the elusive *"IT."* According to scholars John d'Emilio and Estelle B. Freedman, authors of *Intimate Matters: A History of Sexuality in America*, the Beats at least made the *"non-white"* world visible to the WASP ruling class: *"The Beats drew inspiration of sorts from the black hipster of the northern ghettos who moved in a world of jazz, drugs, and sex."* And yet the shared reefers, finger-popping, and good times did not necessarily lead to any political engagement to fight racial injustice, rarely challenged in the novel. "On the Road *is race-blind,*" explains Ray Carney, a professor at Boston University. "On the Road *reflects the time it was created. A post-war America with no recognition of most of the great issues that would come to the forefront of American life in the decade and a half that followed Kerouac's novel. The race problem does not exist. The passage near the beginning of part three of* On the Road, *with its paean to "the happy,* true-hearted, ecstatic Negros of America" captures the complete blindness of Kerouac's novel to the racial issues that deeply divided America. Political and geopolitical issues are not dealt with in Kerouac's novel."

JACK IN THE CLOSET

The narrative describes the fluidity of sexual behavior, its accounts of casual sex for cash, wife-swapping, and bisexuality heralding the erotic explosion of the post-Pill 60s. Carlo Marx, the only homosexual in the novel who is really "out", becomes Moriarty's agitated lover. Later, Moriarty secretly sells his beauty to a "fag" in a hotel room (the novel merely alludes to the scene, but the film treats it more frontally). The homoerotic relationship between Dean and Sal, a literary sublimation of the unresolved sexual tension between Kerouac and Cassady, has elicited much comment. Ann Charters, Kerouac's indulgent biographer, writes: "Kerouac's attitude toward homosexuality was complex and ambivalent. He couldn't accept it in Ginsberg as anything but a weakness." Writer Barry Miles adds: "Kerouac always embraced his parents right-wing ideas: he came out of a French Canadian catholic background, very reactionary, old fashioned and intolerant and he never really changed, he kept quiet about it in the early years and later on he was more outspoken about it. Also he had a gay side to him which he tried to repress and was embarrassed and ashamed of but he did have sex with quite a lot of men. The only one who talks about it is Gore Vidal in Palimpseste." The effort to reconcile his religious convictions with his sexual confusion

"Kerouac always shared the viewpoint of his parents, reactionary , right-wing catholics."
BARRY MILES

drove Kerouac into the classic repressed homosexual-homophobic configuration.

D'Emilio and Freedman see Beat subculture and the gay world overlapping. For example, Allen Ginsberg was transfixed with love for Neal Cassady, although he wrote Howl for Kerouac. The Beats' sexually-liberated artistic practices facilitated the emergence of the gay genre in American literature, a radical departure from the hetero-normativity dominant in the fiction of the time. But although the militant activism of Ginsberg and Burroughs (author of Queer) helped attitudes evolve and contributed to the formation of the LGBT liberation movements, "legitimate" homosexuality was still masculine – to state the obvious.

WHAT WERE THE GIRLS UP TO?

"Marylou, rustle around the kitchen, see what there is." Obviously, the men take it for granted she'll obey. Feminism had yet to rear its rebellious head. Though Kerouac's female characters are not puritanical about their sexuality – already a great step forward in America - On the Road relegates them to the background in a story that associates the cult of the male with the wide open spaces. Despite the many acclaimed women poets on the Beat scene, they are astonishingly invisible in the novel's plot. According to Ray Carney: "The women are not only just 'along for the ride,' as in many Hollywood movies, they are simply not present in the major scenes of his novel. They are purely supporting characters and sex objects: mothers, lovers, and wives; but never intellectual or imaginative equals to the men. This is the side of Beat culture that Cassavetes was critiquing in the second version of Shadows." Kerouac's trip may be revolutionizing America, but the male mentality of the time, condescending and paternalistic, still rules in its macho ethos. Critics like Barry Miles readily point out that On

Despite the many acclaimed women poets on the Beat scene, they are astonishingly invisible in the novel's plot.

the Road and Beat culture in general "were terribly sexist. Women weren't allowed to do anything" besides cook and make babies. The conservative mainstream sexual politics didn't ruffle Kerouac who held such a consumerist attitude about sex that he kept lists of the women he slept with, recording the number of times they made love. Barry Miles call this a "capitalist accumulation" of sex, and admits it is a bit pathetic, worlds away from a Rabelaisian orgy full of joy and energy. Burroughs found Kerouac's sex life depressing. As for Carolyn Cassady, she has written that Neal knew so little about gentleness, sex with him was like being raped.

Kerouac may have given the Beats their young, masculine face, but authors Diane di Prima, Hettie Jones, Joyce Johnson, Joan Vollmer, and Josephine Miles were Beat poets in good standing. A sub-category in a movement that was subterranean itself, they bridged two eras, democratizing literature and opening the horizon of the strait-laced poetry of the 1940s. Poet Anne Waldman says: "It was often a challenge, worrying about Burroughs' misogny, or whether I was being perceived in a sexual way, but that was common in the 50s and 60s milieu." In the words of Hettie Jones: "We weren't at all like the women Kerouac wrote about. (...) When I was married to LeRoi, I was the one working. (...) The men were overpowering and took up a lot of time. The women's movement which happened in the seventies was an inspiration to those of us who had been the first." As practically the only surviving Beats, they are now the voice of a movement that is part of literary history – or should one say 'herstory'? ●

1962

1. Edie — 100   NY, NJ, Detroit, Ontario
2. Jeanie — 25   Washington
2A. ~~Beth Washington~~ — 2
3. ~~Margie — 20   Lowell~~
3A. ~~Ellen~~ — 2
4. Celine — 1   NY
5. Donna — 4   NY
6. Laya — 7   Lowell
7. DeSoto — 2   Sidney, N. Scotia
8. Kitty — 1   Hartford
9. ~~Hannah~~ — 1   Middletown, Ct.
10. Doris M. (of Newton, Mass.) 3   NY
11. Lillian — 2   London, England
12. Sarah — 3   Washington
13. Wash. — 1   Washington (as sailor)
14. Mary Filth 3   Lowell
15. Jean B. — 1   Lowell
16. Laya Jr. — 1   Lowell
17. Red — 1   N.Y.
18. Lucille — 2   N.Y.
19. Kay — 1   N.Y.
20. Raleigh — 1   Raleigh, N.C.
21. Horrors — 1   Boston (194— ?)
22. Spanish — 1   N.Y.
23. Joan — 1   N.Y.
      Adams

         23 — 175
23A. Rita B. — beaver
24. Vicki — 5   N.Y. 15
24½A Girl in Valley
25. Peggy B. — 3   N.Y.
26. Jerry L — 1   N.Y.
27. Ruth S. — 2   N.Y.
       Heaphy
28. Harlem — 1   N.Y. — 28 — 187
28A. Jeanne Fitz 10   NY Philippine
29. June — 3   N.Y. & Calif. 2
30. ~~Celine~~   N.Y.
31. Joan H. 150   N.Y.
32. Merrill J. 4   N.Y.
33. Carolyn C. 30   Calif.
34. Dusty 3   N.Y.
   35. Barnard 1 N.Y. (Joanie)
      36. Renk 4 N.Y.
         37. Lil Harlem 2 Calif.
            (over)

38. Anxck 1 Mexico
39. Luz 1 Mexico
40. Mexico 1950-52 (5)
41. Alene 40 N.Y.
42. Frisco gals Oaklans
   San Pedro
42A. N.Y.U. Junkie
43. Mary ACK 10 N.Y.
44. Esperanza '56
45. Helen W. 25
46. Joyce G. 15
47. Arabs Tangiers
48. Paris Italienne
49. Ellie Paris
49A. Lucille 2nd Ave.
50. (Gita girl)
51. Rose G. book
51. Lois 50
52. Dody 50
53. Gregory girl
54. Sally Teeth
55. DiPrima
56. Helen Elliot Calif
57. Jackie C. Calif
58. Gretchen Mexcity
59. Theodora 1'Givens
60. Yseult

BROOKLYN SOULAS

61. Lee (bryn) 10
62. Penny '56 Frisco
63. Lowell Middlesex room
64. Helen P. Truro 50 2 acts
65. Nancy dukes 10
66. Tropp N.Y.
67. "Rachel"
68. Lee Piano 25
69. Steve Allen girl
70. Carnegie Hall "Balloons"
71. Washington Madame
72. San Pedro
73. Dreaming Bankside
74. In Hel's room (brunettes)
75. Adele 25
76. Kolb's moll
77. Bev Colo & Savio 25
78. Sara Y. 25
79. Ginger
80. Rose Dauphine St.
81. JM
82. Joyce Paris
83. Phd 3
84. Soud'un
85. (Anny) Ross

THE LIST OF JACK'S LOVERS THAT HE COMPILED IN 1962 – THE NUMBER ON THE RIGHT IS THOUGHT TO BE THE NUMBER OF SEXUAL ENCOUNTERS WITH EACH PERSON

HOW THE BEAT PIONEERS REINVENTED THE ROAD TRIP

BEAT IT

BY ÉTIENNE ROUILLON
TRANSLATED BY ANITA CONRADE

★

THE TITLE ALONE GIVES YOU ITCHY FEET. IT IS A MANIFESTO FOR AIMLESSNESS, A MAP THAT KEEPS UNFOLDING. ON THE ROAD SPAWNED A NEW WAY OF HITTING THE HIGHWAY, FOOTLOOSE AND FANCY FREE YET PART OF A NOMADIC COMMUNITY. THE BEATS' GEOGRAPHIC, POETIC, AND PERSONAL JOURNEYS SIRED A MIGRATORY SPIRIT THAT STILL HAS THE POWER TO SWAY TODAY'S WRITERS.

★

He's a hobo. He tells me he started at age 13. Like this: "I've been ridin' the rails for thirty years." Holy shit, you think: "Yeah, thirty years of hopping freight cars!" This guy was the key encounter of my trip, the symbol of transgression, of freedom, of self-fulfillment through and by wandering. When I left for the United States to write Dans les roues de Jack Kerouac, my idea was not to drive the same highways he did, but to go meet people who still cultivate Kerouac's state of mind, the motor behind his journey. To pull up your roots, and never settle down. You can guess a hobo hasn't read

many books. But, Kerouac's On the Road, *he can certainly dig that."* If a coal car rolled past Christophe Cousin at a nice lazy pace, there's no doubt he'd jump on. His propensity for this type of ticket earned him some altercations with police in a Trans-Siberian bisecting Mongolia. Before he became one of the most brilliant French travel writers currently trotting the globe, Christophe lived on his parents' farm in the Loiret, surrounded by 430 acres of fields. He escaped by reading: Jack London for the wilderness, Nicolas Bouvier for the human side, and the atlas for horizons. And the motivation for vagabonding and its poetry came directly from the Beats: Kerouac, Ginsberg, and Burroughs.

LONESOME HIGHWAY

One thing is puzzling: these guys were poets, Baudelairean temperaments capable of imagining *"a hemisphere in a head of hair."* Why would they bother to go clog up their lungs – already damaged by Benzedrine – with dust from roughly paved roads? The Beats obeyed the call of the pioneers, cowboys, and prospectors, blazing trails to the West, even though their conquest established the basis for a

> The Beats obeyed the call of the pioneers, cowboys, and prospectors, blazing trails to the West.

society the Beats are determined to stay on the fringes of. This is the theory developed by Jacqueline Starer, author of *Les Écrivains beats et le voyage* (1977). According to her analysis, the idea of a Beat community is an artificial construct. Although the concept finally won over some followers, it does not account for the individuality of these writers: they may have been friends, but in their artistic pursuits, they were loners. One common denominator remains: the refusal to conform in any way, as creators or social activists. They also share an escape hatch: travel, either imaginary or geographical. The main thing is to move and be moved. *"With their 'New Vision,' they contributed the basis of a New Sensibility that was beginning to sweep America; then, after leaving New York, drawn across the continent by Cassady, they discover their land, seek their identity, and try to*

THIERRY VERNET BETWEEN PRILEP AND ISTANBUL, PHOTOGRAPHED BY THE SWISS TRAVEL WRITER NICOLAS BOUVIER IN 1953

transform themselves." Jacqueline Starer sees Huckleberry Finn as the grandfather of the Beat pioneer, stirred by the need to take in the wide open spaces in order to find a way to belong. An initiatory journey, in other words.

Nevertheless, the Beat's quest has a ferocious originality that endures, inspiring today's backpackers and wanderers. It is an aimless journey, with no particular destination: just a vanishing point in the distance. *On the Road* consists entirely of constant departures, every time Sal Paradise seems to settle down: as a night watchman in San Francisco, a picker in the cotton fields, sonny boy at Mama's house. He stops only long enough to make his decision to move on even more dramatic. But the real journey is elsewhere. According to Christophe Cousin, *"the writing is the second journey. The one that enables you to put together the pieces of the first. I don't know exactly how Kerouac went about it. Of course, I've heard the story of how he typed out the scroll in three weeks, in one fell swoop. Did he take many notes while he was traveling? In any case, to my thinking, Kerouac personifies the boundary between two schools of writer-travelers. There are those who are able to tell a highly accurate story of what they experienced at a specific point in time. And there are others who, like Jack Kerouac, are possessed by another form of writing, which is more poetic because their memory is blurred. It gives rise to a more impressionistic text. That's how I function, because my memory is not that sharp, and yet I take very few notes when*

DAY 24, DENVER-BIG MOUNTAIN, PHOTOGRAPH TAKEN FROM *DANS LES ROUES DE JACK KEROUAC* ("IN JACK KEROUAC'S WHEELS") BY CHRISTOPHE COUSIN AND MATTHIEU PALEY

I'm actually traveling. I get out my notebook only to record the esthetic or emotional poetry of an instant. For instance, I wouldn't write down what we say during this interview, but I would recall the hint of red on the two chairs over there, in the back of the room. Three words could bring the whole scene back to me. And it doesn't matter if the writing distorts the events. When people asked Kerouac, 'Did that really happen to you?' he would answer, 'As soon as I write it down, it becomes a fact.' When my publisher offered me this project, Dans les Roues de Jack Kerouac, *I accepted because the challenge was to write it in less than five weeks. Composition can be torture for me,* unless I'm in an impossible rush. When I got back, I'd sit down at my desk and start writing at nine in the morning. By noon, I'd moved to another spot, and in the afternoon, somewhere else again. The next day, I'd do exactly the same thing. My ten pages a day. The energy, the way of writing by drawing on my memories and the few notes I had... Then, I really felt like I was in osmosis with* On the Road."

BLOG-TROTTER

In the summer of 2008, writer Guillaume Chérel told the tale of his trip from New York to San Francisco online in *Sur les pas de Jack Kerouac* (http://kerouac.blogs.liberation.fr), a blog

"The writing is the second journey. The one that enables you to put together the pieces of the first..."
CHRISTOPHE COUSIN

Almost immediately, *On the Road* soared to cult-novel status. It's an invitation to wander, before you even open the book, before you even know what it's about. Its magnetism undoubtedly lies in its literary uniqueness, but also in its ability to express the need to keep moving.

need to keep moving. The same belief guides the many contributors to online travel forums hosted by alternative guides like *Le Guide du routard* or *Lonely Planet*. Members exchange the exact address of a bar where Jack drank, or of a grave. With handles like 'Kerouac' and 'Sal Paradise,' these connoisseurs are in perfect harmony with the trips they recommend. *On the Road* is cited as a travel contract, if not a Bible. For example, on a thread devoted to *"chauffeur-guides in India,"* on *routard.com*, 'bubu06' rages: *"The real routard is a thing of the past. A Beat Generation wanderer (...) (for those who have read Jack Kerouac) would never have rented a taxi to cross India."*

GYPSY SPIRIT

Almost immediately, *On the Road* soared to cult-novel status. It's an invitation to wander, before you even open the book, before you even know what it's about. Its magnetism undoubtedly lies in its literary uniqueness, but also in its ability to express the need to keep moving. The restless spirit is not the exclusive property of the Beats, however. There were other roads, as well. One path is practically the twin of Kerouac's, taking place at the same time – in fact, they intersected. In 1948, another trio of friends climbed into a Ford Hudson and drove out of New York headed for the West Coast, via Mexico, hoping to land a job at Walt Disney Studios. Fortunately, they returned to Europe, and had monumental careers as comic-book artists: Jijé (*Spirou*), Franquin (*Gaston*), and Morris (*Lucky Luke*). In 2011, the zany odyssey appeared in the pages of the magazine *Spirou*, entitled *Gringos Locos* with a story by Yann and illustrations by Olivier Schwartz.

A few years later, between 1953 and 1954, another pair of travelers set out, on another continent. They drive a Fiat Topolino all the way from Switzerland to Afghanistan, its breakdowns earning the pair new friends. Many readers disappointed in *On the Road* are delighted by the extraordinary psychological and physical journey of *The Way of the World*, by Swiss writer Nicolas Bouvier. Finally, Bouvier reconciles them with Kerouac: Christophe Cousin is one such reader (see the box on page 224): *"You imagine* On the Road *is going to be great, but it doesn't survive the reading. The thing I missed the first time I started it was the idea of a journey to meet the Other. Because that isn't Kerouac's goal."* Sal Paradise is fleeing a world, whereas Nicolas Bouvier and his travel companion Thierry Vernet choose to embrace it. Christophe goes on: *"There's a great generosity in the way Bouvier tells about the people he meets. That's why I made the encounters such an important part of* Dans les roues de Jack Kerouac. *It was a means of going beyond the simple plan of experiencing Jack Kerouac's trip for myself, a way of revealing the universality of the road."* Bouvier or Kerouac, two ways of expressing the same observation, the first sentences of *The Way of the World*: *"You think you're going to take a trip, but soon the trip takes you. And it makes you or breaks you."* ◉

hosted by the Paris daily *Libération* and haunted by Ti-Jean's imprint. Post by post, Chérel narrows down his answer to the question his readers continually hint at in comments (often virulent and exasperated): Why the hell take the same road as Kerouac? Was Chérel embarking on an exhaustive pilgrimage to the landmarks dotting Kerouac's trail? Or was he trying to contrast the rugged individualists of yesteryear and today with the more insidious conformism of contemporary America? Loyal to his Beat mentor, Guillaume Chérel avoided forging an explicit reason for his journey. Like the trip in *On the Road*, it had only one requirement to fulfill: the imperious

THE BOOK

ON THE ROAD

ROCKERS AND BEAT LEGACY

THE ROAD TO ROCK

BY ÉRIC VERNAY
TRANSLATED BY ANITA CONRADE

SEX, DRUGS, NON-CONFORMITY, AND BOHEMIA: THE FORCES THAT DROVE ROCK CULTURE TO ITS CURRENT PINNACLE STATUS WERE ALREADY AT THE HEART OF THE BEAT GENERATION. KEROUAC, IN PARTICULAR, HAS ALWAYS FASCINATED ROCKERS. AS DEMONSTRATED HERE, THE PANORAMA OF ARTISTS PAYING HOMAGE TO HIM NOW STRETCHES INTO ITS FIFTH DECADE...

ack Kerouac, Allen Ginsberg, and William S. Burroughs, the big three of the Beats, had a crucial impact on folk, rock, punk, and hip-hop music well into the 70s, 80s, and 90s. Today, this kinship seems natural and almost logical to us. Nevertheless, it contains a central paradox. Kerouac and his friends were great lovers of jazz, above all (see page 32). The novel *On the Road*, in particular, is a paean of praise to the freedom and improvisational genius of be-bop. It is teeming with references to this particular jazz form, a genre that was flourishing in America's cities in the post-war period. For example, a George Shearing performance sparked these literary fireworks: *"He blew innumerable choruses replete with amazing chords that mounted higher and higher till the sweat splashed all over the piano and everybody listened in awe and fright."*

Charles Carmignac, who plays dobro, guitar, and xylophone in a Franco-American band named after *On the Road* character Dean Moriarty, offers this explanation: *"I think that when Kerouac discovered be-bop, he felt the same way the kids in the 60s and 70s did, when they started listening to rock and folk. For each generation, a different genre broke out of the pop mold and opened new creative perspectives. Like Ginsberg, some of Kerouac's followers were open to the change in musical focus, but Kerouac himself remained loyal to jazz and bebop. It may have been genuine musical sensitivity or Kerouac's contrarian spirit, his refusal to follow fashion."* True, Kerouac lives on in a few later jazz compositions, notes music critic Philippe Carles. For example, singer Mark Murphy recorded *Bop for Kerouac* in 1981, and poet Enzo Cormann collaborated with saxophonist Jean-Marc Padovani on *Chorus by Jack Kerouac from Mexico City Blues* in 2001. But Carles is careful to point out that jazz inspired Kerouac much

> The Beat's impact on folk, rock, punk, and hip-hop seems natural but above all Kerouac and his friends were great lovers of jazz.

more than Kerouac inspired jazz: *"His writing is saturated with its improvisational principles."* As soon as the 60s started gathering steam, folk and rock enthusiasts rediscovered Beat wisdom. Bob Dylan, the Beatles, and the Doors were especially powerful artists who brought Beat poetry and the coffee-shop, hootenanny way of life to the attention of huge audiences.

DYLAN, THE SPIRITUAL SON

Dylan mentions Kerouac several times in his autobiography (*Chronicles*), as well as in *No Direction Home* (2005), the documentary Martin Scorsese made about him. "On the Road *had been like a Bible for me. (...) I still loved the breathless, dynamic, bop poetry phrases that flowed from Jack's pen... I fell into that atmosphere of everything Kerouac was*

"TI JEAN"
JOHN L. KEROUAC
MAR 12, 1922 — OCT 21, 1969
— HE HONORED LIFE —
STELLA HIS WIFE
NOV. 11, 1918 —

ZIMMERMAN REVISITED

BY ANASTASIA LEVY

BEFORE BOB DYLAN EVEN ARRIVED IN GREENWICH VILLAGE WITH HIS GUITAR ON HIS BACK, YOUNG ROBERT ZIMMERMAN WAS ALREADY WILD ABOUT KEROUAC AND THE OTHER DHARMA BUMS. THE MANY PERSONAL AND INTERTEXTUAL AFFINITIES BETWEEN THE FOLKSINGER AND THE POETS DESERVE A SPECIAL SQUARE IN THE GREAT PATCHWORK OF BEAT KINSHIP.

Quoted by Sean Wilentz, author of Bob Dylan in America, the icon reminisced in 1985 about his influences: *"It was Jack Kerouac, Ginsberg, Corso, Ferlinghetti ... I got in at the tail end of that and it was magic ... it had just as big an impact on me as Elvis Presley."* In 1959, when Dylan was still in college in Minnesota, he read *Naked Lunch*, by William Burroughs, and Kerouac's poetry collection *Mexico City Blues* the same year. The *"King of the Beats"* still ruled then, but fifteen years later, Dylan and Ginsberg were visiting his Lowell, Massachusetts grave.

In the Beats, Dylan had finally found a group of American poets with whom he shared a vision, and he enthusiastically blended it with folk. A music scene

BOB DYLAN, GREAT ADMIRER OF THE BEAT GENERATION, HERE IN NEW YORK IN 1962.

including both bebopping beatniks and guitar-strumming folkies gave rise to the 20-year-old who traveled to New York in 1961, hoping to see Woody Guthrie before he died. In his prolific songwriting career, Dylan continued to incorporate Beat poetics into his unique brand of American folk music. *Subterranean Homesick Blues* (1965) is a prime example, with its series of seemingly random words, casually strung together, line by line, to make a poem that somehow expresses all the absurdity of the air-conditioned nightmarish American consumer life. It's even more evident in *Desolation Row*: *"They're selling postcards of the hanging / They're painting the passports brown*

/ The beauty parlor is filled with sailors / The circus is in town." In the opening sequence of D.A. Pennebaker's 1965 documentary of his tour of England, Dylan holds up homemade cardboard signs bearing the last word in each line of *Subterranean Homesick Blues.* Allen Ginsberg, Dylan's living link to the Beat Generation, appears in the background. These links were more personal and literary than political. Dylan refused to march in anybody else's parade: he was no Joan Baez, singing *"We Shall Overcome"* for a crowd of protesters in Washington, DC.

But Dylan and the Beats did share a love for the America of the under-dogs, the abandoned, those still in quest of social justice. The Beats, with their electrifying praise of wandering hobos, homosexual Jewish Buddhist poet geniuses, and highway hedonism, had inspired Bob. As the 60s wore on, the roles were gradually reversed, and Dylan was the one who breathed new life into the Beatnik values that had forged his first songs and early performing persona. He was always the link between the two worlds. For example, the first lines of *I Dreamed I Saw St. Augustine* (1967) paraphrase Joe Hill, written in memory of the Wobbly leader unjustly executed in 1915 – a story Ginsberg put him onto in *America*. Greil Marcus is right when he says *Like a Rolling Stone* owes more to *Howl* than it does to any song.

" TEENAGERS, drunk, disheveled, excited "

On the Road, p. 84, Penguin Classics, 2002

saying about the world being completely mad, and the only people for him that were interesting were the mad people, the mad ones, the ones who were mad to live, mad to talk, mad to be saved, desirous of everything at the same time, the ones that never yawned, all those mad ones, and I felt like I fit right into that bunch." Dylan also met Allen Ginsberg in the 1960s, the beginning of a long friendship Ginsberg recalls with emotion in Scorsese's documentary. But he first heard the new young folksinger on an LP a poet friend, Charlie Plymell, played for him, when he returned from India. The song was *A Hard Rain's A-Gonna Fall,* and Ginsberg says he wept: *"It seemed the torch had been passed to another generation from earlier Bohemian or Beat illumination or self-*

Ginsberg heard *A Hard Rain's A-Gonna Fall* by Dylan and says he wept: "It seemed the torch had passed to another generation."

empowerment." *Mexico City Blues* was another revelation for Dylan. What made Beat literature so eloquent for this generation? Ginsberg reports that when he later asked Bob, the younger man said it was the first poetry to speak his own language. Kerouac's influence is obvious on albums like *Highway 61 Revisited,* released in 1965: Dylan even quotes passages from *Desolation Angels.* On his 1985 release *Empire Burlesque,* Dylan mentions *Mexico City Blues.* Throughout his career, Dylan makes reference to the Bohemian way of life, the perpetual motion esthetic of those just slightly older than he (see *Zimmerman Revisited,* on this page).

THE BEATLES, BEATISH BRITS

John Lennon had also taken Kerouac to heart, albeit more discreetly. In his study *Subterranean Kerouac: The Hidden Life of Jack Kerouac,* Ellis Amburn reports an exchange in which Lennon admitted to Kerouac that the spelling of the name Beatles, initially spelt 'Beetles' was changed to 'Beatles' to include reference to the 'beat.' An outgrowth of beatnik culture, non-conformist and copiously irrigated by the desire to transcend Western materialism, by

Long before they went psychedelic, the Beatles were attuned to the Beat spirit.

the mid-60s the British version of 'beat music,' as produced by George Martin, was tuned-in and turned-on. The song *She Said She Said,* on the album *Revolver* (1966), describes an acid trip in Los Angeles. *Tomorrow Never Knows,* written *"under the influence,"* is suffused with Tibetan Buddhism, expressing the Beatles' affections for opening the doors of perception. Its other-worldly electronic sound effects (guitar solos replayed backwards, reverb, etc.) and lyrics, no longer driven simply by teenage hormones, reflect the Fab Four's experience with Oriental religions. Obviously, the trend emulated Ginsberg and Kerouac's passion for Eastern religious philosophy, along with a little help from artificial paradises. The Beatles were imbibing the same hallucinogenic substances as the Beats, who had pioneered acid as one of the keys to the

In his wistful nasal twang growl, Tom Waits narrates the fragmented wanderings of the dharma bums.

psychological highway. On *Sgt. Pepper's Lonely Hearts Club Band* (1967), the song *Lucy in the Sky with Diamonds* is a cryptic tribute to Dr. Hofmann's 1943 laboratory find: LSD (the initials of which inspired the song's title). The album cover also honors the Beats: with William Burroughs peering out from the crowd. Long before they went psychedelic, the Beatles were attuned to the Beat spirit. From the start, back when they sang simple songs like *I Want to Hold Your Hand* (1963), the British rockers glowed with the *"new consciousness"* promoted by Kerouac and Ginsberg. In *Deliberate Prose*, a collection of essays, Ginsberg reminisced about seeing the Beatles play in New York City. He looked back on the concert as a visionary experience, something that would pierce the dense skull of Western civilization. At last, black dance had been brought to the white West, people would rekindle with their bodies and Americans were going to shake their asses!

THE DOORS AND TOM WAITS

For Jim Morrison, Doors concerts were veritable ceremonies. As the shaman of West Coast rock, he sought to open *"the doors of perception"* (hence the name of the group, from Aldous Huxley's book) via the hypnotic beat, the poetry of his mystical texts, and his incantatory singing. Influenced by William Blake, and encouraged by Beat poet Michael McClure to publish his own writings, Morrison often cited Kerouac – whom he read at age 21 – as one of his mentors. Keyboard player Ray Manzarek concurred. Manzarek began accompanying McClure

reciting his poems in 1988, long after Jim had vanished. Describing this intentional friendship in the documentary *The Third Mind* (1999), Ray Manzarek asserts that *"if Kerouac hadn't written* On the Road, *the Doors wouldn't have existed. We wanted to be Beatniks. We wanted to be poetry and jazz."*

In the 1970s, another singer staked his claim to the Beat heritage: Tom Waits, whose life had changed when he read *On the Road* at the age of 18. In his wistful nasal twang, the Californian narrates the fragmented wanderings of the dharma bums on albums like *Swordfishtrombones* and *Rain Dogs*. Bones Howe, who produced *Nighthawks at the Diner* (1975), compared Waits reading the classified ads aloud during a live jazz show to *"Allen Ginsberg, but with a really, really good band."* Later, Waits worked with William Burroughs, recording *Smack My Crack* on a 1987 spoken word album, and also composing the music for *The Black Rider: The Casting of the Magic Bullets,* a German fairytale Burroughs adapted, staged by Robert Wilson.

PUNK RAPPER WILLIAM BURROUGHS

William Burroughs is undoubtedly the Beat writer who has had the greatest influence on post-modern rock. Patti Smith referenced him constantly on her album *Horses* (1975), and he owned his title as "Godfather of Punk" so thoroughly he was able to dismiss it. Joe Strummer and Richard Hell bowed down to him, and Burroughs himself was fond enough of the Sex Pistols' iconoclast savagery to wire his support for their *God Save the Queen* (1977). But his aura goes well beyond a single subculture. The British progressive rock band Soft Machine owes its name to one of his novels. The American jazz-rock group Steely Dan was named in reference to a dildo that appears in *Naked Lunch*. Burroughs also theorized extensively about the

cut-up literary technique, and this may be his most enduring contribution to rock songwriting, from Steppenwolf to Nirvana, with a nod to Thom Yorke (for the Radiohead classic *Kid A*), and especially David Bowie, in his Berlin trilogy era of the late 1970s. Like Burroughs, the Thin White Duke liked the idea of shattering the world to reassemble it as an even more expressive chaos. Omnipresent on the scene, Burroughs interviewed Lou Reed and Blondie, and recorded with Laurie Anderson, Kurt Cobain, R.E.M., and Sonic Youth – the latter two also honored Jack Kerouac on the spoken-word anthology *Kicks Joy Darkness*. The literary lightning bolts and hypnotic visions that leap forth from the Beat poets' deconstructed texts also energize hip-hop genre. *"I don't think most people in the rap world are hip to the cut-ups, but if they checked out Burroughs and Gysin they'd certainly see the connections between the two,"* explains self-styled "Beatnik rapper" Justin Warfield. Rap, consisting of chanting rhymes onto rhythms and melodic loops, is the child of the militant "spoken word" performances by Gil Scott-Heron – himself beholden to the jazz poetry practiced by the Beats. Just listen to Jack Kerouac reading his *American Haikus* (1958) accompanied by saxophonists Al Cohn and Zoot Sims. Today, Saul Williams, a poet of slam, the latest spinoff from the rap/spoken word genre, openly acknowledges the Beats – but he's got attitude: *"We're the real Beat Generation. Kerouac and Ginsberg had jazz, but we've got the actual beat."* ●

Like Burroughs, the Thin White Duke liked the idea of shattering the world to reassemble it as an even more expressive chaos.

ALLEN GINSBERG (RIGHT) PHOTOGRAPHING SONIC YOUTH'S AMERICAN SINGER AND GUITARIST LEE RANALDO, WHILE READING *ON THE ROAD* AT A BEAT EVENT ORGANISED BY NEW YORK UNIVERSITY IN MAY 1994

IS THERE A BEAT LOOK?

ROAD TO FASHION

BY ÈVE BEAUVALLET
TRANSLATED BY AUDREY CONCANNON

★

AT FIRST, THERE SEEMS TO BE LITTLE IN COMMON BETWEEN KEROUAC AND COCO CHANEL, NO MORE THAN BETWEEN MICHEL HOUELLEBECQ AND LADY GAGA. THE BEAT GENERATION DIDN'T DESIGN CLOTHES YET THEY INVENTED A MODERN WAY OF WEARING THEM. A LOOK BACK TO THE DAYS WHEN THE T-SHIRT SOWED PANIC... AND WHEN ANTI-FASHION BECAME FASHIONABLE.

★
---

ack Kerouac may well have disdained the world of fashion, yet fashion, on the other hand, adored Jack Kerouac for decades. His old blue raincoat was sold for 15,000 dollars to Johnny Depp in 1994. A capsule collection called *"The Jack Kerouac Project"* was launched in 2007 by the Italian label, Hogan. Gap chose a photo of Kerouac in a lumberjack shirt for its 1995 campaign... making him a genuine fashion icon. Seem paradoxical? Well, not really. The Beat Generation, on the back of their anti-materialist values, might have scorned haute couture, but surely not style. Modern street-wear

and the Abercrombie & Fitch stores come from them. The hipsters in Brooklyn, or the Marais in Paris, come from them too. The trend for recycling, salvage and thrift stores all originated with the Beats. Discreet, practical, plain beat-style clothes have today become staple wardrobe basics: jeans, chinos, leggings, leather jackets, and turtlenecks... well worn pieces that may once have had political overtones, liberating bodies and prompting fashion to open up to the postwar lifestyle revolution.

BEAT EFFORT

In the 1940s, with the exception of Jack Kerouac, who appeared a little disheveled, the Beat Generation writers did not yet openly distance themselves from traditional codes of elegance. Fashion dictated suits for men and pastel colors for women. Burroughs, the eldest, wore a hat. Soon however, the writing began to show evidence of a fascination for the cool and roguish figure of the hipster. Young jazz fans, drug users and advocates of sexual freedom advertised their anti-conventional values by wearing *zoot* suits (a parody of trouser suits designed

> The Beat Generation might have scorned *haute couture,* but surely not style.

with very wide legs) and by idolizing the trumpeter Dizzy Gillespie. The latter, among others, personified the whole Beatnik package, as seen in the cartoons from 1950-1960 like in *Mister Magoo,* with his *béret,* goatee and round black tortoise-shell spectacles.

However, the Beat Generation, more than just borrowing accessories from the *zoot* suiters, went further and radicalized the principle by undermining the clothing's original function through a blurring of social status (middle class youngsters appropriating workers' attire), the professional bodies (anti-militarist youth wearing army uniforms in the city like the Royal Navy duffel coat, or the chinos worn by soldiers in World War II) and the distinction between public and private spheres (the T-shirt was still a piece of underwear when adopted by the Beats). Kerouac, John Clellon Holmes and

AUDREY HEPBURN, THE PERFECT BEATNIK IN *FUNNY FACE* (1957), DRESSED BY HUBERT DE GIVENCHY

The adjective "beat" became a sartorial quality: beat the garment to make it better fit the values of a generation.

Joyce Johnson describe young boys sporting old miltary jackets, faded Levi's, threadbare sweaters and chinos. Kerouac even made the adjective *"beat"* into a sartorial quality (*"beat sweater and baggy pants"* and *"beat shoes that flap"*), like the desire to *"tire out"* the garment to make it better fit the values of a generation. Think of Sal Paradise's wool shirts, his three-dollar coat and his canvas bag, or Dean Moriarty's workers' clothes, muscles bulging in his tattered T-shirts...

ALL BLACKS AND DHARMA BUMS

As for women, the designer Clair McCardell designed a casual line based on black jersey in the late 1940s, but it would take until the 1950s before a recognizable style emerged, first developed by the poet and editor Diane de Prima. She used to appear on campus like an alien wearing her hair down to her waist, in ballet shoes, jeans and a black nylon leotard. Black leggings and Capezio ballet shoes entered closets. Black, erasing sexual markers, is adopted in opposition to the saccharine and flowery colors that dominated at the time. Juliette Greco, Miles Davis's mistress and existentialist fashion icon, became the beat styled star in black. More surprisingly, Marilyn Monroe also adopted tapered pants during her time in New York. *"Except for student and arty circles, until 1968 it was still not acceptable for women to wear pants,"* recalls Laurent Cotta, director of the Galliera Museum's contemporary collections in Paris. *"It was therefore far from trivial to see a star*

ZOOT SUIT, *BÉRET*, ROUNDED SPECTACLES: THE TRUMPET PLAYER, DIZZY GILLESPIE, HERE IN THE 1940'S, WAS IDOLIZED BY NEW YORK HIPSTERS

like Marilyn endorse a such a style. This was a well-traveled generation (bear in mind the great transatlantic movement between The Village, U.S.A. and Saint-Germain-des-Prés, France), often painters, making sartorial comfort and simplicity an aesthetic in itself." Soon, sales of jeans had exploded (Levi's, Wrangler, Lee), and the Hanes and Fruit of the Loom stores stocked up on white and striped T-shirts. Donning a smock or *béret* signposted a trip to Paris. Audrey Hepburn was radiant in *Funny Face* in 1957 wearing costumes designed by a young Hubert de Givenchy. The beatnik became en effective marketing product, and anti-fashion became the hippest of styles. Kerouac confided his distaste in vain to *Playboy* **magazine** in 1959. His rant would fail to prevent the beat style from entering, in a most unlikely scenario, the realms of luxury fashion.

YVES SAINT LAURENT, A LITTLE BEAT

In 1960, Dior's young designer, a certain Yves Saint Laurent, was the first to open up the doors

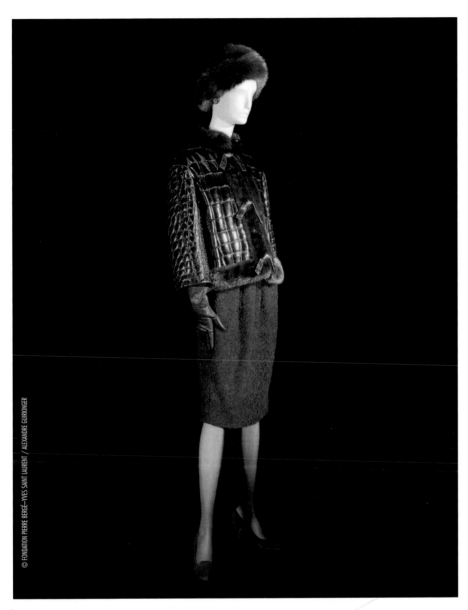

YVES SAINT LAURENT'S DESIGNS FOR CHRISTIAN DIOR'S FALL-WINTER 1960 COLLECTION WAS CALLED "BEAT LOOK".
HERE, "CHICAGO": A FAUX CROCODILE LEATHER JACKET TRIMMED WITH BLACK MINK AND WOOL SKIRT

The *Beat Look* collection has endured as one of the great manifestos for modernity in fashion.

in the army... Of course, it was a huge scandal. Marcel Boussac, a textile manufacturer known for his conservative views, was afraid of losing haute couture clients and had Saint Laurent fired from Dior." Despite the furor, the "Beat Look" collection has endured as one of the great manifestos for modernity in fashion, launching many further adventures in the subversion of conventional modes of dressing.

STYLE VS. FASHION

Unlike its younger, more exuberant hippie cousin, beatnik style never underwent any significant period of disenchantment. Some decades or designers endorse it with lesser or greater degrees of enthusiasm: the ska period of the 1980s, the Helmut Lang silhouette, early collections by Jean-Paul Gaultier with tapered pants and smocks, a 90s minimalist wave and so on... all are indebted to the beat look. *"They were never out of fashion because the clothes established themselves as basics,"* concludes Laurent Cotta. *"With the Beat Generation, it was a logic of style over one of fashion. Themes and variations were created from a limited range of elements. That's how Chanel got the better of her archrival Dior in couture. She thought about the durability of the piece, of what constitutes the basis of a shape, rather that what goes out of style. Similarly, the beatniks succeeded in creating a look from next to nothing"*: values that should be a big hit in 2012. •

of high fashion to the street and counter-culture. His "Beat Look" collection generated severe misgivings. Though made from cashmere the black turtlenecks worn by the models were uncomfortably similar to those donned by the hooligans in the Latin Quarter. Never before had any class other than the upper middle dictated fashion moves. Never before had the color black, traditionally synonymous with elegance, been appropriated by the darkness of anarchy. In short, never before had

politics invaded the catwalk with such a nerve. *"There was a black leather jacket made of crocodile skin in the "Beat Look" collection, which was extremely luxurious as the crocodile scales were huge and lined with mink,"* resumes Laurent Cotta. *"We were still in the middle of a war with Algeria and those wearing black jackets in France would sometimes go and chastise the conscripts leaving for Algeria. Then along comes this young designer, who was born in French Algeria, old enough to be*

THE BOOK ON THE ROAD

FRENCH CONNECTION

BY QUENTIN GROSSET
TRANSLATED BY AUDREY CONCANNON

★

CAN ONE IMAGINE *ON THE ROAD* HAPPENING ON THE ASPHALT OF THE CORRÈZE REGION OF FRANCE? OBVIOUSLY NOT, YET THE BEATS' TRIP TO PARIS LEFT ITS MARK ON FRENCH LITERATURE AND WRITERS, SUCH AS JEAN-JACQUES LEBEL, PHILIPPE DJIAN, AND F.J. OSSANG, INSPIRED BY *THE DHARMA BUMS'* VOLATILE SPIRIT AND THIRST FOR FREEDOM..

★

The beat poet, Gregory Corso, landed in Paris at the swanky terrace of Les Deux Magots, a café in the capital's 6th arrondissement, brandishing a pistol while insulting what remained of the existentialists. It was 1957 and the Parisian intelligentsia was unsettled by the beat writers' take on poetry as a way of life. The Beats were fleeing American conformism to embrace the Parisian myth and followed in the footsteps of their idols who had trodden French soil before them (John Dos Passos, Henry Miller, Ernest Hemingway, F. Scott Fitzgerald etc.). They crashed in a seedy nameless hotel in the Latin Quarter, later dubbed the "Beat Hotel."

Allen Ginsberg sat by Apollinaire's tomb in the Père Lachaise cemetery to engage in a conversation from beyond the grave: a literary dialogue between the French and the Americans uninterrupted ever since, as the Beats' fascination with France is reciprocated in kind today.

INCANDESCENT POETS

During his stay in France, Jack Kerouac received what he called a *"satori",* a Japanese word denoting *"sudden illumination, sudden awakening or simply kick in the eye."* This resembled the atmosphere in the "Beat Hotel," where his friends Ginsberg, Burroughs and Corso shook the sleepy district by getting high on Antonin Artaud's intoxicating poems.

It was Jean-Jacques Lebel who introduced them to French free verse, an artist with many strings to his bow (artist, activist, and organizer of happenings), and the first to translate the Beat Generation. In his huge apartment crammed with African masks and Dada paintings, he serves us a whiskey and revisits this French period that he considers wrongfully overlooked by historians. *"It's unfair*

In 1957, the Beats were fleeing American conformism to embrace the Parisian myth.

that the American academics, still so dumbly nationalistic and patriotic, continue to ignore these intense years. After all Ginsberg wrote Kaddish *here, a very personal text on the history of his mother's insanity, and Burroughs finished* Naked Lunch *at the Beat Hotel."*

The meeting with the Beats happened quite naturally, says Lebel. He used to visit the English bookshop on 42, rue de Seine, frequented by the Beats. He ended up translating *Howl*, Ginsberg's masterpiece. *"Good things have been said about the Ginsberg translations I did, but this was due to our collaboration. It's a privilege to work with a great living poet on the translation of his own works."* Lebel played a fundamental role in disseminating the beat works in France, especially with his anthology *La Poésie de la « beat generation »* (*The Poetry of the "Beat Generation"*) published in

"

UP
EIFFEL
TOWER
BEAUTIFUL
dream-machine in sky

ALLEN GINSBERG

EXCERPT FROM A LETTER TO JACK KEROUAC
CITED IN *BEAT HOTEL* BY BARRY MILES (2000)

"

> *"Corso cut off Duchamp's tie because he'd read that the Dadaists had done that."*
>
> JEAN-JACQUES LEBEL

1965 and reprinted on several occasions.

Lebel was also behind the comical encounters between these poets and French authors such as Henri Michaux and Marcel Duchamp. *"I organized an epic night with the Beats, Duchamp, Man Ray, and Octavio Paz. It was very important for them to meet these brilliant precursors. Gregory Corso was drunk and cut off Duchamp's tie because he'd read that the Dadaists had done that. And Ginsberg kissed Duchamp's knees."*

INVITATION TO TRAVEL

Four stars have replaced the rats, and the current premises of the Beat Hotel has nothing in common with the insalubrious dive where the Beats devoted themselves to drugs and free love. Occupying a plush chair in the Relais du Vieux Paris, Philippe Djian, author of the recent *Vengeances*, speaks of what's left of this cultural context. *"We're in a crappy era, where no one even stands comparison with them. The legacy is too much for anyone to bear: when the Italians do a piece on me with a photo montage of me on a Harley Davidson setting me up as an heir to Kerouac, it just makes me laugh."* Yet in a collection entitled *Ardoise* ("the bill"), Djian wrote about what he owed Kerouac, whose writing, he says, had a physical effect on him: *"The most important thing is the style. Kerouac's very musical writing taught me that as with infrasound, there is an infra-literature whose melody and rhythm must be in tune with the times."*

It's clear to Djian that there are no heirs in France. Some critics have agreed, however, to appoint Claude Pélieu, another fellow traveler of the Beats, as *"the only French-speaking beat poet."* Author of *Automatic Pilot*, and a translator of Burroughs and Ginsberg, he was the first to borrow the cut-up technique, in which words in a text are cut out and disordered to generate a new text. Burroughs also lent his voice to the track *Long Song for Zelda* in 1971, an ode to Zelda Fitzgerald on the legendary *Obsolete* album, by the musician, poet and writer Dashiell Hedayet (aka Jack-Alain Léger), who translated Leonard Cohen and Bob Dylan.

The poet/musician/filmmaker F.J. Ossang, also hiding behind a pseudonym, is even more versatile. The latter reserves his ire for the hippie offspring of the beatniks, but claims that the beat spirit lives on in the punks. Cineaste of metaphysical wanderings, close to Pélieu, Ossang obviously considered adapting *On the Road*. *"My idea was to cross* On the Road *with* Visions of Cody, *as well as using* Some of the Dharma, *a huge collection of poems and prayers from Kerouac's Buddhist period. Eventually the project fell through. Looking for a secret name for a company for a new film project, I later naturally thought of 'Dharma Guns' from* The Dharma Bums... *Ultraviolet humor..."*

The French heard the beat works as a call to spatial and sensorial wandering. In the words of Burroughs, Michel Bulteau is an *"explorer of untouched psychic areas."* The dandy author of the *Manifeste Électrique Aux Paupières de Jupes* (*Electrical Manifesto of Skirts with Eyelids*) was introduced to the New York underground in 1976 by Ginsberg, who showed him a city on the boil with the beginnings of punk, the Warholian mythology and the ever restless Beats. *"They were the synthesis of Arthur Rimbaud and Charlie Parker, both of whom always believed that art could change lives,"* says Bulteau.

Formerly a journalist with *Libération*, Philippe Garnier expatriated to the States and also went on the road, the romance of Kerouac-style hitchhiking in mind, *"I had this dog-eared paperback copy of* On the Road, *a secondhand Signet edition picked up in Amsterdam. I think I still had it in my bag the first time I crossed the U.S. in 1971."* His long articles irritated the editors at *Libération*, but Garnier always landed on his feet thanks to the colorful style in his column *L'Oreille d'un sourd*. He described a changing America in the 80s: *"In the late 1970s, young people had been 'demonized' by the Charles Manson case. Paranoia and fear were the norm now. There were fewer people on the road."* Had the roaming spirit disappeared for good?

Yves Simon was also nostalgic for his youthful readings of the Beats, *"As you grow older, you try to realize old dreams so as to have as few regrets as possible before dying,"* he wrote in his penultimate novel, *La Compagnie des Femmes*, where he recounts how, for no reason, he left Paris for a tour of the South. The solitary backpacker accesses this feeling particular to road-novels where every encounter with a woman is experienced as a journey within the self.

More down to earth, the author Jean-Jacques Bonvin, from Geneva, distances himself from the mythology by dealing in his book *Ballast* with the Beats' contrasting deaths. The extremely dense prose focuses on the figure of Neal Cassady: *"Cassady was the only one who went all the way, that is to say straight to the wall. They all saw the wall, but Ginsberg and Kerouac negotiated their corners so as to postpone death. Ginsberg found a kind*

The French heard the beat works as a call to spatial or sensorial wandering.

"

Remi was an old prep-school friend, a Frenchman brought up in Paris and a really MAD GUY

"

On the Road, p.26, Penguin Classics, 2002

of comfort in life and in death, and Kerouac drank beer to the point of exploding his system, while uttering insanities. Meanwhile Cassady raced ahead, possessed by the breakneck pace at which he lived life," asserts Bonvin. Hence, the Beats became material for fiction, surely the best clue behind the Beat revival in France.

FAN SERVICE

A pack of American Spirit cigarettes on the desk and a portrait of Kerouac on the wall, the 13e Note publisher's premises perpetuate the Beat spirit along with a more contemporary Punk dog look (*i.e.* the dog that keeps brushing between my legs during the interview). Having knocked about the world in shipping, Éric Vieljeux created this publishing company in 2008 with an editorial line mainly devoted to the paragons of American counter culture, tuned into 8.6, nomadic culture and chaos. *"Much of the catalogue is made up of neo-Beats like Dan Fante, Nick Tosches... heirs to marginal literature, but television and*

computers too," explains Sandrine Belehradek, the editorial director. *"The latter are rawer and less literary. On the Internet, the younger ones get together on social networks to show and spread their work."*

Another French publishing house has also laid claim to the Beat revival: Derrière la Salle de Bains Editions was created in 1995 in Rouen by Marie-Laure Dagoit who says, *"I am touched by the lesser known Beats. And by the writings of Peter Orlovsky, who represents love in the group. I devoured all available Beat literature. Reading fast at night. And by day I dreamed of recreating the Beat Generation in my publishing company."* Boasting an editor's dream catalogue (including Ossang, Bulteau, Tosches and unpublished Beat pieces), Dagoit has benefited from great contacts: *"Claude Pélieu gave me some addresses, in particular Ginsberg's and Burroughs' addresses. I wrote to them on behalf of Pélieu, and they sent me some pieces."*

Given the proliferation of these French cousins, it would seem that Philippe Djian's pessimism about the

The 13e Note publisher's premises perpetuate the Beat spirit along with a Punk dog look.

Beat Generation's legacy in France is perhaps not wholly justified.

Stephan Eicher's lyricist declared, in the overdone lobby of what remains of the Beat Hotel, that *"France is a pain in the ass,"* though he'd been given a copy of *Polichinelle* by Pierric Bailly that happened to be in our bag. In an attempt to make the most of the apathy in the book, Bailly remixes the peasant expressions of a bunch of troubled teens in the Jura with an energy close to rap, a bit like the Beat writings married to the spontaneity of jazz. In delivering his own conception of French beat, he states, *"Beat is retarded, naïve, made out of plastic."* ●

THE BEAT GENERATION AND CINEMA

TRACKING IN

BY LAURA TUILLIER
TRANSLATED BY AUDREY CONCANNON

★

KEROUAC SAID THAT HE WAS FASCI-NATED BY *"HOLLYWOOD STARLETS"*. IN TURN, THE CINEMA INDUSTRY FELL UNDER THE SPELL CAST BY THE BEAT GENERATION. A LOOK BACK ON FIFTY YEARS OF FLIRTING: FROM THE BEATS' OWN FILM-MAKING TALENTS, TO THE DARING ROAD MOVIES OF THE SEVENTIES, AND UP UNTIL HOLLYWOOD'S EXAGGERATED PORTRAYALS OF THE MOVEMENT.

★

n November 11, 1959, two films are screened as part of a double bill in New York: *Pull My Daisy*, a short film by Alfred Leslie written by Kerouac, and *Shadows*, the first feature directed by John Cassevetes. Both were shot in 16mm with no budget, on location and in all spontaneity. Jonas Mekas wrote in *Film Culture* that the Cassevetes movie *"destroys the myth of the one million dollar production."* *Pull My Daisy* doesn't even trouble itself with such considerations. With an extremely low budget, the short film was part of the ongoing Beat gesture. Kerouac supplied the voiceover and abandoned himself with obvious enjoyment to a syncopated prose in the flow of words set to Frank Leslie's images. Allen Ginsberg, Gregory Corso, and Peter Orlovsky have fun onscreen exasperating a clergyman who has the misfortune of visiting their friends, a couple (the man, a railroad employee and the woman, a painter).

FOR A FEW DOLLARS LESS

"Pull my Daisy *is nothing other than a liberation movement,"* explains Bernard Benoliel, director of the French Cinémathèque's cultural activities and co-author with Jean-Baptiste Thoret of the book *Road Movie, USA*. The freethinking Beat Generation authors naturally preferred writing, which required nothing more than reams of paper and some inspiration. Hence, the few beat films are always no-budget affairs (not like those that Cassavetes would go on to make, though his budgets would always be modest), and shot between buddies. *Guns of the Trees* (1961) by Jonas Mekas based on a poem by Allen Ginsberg, depicts a generation intoxicated by life without rules, clashing with bleak postwar realities such as mixed couples faced with racial intolerance, and renewed

> Kerouac supplied the voiceover on *Pull My Daisy* and abandoned himself with obvious enjoyment.

peace up against the atomic threat.

William Burroughs in turn makes some interesting appearances as an actor, notably in Gus Van Sant's *Drugstore Cowboy*, and he inspired Cronenberg's *Naked Lunch*. If the Beat filmmakers (Ron Rice, Vernon Zimmerman, Gordon Ball, etc.) are confined to the ultimately sedentary New York underground, those nicknamed beatniks in the West are of special interest to Hollywood.

FREAKS & BEATS

The folkloric charisma of the Beats (bearded, joint in mouth, and the singular slang) soon attracted the majors, determined to exploit the rich vein of Beatnik fashion, Kerouac refused the title "King of the Beats" and many beatniks were committed to political causes, far removed from the naïve popular image of the

ON THE SET FOR *PULL MY DAISY*, ROBERT FRANK FILMS ALLEN GINSBERG SHARING A BEER WITH GREGORY CORSO, IN 1959

TWO LANE BLACKTOP BY MONTE HELLMAN (1971)   EASY RIDER BY DENNIS HOPPER (1969)   THELMA AND LOUISE BY RIDLEY SCOTT

"The depiction of the Beats on mainstream television inevitably focused on caricature and denigration."

poet gently floating along to a bebop melody. Two movies are symbolic of this tendency to caricature: *The Beatniks* and *The Wild Ride*, made in 1960 by two unknown directors, Paul Frees and Harvey Berman. The first employs an insipid plot pitting a band of degenerate beatniks against Universal Records. Although the label spots one of them, his noisy and oblivious friends make him miss the opportunity of a lifetime. In *The Wild Ride* (produced by Corman, starring Jack Nicholson), the references are all about accessories (the car, jazz records etc.), and the pattern is identical. The brightest of the beatniks really wants

to enter society's ranks and live the fashionable American Dream, but his dissolute friends lead him astray. As noted by Ray Carney, professor at Boston University and co-author of the exhibition catalog, *Beat Culture and the New America -1950-1965*, "the depiction of the Beat Generation by mainstream television and cinema inevitably focused on caricature and denigration."

Vincente Minnelli's *The Sandpiper* (1965) painted an empathetic, but vapid and typical, portrait of a band of beatniks (clustering around Liz Taylor) making merry on a Big Sur beach. The years went by, but Hollywood didn't change. *Heart Beat*, released in 1980, was a sluggish adaptation of Carolyn Cassady's memoirs starring Nick Nolte and Sissy Spacek. Though the movie has the virtue of adopting a female perspective and evokes Neal's resentment when Kerouac "steals" his life to turn it into a bestseller, the moviefails to find a particular aesthetic form and confines itself,

despite the tantalizing slogan ("*They didn't do anything wrong. They just did it first*"), to the rather safe ranks of TV drama.

The Beats were talked about on the small screen too. In the 90s the high school slackers in *Freaks and Geeks* painfully slogged through Kerouac's masterpiece, *On the Road*. And more recently *Mad Men* took an ironic and condescending slant on the Beat Generation. The hero Don Draper's first mistress is friends with beatniks. 'Midge' works, takes lovers and lives alone in Greenwich Village. She's an independent and admired woman, yet she gradually sinks into poverty and addiction. The implication is that her beatnik friends are to blame, for living by the motto "*Let's get high and listen to Miles*." The series writers subtly lampoon them. Don Draper, a past master in controlling appearances, criticizes the beatniks in their own terms, making 'Midge' smile with his assessment.

HOWL BY ROB EPSTEIN AND JEFFREY FRIEDMAN (2010)   VANISHING POINT BY RICHARD C. SARAFIAN (1971)

Like Sal et Dean, many legendary cinematic pairs have found going on the road a sure route to friendship.

For him, they boil down to their pre-hipster look. And for audiences, yes, the Beats can easily be reduced to mere appearances, but only when cinema fails to capture what constitutes the uniqueness and beauty of this generation. And that hasn't always been the case.

JUST AN ILLUSION

"Cinema got its On the Road with Easy Rider," says Olivier Assayas in his article "Notes on American Space," in Cahiers du Cinéma, April 1982. Easy Rider by Dennis Hopper blazed a trail for road movies in 1969, independent cinema's main genre of the 1970s. The glorious bikers, Wyatt and Billy, roam (crossing West to East this time) a still mythical America, but on the brink of collapse. "The thing common to On the Road and the road movie, which maybe comes from Westerns is that you usually go on the road in pairs," comments Bernard Benoliel. Just like Sal Paradise and Dean Moriarty, many legendary cinematic pairs have found going on the road is the surest route to friendship: 'The Mechanic' and 'The Driver' in Two-lane Blacktop, 'Kowalski' and his DJ guide 'Super Soul' in Vanishing Point, the anarchist free lovers in Zabriskie Point, and later on, the eponymous friends in Thelma and Louise and the stray kids, 'Mike' and 'Scott', in Gus Van Sant's My Own Private Idaho. But though the movie heroes roam the same dusty roads as the Beats by pairs, things had changed in America and the promise of the fifties turned into the depression of the seventies. "The paranoia,

INDIANS IN THE CITY

Kent Mackenzie's first movie – he would go on to direct documentaries – The Exiles (1961) follows the rowdy night in the life of a group of unemployed Native Americans in Los Angeles' Bunker Hill district. The film took three years to shoot using borrowed equipment and a volunteer crew. Most of the actors play themselves, people in a marginalized community living alcohol fuelled nights to a sound track of rock'n'roll. Bunker Hill is the wretched refuge of Yvonne, an abandoned pregnant wife, a headstrong character reminiscent of Camille, Kirsten Dunst's character in On the Road. Walter Salles, who screened The Exiles for his crew, comments: "The film vanished for 40 years and was restored shortly before our shoot. The combination of documentary footage with fictional scenes about a community of young Native Americans is fascinating." L.T.

> ## "
> # Remi had flown down to HOLLYWOOD (...) taking my sad silly movie original, and nothing had happened
> "
>
> *On the Road*, p. 109, Penguin Classics, 2002

terror and violence of Easy Rider *are very different from the hope filled reveries of* On the Road," says Ray Carney. While Kerouac could naively celebrate the fellowship between blacks and whites based upon a jazz background, the Los Angeles race riots, Martin Luther King's assassination and the often-violent struggle for civil rights signaled the end of innocence. The road movies of the 1970s are disillusioned, often absurd. Characters go round in circles and people die. The final images of *Easy Rider*, *Two Lane Blacktop* (the film bursting into flames like a burning road) and *Vanishing Point*, say it all: America was a dream that turned into a nightmare, a dead end road.

Bridging the *"dharma bums"* celebrated by Kerouac and the cinema would be the state of dream, the ideal shortcut to attaining the *"visions"* so dear to the writer. Could the *"road movies of sleep,"* as defined by Bernard Benoliel and Jean-Baptiste Thoret, be distant cousins to Kerouac and his followers? Take for instance the psychedelic spirals of *The Trip* in 1967 (another Corman production, written by Nicholson and Peter Fonda) with a copy of Allen Ginsberg's *Howl*

positioned in the foreground of a shot like a spiritual compass. Then again in the 1990s with *My Own Private Idaho* and its narcoleptic hero falling asleep right in the middle of the road between the white lines pondering parallel trips. Like William Blake in Jim Jarmusch's *Dead Man*, who in long, drawn-out death throes navigates between waking hallucinations and shifting reveries. Maybe it's these explorers of an America composed of parallel roads who open the *"doors of perception"* dear to Blake, with - like the Beats before them - recourse to a lot of illicit substances. As noted by Bernard Benoliel, *"space is the only true American novel, but who can write or film it?"* Roaming the North American continent without being able to get a handle on it drives Kerouac and the drowsy heroes of these few poetic fictions to take a fork in the road: *On the Road*'s America is dreamt up, and one travels across it with eyes wide shut.

"Isn't America an invention of cinema?" wonders Wim Wenders in *Emotion Pictures-Reflections on Cinema.* Kerouac himself, when writing *On the Road,* drew upon filmmakers like Preston Sturges (*Sullivan's Travels*) and John Ford (*The Grapes of Wrath*) who

> The America of *On the Road* is a dream that is traveled with eyes wide shut.

had already depicted roads, skylines, and vagrants before the appearance of the road movie, images constantly recurring in Kerouac's work. Kerouac even references Charlie Chaplin, the founding father, as Bernard Benoliel points out: "'Setting our course for the American continent. Holding hands, we walked several miles down the road,' *a description that could be mistaken for the famous last shot of* Modern Times." Already a movie buff's trip, *On The Road* built imaginary bridges crossed by the most adventurous of the American filmmakers. ●

EXPLODING FROM ALLEYWAYS AND IVORY TOWERS...

The BeaTniks

LIVING BY THEIR CODE OF REBELLION and MUTINY!

starring
TONY TRAVIS KAREN KADLER
co-starring
PETER BRECK and JOYCE TERRY

| Written and Directed by **PAUL FREES** | Production Supervision **KEN HERTS** | From an original story by **JOYCE TERRY** and **KEN HERTS** |

A Barjul International Pictures Release

THE BEATNIKS (1960) IS ABOUT A GROUP OF DEGENERATE, NOISY, DANGEROUS AND IRRESPONSIBLE BEATNIKS

CAROLYN AND NEAL CASSADY IN SAN FRANCISCO, 1947

FAMILY

DIARIES

COMMENTARY BY: **KRISTEN STEWART | AL HINKLE | CAROLYN CASSADY | JOHN COHEN |**

We all know that the mythical characters of *On the Road* are more or less faithfully based on people close to Jack Kerouac — friends, lovers, and parents. Thus, Dean Moriarty, *"the side-burned hero of the snowy West,"* Camille, the *"brunette,"* Marylou, the *"beautiful little sharp chick,"* *"big tall"* Ed Dunkel and his wife Galatea, who *"looked like tears all over,"* were really called Neal and Carolyn Cassady, LuAnne Henderson, Al and Helen Hinkle. This portfolio represents a chronological and subjective immersion in their everyday lives. When possible, we showed these pictures to the people who took them and to those who feature in them. Accordingly, Carolyn Cassady, Al Hinkle and the photographer John Cohen consented to share their memories with us. Kristen Stewart, who plays her in the film by Walter Salles, provides commentary on the images of a very young LuAnne Henderson. A family album.

BY JULIETTE REITZER

TRANSLATED BY AUDREY CONCANNON

THE KEROUAC FAMILY IN CANADA CIRCA 1930. FROM LEFT TO RIGHT: ARMAND GAUTHIER, A FRIEND OF THE FAMILY, CAROLINE ALIAS "NIN", LÉO, JACK AND GABRIELLE KEROUAC

| LUANNE PRESENTING TROPHY AT MIDGET AUTO RACES, DENVER, CIRCA 1945

| PIN-UP PHOTO OF LUANNE CIRCA 1945, BY HER STEPFATHER STEPHEN HENDERSON

LUANNE HENDERSON (MARYLOU IN "ON THE ROAD")

Kristen Stewart: "To be honest, at first, I asked myself: *"Oh my god, how am I going to play such a bubbly person?"* I felt very different from her, especially from her outward self. She was constantly smiling, she shined. As soon as I knew where that smile came from, it became much easier for me. It's not a vanity thing. She was aware of herself physically but at the same time she was able to set that aside. Whereas most girls who smile are smiling to themselves, she's truly smiling at you." **A. T.**

AL HINKLE (ED DUNKEL IN "ON THE ROAD")

"Neal Cassady and I worked the railroads and lived in San Jose, California. My wife Helen and I had two children, and Cassady had three. Helen (here in San Francisco with our son Mark in 1952) helped me a lot so that I could study during the annual vacation at Southern Pacific. That's me on the left in the bottom photo, taken in 1954."

CAROLYN CASSADY (CAMILLE IN "ON THE ROAD")

"These photos were taken in 1952 in San Francisco before we moved to San Jose. We rented a small house on Russian Hill where we lived for five years. Jack Kerouac lived with us. He took the photo of Neal with his arms around me. On the top photo on the right hand page, Neal and Jack are posing with my daughter Cathy."

 © JOHN COHEN, COURTESY L. PARKER STEPHENSON PHOTOGRAPHS, NYC

JOHN COHEN, PHOTOGRAPHER

"In 1959, Robert Frank had asked me to take pictures of the production of his first film *Pull My Daisy*. Kerouac visited one day, and later was at the party after the filming was done. It was during that party he tuned in to listen to himself on the radio. Poets and writers were rarely heard over the airwaves at that time. The image in the coffee shop includes the painter Larry Rivers, Jack Kerouac, musician David Amram, Allen Ginsberg, and the back of Gregory Corso's head. "

PETER ORLOVSKY, ALLEN GINSBERG AND GREGORY CORSO ON THE SET OF *PULL MY DAISY*

ARTISTS'

DIARIES

WORKS BY: WALLY HEDRICK | BRION GYSIN | RICHARD PRINCE | DENNIS HOPPER | STEPHEN SHORE | WALLACE BERMAN | ED RUSCHA

Originally a literary movement, but endowed with an extraordinary visually evocative power, the Beat Generation has proved a rich source of inspiration for the visual arts. The gas station, the recurring motif of beat iconography to the point of becoming a cliché, could be the symbol of this "lost generation," who embarked on a quest for powerful excitement and the discovering new places. The eye readily wanders while touring the wide-open spaces. Coupled with the use of photographic equipment, a road trip is the perfect opportunity to capture the spirit of the places passed through. On a psychedelic wave fueled by hallucinogenic drugs, the trip is not just physical… Many artists attempted to "*open the doors of perception*" through their work and to push back boundaries. Criticism also found expression, by more or less subversive means, against war, consumerism, communications and intellectual property. The Beat Generation artists played their part in some of the mythologizing of the United States, even as they called attention to the impending decline of the "*American way of life*" in the "*global village.*" Have a nice trip!

BY ANNE-LOU VICENTE   TRANSLATED BY AUDREY CONCANNON

WALLY HEDRICK

Autobiographical and sometimes flirting with the erotic, the Californian painter Wally Hedrick's creations are also politically charged anti-war pamphlets. The *Vietnam Series* figure amongst this Korean War veteran's major work, and are composed of colorful oid paintings many of which were painted over with black during Hedrick's protest against the Vietnam War, including the American flag painting entitled *Burn Me!* | *BIG DICK (NIXON) FOR PRESIDENT, 1960, OIL ON CANVAS*

BRION GYSIN

Writer, poet, performer and painter, Brion Gysin invented the "cut-up technique," later developed by William Burroughs. He created the *Dreamachine* in 1961 put together with a cylinder of paper, a hub and a bulb. The aptly named *Dreamachine* facilitated the production of colorful visions echoing the perceptual trips of the time. In 2011, the Galerie de France in Paris presented *Alarm*, the masterpiece of concrete poetry: a series of poems in calligraphy, printed from the original version created thirty-five years earlier by Gysin. | EXTRACT FROM *ALARM*, 1975, INK ON PAPER

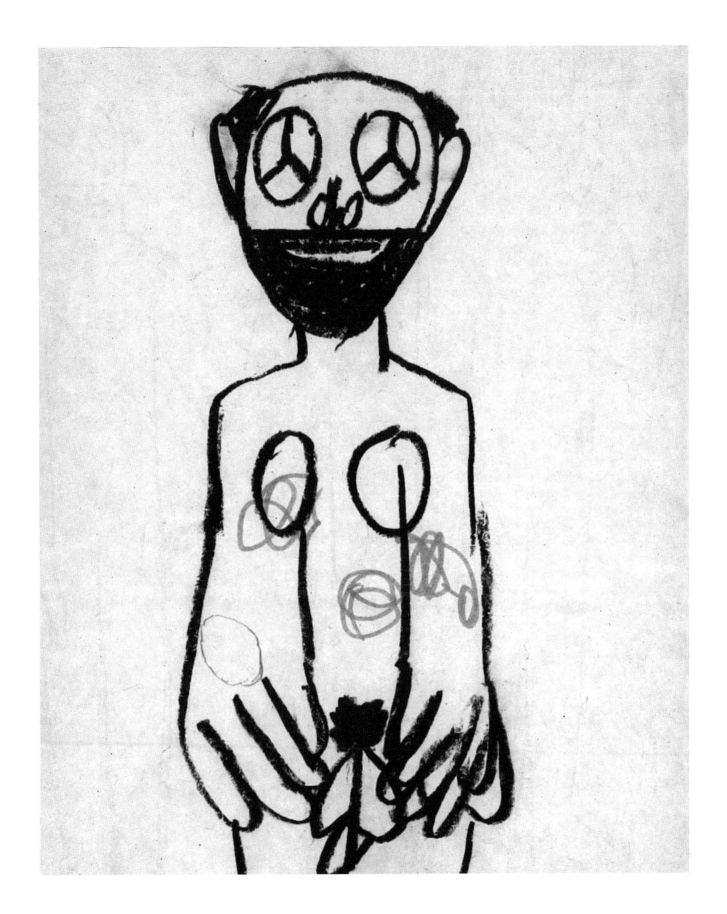

RICHARD PRINCE

Richard Prince has mastered the art of appropriation through photography and photographic collage. Questioning the copyright and authenticity of images, he faced several lawsuits, notably for having used a controversial photo by Garry Gross of the child actress Brooke Shields. A fan of Marlboro advertising's cowboys, masked nurses and busty blonds, Prince also creates hippie drawings like this portrait of Allen Ginsberg. | *UNTITLED (HIPPIE DRAWING, ALLEN GINSBERG)*, 2000-2005, PENCIL AND FELT TIP ON PAPER

DENNIS HOPPER

Dennis Hopper is best remembered as the actor and director of the cult hippie movie *Easy Rider*, released in 1969. "Born to be wild," this American counter culture icon was a poet, painter, and photographer. Just a few months after his passing in 2010, the prestigious Museum of Contemporary Art in Los Angeles devoted a retrospective to Hopper, with its title *Double Standard* borrowed from this photograph showing two gas station signs through the front windshield of a car.

DOUBLE STANDARD, 1961

STEPHEN SHORE

Stephen Shore's work marked a major turning point in photography, especially through the introduction of color, mainly used for advertising at the time. Taking his cue from Jack Kerouac, he embarked on a trip across the United States in 1973 with a photographic dark room in the trunk. Wide open spaces dotted with motels, parking lots and gas stations... his photographs document places that exist to be passed through, while painting a detailed portrait of a country and an era.

BEVERLY AND LA BREA, 1975

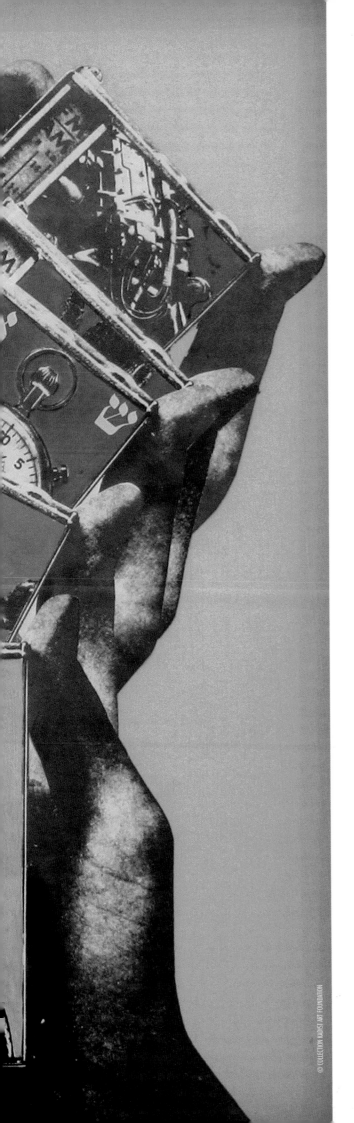

WALLACE BERMAN

"Art is Love is God" was the motto of this Kabala follower, considered the father of assemblage art. Wallace Berman worked discreetly but made a significant contribution within the Beat Generation, including self-editing his fanzine entitled *Semina*. His favourite equipment from 1964 was the Verifax, a forerunner of the photocopier derived from photographic principles. In appropriation and serial mode, his *Verifax Collages* demonstrated his ability to manipulate mass icons.

UNTITLED (SHUFFLE), 1968, COLLAGE OF VERIFAX COPIES AND ACRYLIC ON PANEL

ED RUSCHA

Originally a painter, Ed Ruscha also produces drawings, engravings, photography and films. He began a series of artist's books on subjects/objects with *Twentysix Gasoline Stations* published in 1963: gas stations, aerial views of Los Angeles parking lots, swimming pools, business cards, birthday cakes and so on. Combining Jack Kerouac's text and Ed Ruscha's photographs, the eponymous *On the Road* constitutes a double road trip, both visual and literary.

ON THE ROAD: AN ARTIST BOOK OF THE CLASSIC NOVEL BY JACK KEROUAC, 2009

WRITER'S

DIARIES

WITH: ANTONIN ARTAUD | MARCEL PROUST |
ARTHUR RIMBAUD | JOSÉ RIVERA

The famous *On the Road* scroll is crossing the Atlantic for the first time. Hidden away for years, it was recently purchased for several million dollars by a collector who has authorized a few rare peeks at it. They were always stateside, though. For the French release of *On the Road*, the film crew searched Paris high and low, seeking an appropriate temporary shrine for the scroll. They found the Musée des Lettres et Manuscrits. Opened in 2004, it is the only French museum offering a permanent exhibit of autograph documents by writers or historical figures to the general public. These include annotated proofs and manuscripts by Marcel Proust, Victor Hugo, and Charles Baudelaire... "*I created this museum because I'd observed that the works of all the painters were visible, but one could never see the handwriting of kings, emperors, and poets,*" Gérard Lhéritier, the museum founder and director, told us. For the first time in France, the upcoming Kerouac exhibition will feature the scroll and José Rivera's screenplay annotated by Walter Salles, along with documents from Kerouac's archives and those of the French writers who influenced him. We toured the premises with curator Estelle Gaudry, who commented on some of the key pieces for us.

BY ISAURE PISANI-FERRY   TRANSLATED BY ANITA CONRADE

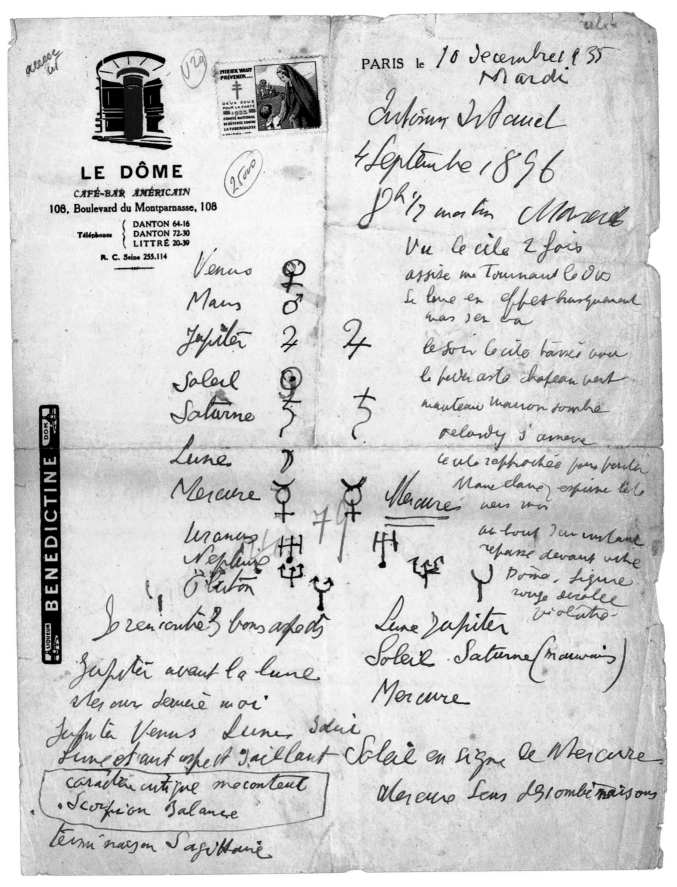

ANTONIN ARTAUD

"Kerouac and Artaud shared a passion for travel. Both were attracted to esoteric religious beliefs, off the beaten track. Kerouac was fascinated by Buddhism. Artaud studied astrology, among other things. On this document, he noted his date and place of birth, and drew an ideogram opposite each planet. The back of the page, covered with nearly illegible scribbling, is a kind of incantatory prosody Artaud spouted, inspired by his astrological chart."

ANTONIN ARTAUD'S HOROSCOPE, DRAWN AND SIGNED BY HIMSELF, PARIS, DECEMBER 10, 1935

Pas immédiatement pourtant.

avait cependant été si forte qu'il ne pouvait se figurer alors qu'il s'en délivrerait jamais et que la mort d'Odette lui semblât seule capable de lui faire le chemin libre pour qu'il pût continuer à vivre; c'est ainsi que souvent un effet de perspective nous fait croire qu'une hauteur qui est devant nous barre entièrement la route; mais Swann avait continué d'exister et s'était aperçu que le chemin contournait l'obstacle mais n'en était pas obstrué Et pourtant cette angoisse qu'Odette avait fait éprouver à Swann (pareille à celle avec laquelle j'avais connaissance à Combray le soir où il venait à la maison) lui était réservé — et, d'après ce que me raconta M. de Charlus ce ne dut pas être longtemps après que j'eus commencé à aller chez eux — de la ressentir encore, non à propos d'Odette, mais d'une autre femme. C'est que cette angoisse, Swann était arrivé à l'âge, où elle se constitue en nous à titre de maladie chronique dont le principe est en nous, et qui cherche seulement dans le monde extérieur, indépendamment duquel elle se développe, des occasions pour déclancher et justifier ses crises. A partir d'un certain âge nous ne sommes plus amoureux d'une femme, mais à propos d'une femme. Nos amours ne sont, malgré la diversité des amantes, qu'un même amour latent, expectant, toujours en imminence de crise et que le plus petit trait d'un visage qui a pu y donner prétexte fait entrer en éruption. De même cette angoisse, un peu plus rare pourtant, qui demande pour se produire des circonstances

MARCEL PROUST

"Kerouac wanted to do the same thing as Proust, but "fast." Here are Proust's legendary corrections to his galley proofs. The corrections to *Within a Budding Grove* attest to the extraordinary care Proust applied to rewriting his novel. Kerouac was a little less careful, but he shares many themes with Proust: time, memory, and... dependence on his mother, the only real woman in both men's lives." | *WITHIN A BUDDING GROVE*, CORRECTED GALLEY PROOF, 1914

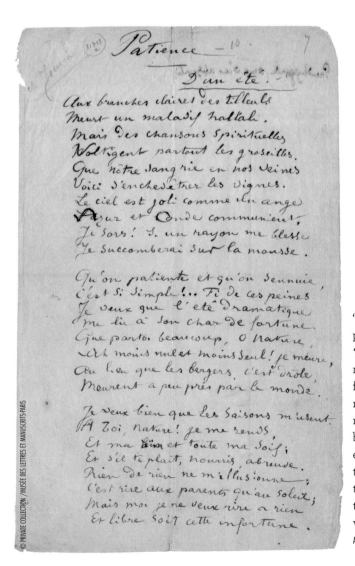

ARTHUR RIMBAUD

"1872 marks the dawn of the modern period in Rimbaud's poetry writing, that of *'the jumble of all the senses.'* Such disorder notably involved shattering the rhyming form he had hitherto respected. Instead of rhyme, Rimbaud uses alliteration, and the result is free verse. Like Rimbaud, Kerouac blasted away the barriers of style, in an expression of his opposition to conventional Western values and ways of life. For the American writer, Rimbaud was a hero, the first to have taken to the road and traveled." | *PATIENCE D'UN ÉTÉ*, AUTOGRAPH POEM SIGNED BY ARTHUR RIMBAUD. SPRING, 1872

FADE IN:

INT. PAPA'S BEDROOM, PARADISE APARTMENT, OZONE PARK, QUEENS - DAY

A humble, neat, working-class bedroom. Small crucifix, portrait of Jesus, photo of racehorse MAN-O-WAR, small RADIO.

CARD: May 1946. Ozone Park, Queens.

In a large brass bed: "PAPA" PARADISE, 57, nearly 300 pounds, a proud, once-wild, French-Canadian printer, thick eyebrows, bulbous nose, moist, luminous eyes. Dying of cancer of the spleen. *The Daily Racing Form* lies next to him.

SAL (V.O.)
I first met Dean not long after my father died.

muito bom isso vir antes da morte do pai

A DOCTOR drains BLACK LIQUID from Papa's huge belly, through a catheter, into a bucket on the floor. Papa's ink-stained hands are yellow from cirrhosis.

Watching this is SAL PARADISE, 24, a well-built former college football star, 5'8", now a struggling novelist.

Sal has clear-blue eyes, a sensitive mouth, jet-black hair. Hanging over him is the loneliness of the perpetual outsider and the passions and burdens of a restless mind. Physically Sal is a bit awkward and self-conscious.

He can't stand to see the pain his father is in, but he can't look away either: he *forces* himself to watch and remember every awful second. Takes a long drag of an Old Gold.

SAL (V.O.) (CONT'D)
I had just gotten over a serious illness that I won't bother to talk about except that it really had something to do with my father's death ...

what if Papa silently asks for a cigarette, doctor disappears, ~~Papa~~ Sal lights the old Gold

Papa looks at Sal, his eyes begging for that cigarette. Over the Doctor's disapproving look, Sal hands Papa the cigarette.

Sal and Papa pass the cigarette back and forth. Blue haze encircles their heads. There's something almost religious about the way they enjoy this smoke together.

The black, foul-smelling goo from Papa's stomach drips into the metal can.

Excellent start

— Should we include a photograph of the whole family in the room? (The one in the bar) — and Gerard's photograph?

JOSÉ RIVERA

ON THE ROAD SCREENPLAY BY JOSE RIVERA, DATED APRIL 22, 2008, ADAPTED FROM THE NOVEL BY JACK KEROUAC. HAND-WRITTEN COMMENTS BY WALTER SALLES

                    SAL (V.O.) (CONT'D)
           ... and my awful feeling that
           everything was dead.

Stabbing pain forces Papa to shut his eyes. Tries hard to
breathe. Sal holds him as if holding his own son. Kisses
Papa on the forehead.

EXT.   CEMETERY, QUEENS, NEW YORK - DAY

A gloomy, overcast day. All grey. At the side of the OPEN
GRAVE:

Sal and his mother "MA" PARADISE, 51, a stout, intense, earth-
mother with shrewd, peering eyes: fingers permanently
DARKENED from years cutting leather in a shoe factory. She
clutches rosary beads.

With them are Sal's sister NIN (22, pretty, petite), Nin's
husband PAUL (28, solid, ex-soldier), and their many FRENCH-
CANADIAN RELATIVES.

All are down-to-earth, working-class drinkers and brawlers,
somber, sturdy, modest and sorrowful. Not much poetry here.

In contrast is Sal's college friend CARLO MARX. The waif-
like Carlo is 21, intense, brooding, intellectual, a lonely
soul, a kind one, slim, with thick black hair, wide full
lips, and eager, dark eyes under round, owlish glasses.

As Ma stoically stares at her husband's grave, Carlo goes to
the shell-shocked, motionless Sal. Carlo quietly sings a
gentle, melancholy Jewish FUNERAL SONG in his ear ...

                                        FADE TO BLACK.

A RAPID SERIES OF IMAGES OF EVENTS FROM MAY 1946 TO OCTOBER
1946:

-- The explosion of a 20-kiloton ATOMIC BOMB over the Bikini
Islands. -- HERMAN GORING on trial in Nuremberg, Germany. --
The chrome-laden grille of a 1946 Plymouth. -- U.S. Navy BLUE
ANGELS fly in formation over Jacksonville, Florida. -- HO CHI
MINH arrives in Paris for talks on Vietnamese independence. --
DR. SPOCK's *Common Sense Book of Baby and Child Care* in
stacks at bookstores next to CAMUS's *The Stranger*. -- Miles
and miles of new IDENTICAL AMERICAN SUBURBS look like surreal
scars on the landscape.

[handwritten margin note: We may be able to do this differently]

                                        FADE IN:

3

INT. KITCHEN, PARADISE APARTMENT, OZONE PARK - NIGHT

In a corner: a wooden DESK, a neat stack of blank paper, an old Underwood TYPEWRITER, a copy of Goethe's *Poetry and Truth*. Pinned to the wall are little hand-written HYMNS on notebook paper.

CARD: "The great home of the soul is the open road." -- D.H. Lawrence.

CARD: October 1946.

Sal hasn't fully recovered from the death of his father. He sits at the desk, faces the silent typewriter, quietly sings Gershwin's "Why Was I Born?" to himself.

Nothing comes. Through the open window, Sal hears SOME STRANGER WHISTLE "Zip-a-Dee-Do-Dah." Annoyed by the silly optimism, Sal takes a drag from his cigarette. Nothing comes. Pours some Tokay, downs it. Nothing comes.

Frustrated, he crushes the cigarette in an ashtray and gets up from his desk.

[handwritten: - what if we cut to the "how to be a good girl" on a TV on the streets? Sal watches it with Carlo, gets away.]

INT. COFFEE SHOP NEAR COLUMBIA UNIVERSITY, NEW YORK - NIGHT

Filled with COLUMBIA STUDENTS in intense discussions. Cigarette SMOKE, coffee, collegiate posturing. A wall poster advertises Ethel Merman in *Annie Get Your Gun*. One STUDENT reads a New York Times: an article about a BLACK COUPLE being lynched in Monroe, Georgia. *[handwritten: Excellent]*

ANOTHER ANGLE reveals Sal and Carlo in a BOOTH filled with cups of coffee, butt-filled ashtrays. Sal looks different from the effete intellectuals around him: he dresses like a lumberjack and his weary eyes possess a sly, working-class skepticism.

Carlo's clothes are ragged, Chaplinesque; he wears a paisley scarf and smokes a cigarette in a red holder; he clutches copies of Blake and Celine. In mid-conversation: *[handwritten: see pg 2A]*

> SAL
> -- To do it *right*, you have to take your consciousness and spread it out on the page so the words look like, you know, music -- *jazz* -- that's the way consciousness really *digs* everything that happens. You getting me, Carlo? That's what I'm trying to find in *art* but --

[handwritten left: this is yet to be discovered -- writing / jazz.]

[handwritten left: Too soon]

[handwritten right: maybe too explicit... at least for the beginning of the film]

[handwritten bottom: This is the answer to his question. Don't solve it now!!]

CARLO
Hand over them fries, young
Melville, they're going to waste as
you blah-blah-blah.

Great!

SAL
The thing is, I'm not finding it
here, in New York. I'm telling
you, New *York* ... just call it dead
and summon all the undertakers.
It's stultified with all these old
forms borrowed from the tombs of
Europe where nobody writes from
their *sweat* and their *balls* --

Plot's too
direct.

CARLO
Except for Celine and Rimbaud and
Artaud and Joyce and Genet --

) Carlo is perfect

SAL
I know, I know -- I don't know what
I want -- no -- I *know* what I want:
I want uninterrupted rapture. I
mean why should I compromise with
anything, or with the bourgeois
calm of the backyard lawn?

CARLO
Careful or they'll get you for
being a Bolshevik.

SAL
Shit on Russians, shit on
Americans, I'm going to live in my
own lazy no good way, *that's* what
I'm going to do.

Sal should
still the
mourning
his
father's
death at
the beginning
of the
film.
Make him
more active
later.
That would
be the arch

Before Sal can respond, a handsome, young, bright Columbia
student, tall and blonde, CHAD KING, runs up to the booth,
cigarette dangling from his lip.

CHAD
Guys! You remember that jailhouse
friend of mine, Dean, from Denver?
Read all of Schopenhauer in the
State pen?

SAL
Stole a million cars and laid a
million girls?

CARLO
Cocksman of the West!

SKETCHES

DIARIES

COMMENTARY BY **CARLOS CONTI**

Kerouac's road trip featured a repetitive series of geographical markers like gas pumps and seedy motels. The issue was how to faithfully render the weathered facades and vintage cars. The reconstitution of *On the Road* was a logistical nightmare for Walter Salles' crew that entailed printing the patina of time onto the film without succumbing to nostalgic caricature. Under the watchful eye of the cinematographer Eric Gautier, the image also owes some of its visual qualities and corroded look to Carlos Conti, Head Production Designer on *The Motorcycle Diaries* and *Betty Blue*. He designed the movie's different sets mixing vintage pieces and crafts, with the aid of the artist Maud Gircourt. He comments on his preparatory sketches: "*Making* On the Road *was an exciting and complex job. To depict this 'road' meant traveling around four countries and dozens of cities coordinating separate crews in the United States, Canada, Mexico and Argentina.*" A portfolio through the rearview mirror.

BY CLÉMENTINE GALLOT | TRANSLATED BY AUDREY CONCANNON   DRAWINGS BY CARLOS CONTI

"

2. "In the novel, Sal Paradise lives on the first floor of a small building above a drugstore. So we transformed a Laundromat into a drugstore. The interiors were shot in different locations."

"

3.

4.

"

3. "We recreated the Blackstone Hotel exterior, which is located in San Francisco in the film, using a street in New Orleans with streetcar tracks. We added a fake façade and altered the other stores."

"

"

4. "After the scene in the bus station, the character Sal stops in front of a few stores. The window of a bridal store was converted into an electrical goods store."

TRAVEL
DIARIES

"THE END OF THE ROAD: THE SECOND UNIT TEAM IN FRONT OF AN ABANDONED GAS STATION, IN THE COLORADO DESERT. ALL THE PHOTOGRAPHS WERE TAKEN IN SCOPE (2.35) WITH A HASSELBLAD XPAN CAMERA."

WITH:

WALTER SALLES | GARRETT HEDLUND | GREGORY SMITH | ÉRIC GAUTIER | CARLOS CONTI

Walter Salles is an all-round artist. Brazilian of Spanish descent, raised between Rio de Janeiro, Paris and California and an accomplished multi-linguist, Walter Salles travels across continents and between fields of interest with ease. After having directed documentaries on filmmakers (Akira Kurosawa), musicians (Chico Buarque, Marisa Monte) and visual artists (Frans Krajcberg), he specialized in road movies with *Foreign Land* (1995), *Central do Brasil* (1998) and *The Motorcycle Diaries* (2004) while exploring the thriller (*Exposure* in 1991, *Dark Water* in 2005) and drama genres (*Broken April* in 2001, *Linha de Passe* in 2009). On The Road reminds one of a compendium: by combining his multiple identities and interests, such as music, sports and cars, Walter Salles who is fine-tuned in the art of adapting literature to the big screen, managed to fully grasp the novel's essence. Photography being one amongst many of his interests, he was enabled to document the great adventure of shooting the film by taking pictures from behind the scenes, from Garett Hedlund's first screen tests in 2007 to the second unit's journey in 2011 (they were in charge of shooting aditionnal sequences). He has exclusively selected and commented on ten key shots for us to enjoy.

BY AURELIANO TONET   TRANSLATED BY LAURA HUGO WESTERHOUT – PHOTO BY WALTER SALLES

"AN IMPROMPTU STOPOVER ON THE TEXAS - NEW MEXICO BORDER: AFTER 400 KMS AT FULL SPEED, THE HUDSON IS OVERHEATING."

"ON A ROAD IN TEXAS. GARRETT IS PLACING THE CIGARETTE PACK 'UNDER HIS T-SHIRT', A DETAIL MENTIONED TO HIM BY CAROLYN CASSADY."

"GARRETT AND THE PHOTOGRAPHER GREGORY SMITH, BETWEEN TWO TAKES ON THE BORDER BETWEEN ARIZONA AND CALIFORNIA."

"NEAR TEXARKANA, BETWEEN TEXAS AND ARKANSAS: "TWO BENNIES A DAY KEEP THE COPS AWAY…" " (IN REFERENCE TO A PASSAGE FROM *ON THE ROAD* BY KEROUAC.)

"ONE OF THE FIRST SHOTS OF GARRETT AS DEAN, NEAR LOS ANGELES IN 2007. PRESS (ON HIS RIGHT) IS A HUDSON COLLECTOR AND OUR CONSULTANT FOR EVERYTHING THAT INVOLVED THE CAR IN THE FILM. UNLIKE THE OTHER PHOTOGRAPHS, THIS ONE WAS TAKEN IN I.50 WITH A LEICA M7 CAMERA."

"DEAN IN SEARCH OF A FATHER, IN DENVER."

"GARRETT AND THE HUDSON, ON THE LAST DAY OF SHOOTING, AFTER A THREE WEEK LONG TRIP FROM NEW YORK TO CALIFORNIA."

"AN ABANDONED TOWN IN THE HEART OF MISSISSIPPI. WAL-MART IS DOWN THE ROAD."

"LAST DAY OF SHOOTING WITH THE SECOND UNIT. NEAR TWENTY-NINE PALMS, IN CALIFORNIA."

SAM RILEY, KRISTEN STEWART AND WALTER SALLES ON THE SET OF *ON THE ROAD*

TITLE	*ON THE ROAD*	RELEASE DATE
DIRECTOR	WALTER SALLES	2012

THE FILM

GENRE	ROAD MOVIE	ORIGIN	FR.	U.K	U.S.A.

WITH	SAM RILEY	GARRETT HEDLUND	KRISTEN
	STEWART	TOM STURRIDGE	KIRSTEN DUNST
	VIGGO MORTENSEN	AMY ADAMS	ELISABETH
	MOSS	DANNY MORGAN	TERRENCE HOWARD
	STEVE BUSCEMI		

Jack Kerouac
1418½ Clouser St
Orlando, Fla

Dear Marlon

I'm praying that you'll buy ON THE ROAD and make a movie of it. Dont worry about structure, I know how to compress and re-arrange the plot a bit to give perfectly acceptable movie-type structure: making it into one all-inclusive trip instead of the several voyages coast-to-coast in the book, one vast round trip from New York to Denver to Frisco to Mexico to New Orleans to New York again. I visualize the beautiful shots could be made with the camera on the front seat of the car showing the road (day and night) unwinding into the windshield, as Sal and Dean yak. I wanted you to play the part because Dean (as you know) is no dopey hotrodder but a real intelligent (in fact Jesuit) Irishman. You play Dean and I'll play Sal (Warner Bros. mentioned I play Sal) and I'll show you how Dean acts in real life, you couldnt possibly imagine it without seeing a good imitation. Fact, we can go visit him in Frisco, or have him come down to L.A. still a real frantic cat but nowadays settled down with his final wife saying the Lord's Prayer with his kiddies at night...as you'll seen when you read the play BEAT GENERATION. All I want out of this is to be able to establish myself and my mother a trust fund for life, so I can really go roaming around the world writing about Japan, India, France etc. ...I want to be free to write what comes out of my head & free to feed my buddies when they're hungry & not worry about my mother.

        Incidentally, my next novel is THE SUBTERRANEANS coming out in N.Y. next March and is about a love affair between a white guy and a colored girl and very hep story. Some of the characters in it you knew in the Village (Stanley Gould? etc.) It easily could be turned into a play, easier than ON THE ROAD.

        What I wanta do is re-do the theater and the cinema in America, give it a spontaneous dash, remove pre-conceptions of "situation" and let people rave on as they do in real life. That's what the play is: no plot in particular, no "meaning" in particular, just the way people are. Everything I write I do in the spirit where I imagine myself an Angel returned to the earth seeing it with sad eyes as it is. I know you approve of these ideas, & incidentally the new Frank Sinatra show is based on "spontaneous" too, which is the only way to come on anyway, whether in show business or life. The French movies of the 30's are still far superior to ours because the French really let their actors come on and the writers didnt quibble with some preconceived notion of how intelligent the movie audience is, the talked soul from soul and everybody understood at once. I want to make great French Movies in America, finally, when I'm rich ...American Theater & Cinema at present is an outmoded Dinosaur that aint mutated along with the best in American Literature.

        If you really want to go ahead, make arrangements to see me in New York when next you come, or if you're going to Florida here I am, but what we should do is talk about this because I prophesy that it's going to be the beginning of something real great. I'm bored nowadays and I'm looking around for something to do in the void, anyway——writing novels is getting too easy, same with plays, I wrote the play in 24 hours.

        Come on now, Marlon, put up your dukes and write!

            Sincerely, later, Jack Kerouac

ADAPTATION TIME

★

FROM BOOK TO FILM, THE TALE OF A TORTUOUS ADAPTATION

TOO LONG, OVERWRITTEN AND OVER-ELABORATE. ERRATIC, FRAGMENTED, DATED AND EXPENSIVE WITH TOO MANY ROADS: IMPOSSIBLE TO ADAPT. BELOW HOLLYWOOD'S LETTERED HILL, PAGES UPON PAGES HAVE BEEN INKED WITH SYNOPSES, EXCLUSIVE CONTRACTS, PROJECTS SCRIBBLED ON PAPER TABLECLOTHS... ALL OF THEM TORN UP IN THE END. *ON THE ROAD*'S OPENING CREDITS WOULDN'T ROLL FOR ANOTHER 60 YEARS. NOT UNTIL *THE MOTORCYCLE DIARIES* BY WALTER SALLES MADE IT POSSIBLE TO WRITE THE END OF THE STORY AT LONG LAST. THE PRODUCERS GIVE THEIR ACCOUNT OF THIS FINAL CHAPTER.

BY ÉTIENNE ROUILLON | | TRANSLATED BY AUDREY CONCANNON

He wrote to Neal Cassady, *"I'll revolutionize American letters and drink champagne with Hollywood starlets."* He delivered on the first part but was stuck with plain water for the second. Yet, it wasn't for lack of trying from the outset. With copies of *On the Road* hot off the press in 1957, Kerouac confidently put pen to paper in a letter (found in 2005) addressed to Marlon Brando. He has a great idea for him: Brando buys the rights to *On the Road* to make a film. Marlon plays Dean and Jack plays Sal. In fact, Kerouac is bored: *"writing novels is getting too easy, same with plays, I wrote the play in 24 hours. Come on now, Marlon, put your dukes up and write!"* And he already has clear ideas on directing it: *"I visualize the beautiful shots that could be made with the camera on the front seat of the car showing the road (day and night) unwinding into the windshield, as Sal and Dean yak."* The tone is certainly pretty gutsy, but this is no wonder writer's faddish whim puffed up by the recent publication of his novel.

URBAN LEGENDS

As a child, Kerouac had a passion for theatre and loved staging backdrops. That's why he immediately took care to reassure Brando on the big black cloud that cast a long shadow on the adaptation projects to come: this book is a real pain to adapt. *"Don't worry about structure, I know how to compress and re-arrange the plot a bit to give perfectly acceptable movie-like structure: making it into all one-inclusive trip instead of the several voyages coast-to-coast in the book."* Roman Coppola, head of the American Zoetrope production company with his sister Sofia, has seen a lot of people struggle with it: *"Ah yes, the famous letter to Brando! But isn't that a myth? You managed to get hold of it? It's just that there are so many myths about* On the Road *and beat culture (see p. 222). For instance, I heard about a project with Montgomery Clift. In my opinion, Hollywood was fascinated by the idea of making a movie from the start. The book was very popular there. But there was a catch. Movies are usually built*

"ON THE ROAD" HAS PASSED THROUGH MANY ILLUSTRIOUS HANDS OVER THE YEARS. IN THE LATE 1970S, FRANCIS FORD COPPOLA SUGGESTED TO JEAN-LUC GODARD THAT HE DIRECT IT, WITH NO FOLLOW THROUGH. LATER, GUS VAN SANT WAS IN THE RUNNING.

around the classic 'beginning-middle-end' plot structure. On the Road *is famous for being absolutely unconventional in this respect. Most of the adaptation projects contemporaneous with Kerouac focussed on that and the results have never been satisfying."*

Indeed, Roman admits that he too tried to develop a screenplay of the book with himself slated to direct. In fact, the book and its adaptation to the big screen haunted the Coppola family for decades. *"We set to work in 1979,"* resumes Roman Coppola. *"My father, Francis Ford Coppola, was very interested in the story and bought the movie rights to the book. In most cases, when it comes to rights in Hollywood, in actual fact, you're really buying an option. Meaning that you buy exclusive adaption rights on the project for two or three years. So the longer a project drags on the more you have to pay. I don't exactly know how it happened, but my father was actually able to buy the book. No business about options. It was his. Otherwise, he would eventually have dropped the project. He always believed that it would make a wonderful film. Everything was just a matter of timing and meetings. And then Walter Salles came along eight years ago."*

FRENCH TOUCH
Walter Salles recalls, *"An adaptation*

of On the Road? *I had never thought about it before the end of* The Motorcycle Diaries. *The book had such an iconic quality to me that the idea of adapting it never even crossed my mind. It was only after* The Motorcycle Diaries *was presented at Sundance in 2004 that the idea started to take shape."* Francis Ford Coppola was so impressed with the film, he zeroxed in on Salles as the missing link in his plans. *On the Road* has passed through many illustrious hands over the years. In the late 1970s, Francis Ford Coppola suggested to Jean-Luc Godard that he direct it, with no follow through. Later, Gus Van Sant was in the running, as the writer and screenwriter Barry Gifford (*Wild at Heart*) tells us: *"Francis hired me to write the screenplay for the movie in 1995. The director was Gus Van Sant. For a variety of reasons we were in the dark, we weren't able to finalize the project. I'm delighted that Walter Salles has been able to pull it off. We've become friends as we have a lot in common. He called and invited me to be a consultant on his movie, which I accepted with pleasure. Walter used my book* Jack's Book *like a bible. It was the first object of its kind, a written chronological documentary, constructed like a video, a 'bookmovie' as Kerouac said. There are obviously many ways to adapt a novel to the screen. What I know for sure is that Walter's version is*

true to himself."

Salles' profound personal commitment is key to understanding why this project at last came to fruition. It had yet to sign a company able to engage wholeheartedly in what for any executive producer constitutes a nightmare project: the period road movie. The MK2 producer Charles Gillibert, who is credited with accelerating the main production process, describes how he was taken over by Walter Salles' contagious enthusiasm. *"In early January 2010, Marin Karmitz, Nathanaël Karmitz and I had a meeting with Walter Salles at MK2 headquarters in Paris to discuss another project he was working on. After a good hour of discussions on the screenplay, directing, cinema... we were just about to leave. Walter pulled out a manila envelope with the title hand-written in pen: 'On the Road.' He handed it to us, saying: "– And there's this as well.*
– On the Road, like the book?
– Yes!"
The tone of his voice betrayed the fact: as we parted we were broaching a subject of much greater magnitude. Walter headed for the airport to fly back to Brazil. We called him back the next day. He returned to Paris two weeks later with all sorts of documents accompanied by Carlos Conti, the production designer. We began by viewing screen tests of Garrett Hedlund, who'd refused all the roles he was offered for two years for fear of missing out on On the Road, *as well as tests with Sam Riley. We also talked to Kristen Stewart, whom we'd met before the release of the first* Twilight *film. Miles and miles of location scouting, photos, videos, script meetings, gathering the technical crews and so on. Walter had already traveled the route taken by Kerouac and met all the figures involved in the Beat adventure and the book. He was completely possessed by* On the Road. *The film already existed, we just had to find it."* They did find it in California. *"Ten days later, Nathanaël and I*

WALTER SALLES, SAM RILEY, DANY RACINE (FIRST ASSISTANT CAMERA) AND THE DIRECTOR OF CINEMATOGRAPHER ÉRIC GAUTIER ON THE SET OF *ON THE ROAD*

"THE FILM ALREADY EXISTED, WE JUST HAD TO FIND IT."

CHARLES GILLIBERT

arrived in Los Angeles to discuss the film rights with Roman Coppola and Rebecca Yeldham, Walter's producer (who worked with him on The Motorcycle Diaries and Linha de Passe.) We gave ourselves one week to reach an agreement as shooting was due to start in the summer."

BEAT IT

"*Profoundly harmonious,*" recalls Rebecca Yeldham, in every possible way – rapturous, amazing, nostalgic, and poetic – when asked to tell us about this summit meeting after five decades of thwarted adaptations. "*I knew of MK2 as I am very involved in the promotion of foreign films in the United States. When we met them, we'd already been working on the project for 6 years. We'd already struggled with the notion of adapting the quintessential American novel as a foreign crew – Walter is Brazilian, I'm Australian, Jose Rivera is Puerto Rican, Éric Gaultier is French and Carlos Conti is Argentine. This led us to seek increased legitimacy on the project, which is why we did all this research, the interviews and the trips. So when MK2 came onboard, we already had this sense of trust in the universality of the book's resonances. Nathanaël and Charles were on the same page as us. Their enthusiasm and courage gave us such a boost that it soon became clear that they were the ideal partners. Sometimes the fact that a film gets* made is a sheer alchemical miracle." Then, after the first six days everyone's ok and its all systems go. "*I don't think Walter ever wondered: 'How would Kerouac have shot it?' On the other hand, I do think he was conscious of another question: 'Would Kerouac approve of what I'm doing?' He also knew that it had to be his adaptation, faithful yet creative too. Throughout this eight-year adventure, Walter worked hard to learn about everyone and everything associated with* On the Road *and the culture surrounding it. I think the film is the fruit of these efforts and our shared dedication to honor this beloved text. And with respect to Kerouac, I think that we can be confident about how he would have received our movie, given what he wrote in the letter to Marlon Brando, '…it's going to be the beginning of something real great.'*" ●

INTERVIEW

WALTER SALLES

MASTER CRAFTSMAN

SINCE HIS FIRST FEATURE *EXPOSURE*, IN 1991, WALTER SALLES HAS BECOME A MASTER IN THE ART OF STEALTH. HIS FILMS ARE PEPPERED WITH THEFTS, DODGES, AND ESCAPES, AS IF SUCH PURSUITS WERE NECESSARY STOPOVERS ON A LONG-HAUL QUEST FOR IDENTITY, SENSITIVE AND SURPRISING. THE FISTFUL OF ROAD MOVIES SALLES HAS MADE (*FOREIGN LAND* IN 1995, *CENTRAL STATION* IN 1998, AND *THE MOTORCYCLE DIARIES* IN 2004) INTELLIGENTLY RENOVATED THE GENRE. NOW FRANCIS FORD COPPOLA HAS ENTRUSTED HIM WITH *ON THE ROAD*. AFTER FIVE YEARS OF CAREFUL RESEARCH, THE BRAZILIAN HAS TAKEN HOLD OF THE NOVEL IN HIS OWN WAY, SKILLFUL AND HUMANISTIC, THOUGHTFUL AND SPONTANEOUS, *"BETRAYING IT TO BE EVEN MORE FAITHFUL TO IT."* HERE IS OUR HIGH-FLYING INTERVIEW WITH THE HIGHWAYMAN RIDING ON URGENCY AND CONTEMPLATION.

BY AURELIANO TONET | TRANSLATED BY ANITA CONRADE

WALTER SALLES, SAM RILEY (SEEN FROM THE BACK) AND VIGGO MORTENSEN ON THE SET OF *ON THE ROAD*

Do you remember how you felt the first time you read *On the Road*?

I read the book during a rough period in Brazil, the years of the military regime. Censorship affected the press, the publishing houses, music, theater and cinema, all forms of cultural expression. *On the Road* wasn't published in Brazil at the time, so I had to read it in English. I was immediately taken by those characters seeking different forms of freedom, by the jazz-infused narrative, by the way sex and drugs were seen as instruments to expand our understanding of the world. It was the exact reverse angle of what we were going through. So Kerouac's vision made a profound impression on me, and on many other people of my generation as well. Symbolically, *On the Road* was published in Brazil in 1983, when the country was moving back towards democracy. The book was so emblematic for me that the idea of adapting it for the screen didn't occur to me until much later.

More largely, what are your affinities with the Beat Generation?

I was a teenager in the early 1970s. For people of my generation, it wasn't difficult to understand that most of the

THE SEARCH FOR A FATHER IS A VITAL THEME IN THE ORIGINAL SCROLL, EVEN MORE SO THAN IN THE 1957 VERSION, AND IT BECAME ONE OF THE MOTORS DRIVING THE ADAPTATION.

need the sense of a future. And we need freedom, we need to get beyond ourselves, or in states of mind that allow us to travel to other worlds, to rise above our immediate surroundings." For me, this is what the Beats made possible. They radically changed the way we live.

In your work-in-progress documentary *Searching for* On the Road, you talk about all the research you did before starting the shoot. Why was this such an important step for you?

When the initial conversations with American Zoetrope took place in 2004, I didn't feel ready. The possibility of undertaking the adaptation was so complex that I proposed to shoot a documentary first, following Kerouac's steps in *On the Road,* trying to better understand the odyssey described in the book. I was also aiming to gain a more in-depth perspective on the issues facing that generation, the socio-political context of the late 1940s, early 1950s. We shot this documentary for five years...

Which version of *On the Road* did you and your co-writer Jose Rivera use for the screenplay?

In Lowell, Massachusetts, the town

where Kerouac spent much of his childhood and adolescence, we had the privilege to meet John Sampas, Jack's brother-in-law. We were starting to shoot the documentary. John was very generous and showed us a copy of the original scroll, three years before it was officially published in 2007.

I was immediately struck by the urgency and immediacy of this version. The first sentence already heralded a different type of narrative. The version published in 1957 began: *"I met Dean not long after my wife and I split up."* The scroll begins differently, *"I first met Neal not long after my father died."*

The hero of the scroll has just suffered a loss that compels him to go forward. The search for a father is a vital theme in the scroll, even more so than in the version published in 1957. This is a theme that has always interested me, and it became one of the motors driving the adaptation. For five years, Jose Rivera and I worked through and talked about many different versions of the screenplay. We tried to respect the book as much as possible. Sometimes we deviated from it – bifurcating in order to be more faithful to it. Since *The Motorcycle Diaries* days, I strongly believe that an adaptation should incite the audience to return to the book, the original version. In this process, our hope is that audiences will be inspired to construct their own versions of *On the Road.*

Kerouac writes in a lush, lyrical, and opulent style. How far did you stray from Kerouacian language?

On the Road is often seen as a narrative circumscribed to what has been lived. But, like some of Kerouac's fans, I believe that the book's unique resonance and originality lies in its ability to straddle the coexistence of what has been experienced, and what has been imagined. Here's an example: Kerouac describes William Burroughs' house in New Orleans as an old, decaying, Southern colonial mansion. In reality,

liberation movements we were witnessing or taking part in when we were 20 had their roots in the generation of Ginsberg, Kerouac, Snyder, di Prima, McClure or Baraka. They had quite simply redefined the culture from within. Recently, I read a very resonant piece written by Oliver Sacks in *The New Yorker,* in which he said that *"to live on a day-to-day basis in insufficient for human beings; we need to transcend, transport, escape; we need meaning, understanding and explanation. We*

VIGGO HAS DONE EXTENSIVE RESEARCH ON BURROUGHS. THE IMPROVISATION ON CELINE IS A SUGGESTION BROUGHT BY HIM. HE'S ONE OF THE CO-AUTEURS OF THE FILM.

VIGGO MORTENSEN AND WALTER SALLES

the house where Burroughs hosted Kerouac and Neal Cassady in Algiers is quite different: a small wooden structure, nestled on a calm street. It didn't have an orgone accumulator as described in *On the Road*. But it doesn't matter, because the old mansion and the orgone accumulator were derived from tales about Burroughs that Kerouac had heard from Ginsberg, when Allen and Neal went to his farm in Texas: mythologies he integrated into *On the Road*. The book transcends the factual report. It is the product of a rare ability to link what has been experienced with elements created by an endlessly creative imagination. This is the spirit we tried to be faithful to.

On the Road is full of contradictions. Radical freedom is touted on one page, whereas the next may be far more conservative. In particular, the book has been criticized for misogyny. How did you overcome this dichotomy?

Like all great books, *On the Road* elicits different reactions, depending on the reader's point of view. If you read Barry Gifford's wonderful oral biography of Kerouac, *Jack's Book,* you'll see how the same scene allows for different interpretations, like Kurosawa's *Rashomon*. Yes, some believe that the book can be seen as misogynistic. But I also spoke to young women who see Marylou's character as a woman who's way ahead of her time, a teenager who

shatters the sexual taboos of the 1950s, and acts in a manner that was forbidden in puritanical post-war America. If the female characters are more present in the film than in the book, it is precisely because this was our interpretation of the book.

Your films, like many other road movies, often involve two people travelling together. How did you set up the Sal-and-Dean duo?

Kerouac gives you a clear understanding of their relationship. Dean is the instigator, the incendiary, the *"Western wind"* who upends all the convictions held by the group of New York intellectuals that Kerouac and Allen were part

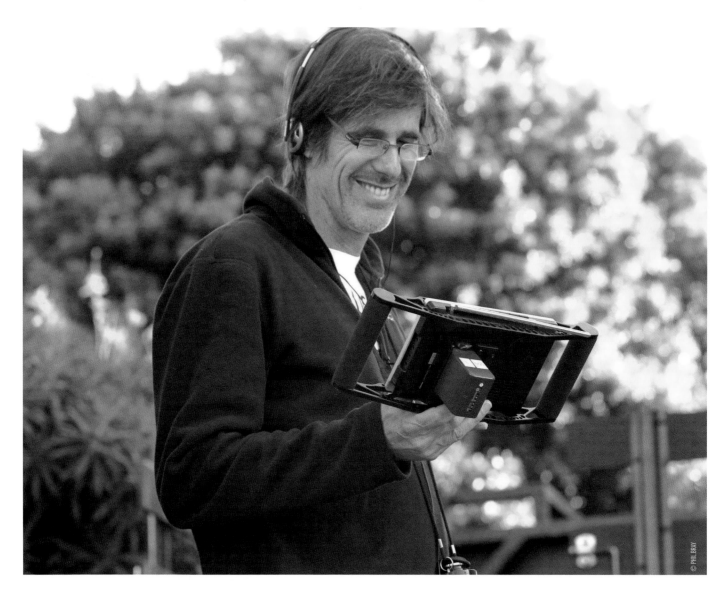

of before Dean landed in New York. Neal/Dean was such a compelling character that he not only served as the central protagonist in several of Kerouac's books, but also in *Go* by John Clellon Holmes, and of several of Ginsberg's poems. Sal is a sensitive observer, one who expresses in words the breath of freedom Dean brings, enabling us to share it. When I was making the documentary, I sometimes heard people criticize Neal for selfishly taking advantage of his friends. But one might wonder who ultimately took advantage of whom. In fact, this fascinating question underlies the narrative of the film.

The wide open spaces are a prominent part of *On the Road*. How did you and Eric Gautier plan the cinematography?

Physical geography is at the heart of the book, but to a lesser extent than what might be called the characters' internal geography. In her insightful introduction to *On the Road*, Ann Charters says that Kerouac's novel can

WE WERE INTERESTED IN FILMING THE CHARACTERS' DESIRE TO REVEAL WHAT WAS UNKNOWN TO THEM, ALONGSIDE THEIR INNER CONFLICTS.

also be seen as a story about the end of the road. The United States were defined by the historical impulse of this westward journey. It's no accident that the Western is the quintessential North American film genre. The end of the conquest of the West signalled the beginning of the end of the American dream, and the characters in *On the Road* carry this dichotomy within themselves. We were especially interested in

filming this desire to reveal what was unknown to them, alongside their inner conflicts. From the beginning, Eric Gautier, with his brilliantly sharp eye, understood the paradox. He is on the lookout, camera in hand, for the characters and their oscillations. As Eric pointed out, shooting *On the Road* in black and white would have been mere fulfilment of expectation, a citation of Robert Frank's *The Americans*. I'd rather keep black and white for a contemporary film – something I did in *Foreign Land* a film about the 1990s in Brazil.

Your adaptation of *On the Road* follows a rhythm similar to the one in the book, alternating moments of introspection and acceleration. Could your film be regarded as a "making-of" about itself?

The book contains the same duality. On the one hand, you have the urgency of a generation exploring all the senses, living to be-bop and Benzedrine tempos. The improvisational quality of jazz resonates throughout the book. On the other hand, you have the contemplation and introspection that are unique to Kerouac. We've tried to express this to-and-fro motion in the film. But a film is also impregnated by what we experience during the shoot as a family: moments of happiness, doubt, joy and despair. Shooting *The Motorcycle Diaries* was not easy, but *On the Road* was ten times harder. For one thing, South America is still a last frontier, whereas the North American frontier has been congested with Wal-Marts and suburban sprawl. We had to go a long way, sometimes a very long way, to achieve the sensation of finding new territory.

Although jazz is the lifeblood of *On the Road*, it has influenced generations of rockers. Do the characters in your film do the jitterbug, or pop their fingers to be-bop?

For *The Motorcycle Diaries*, composer Gustavo Santaolalla had worked

from the onset of production, composing themes that inspired us throughout the shoot. *On the Road* got off to a sudden start thanks to MK2's young producers Nathanael Karmitz and Charles Gillibert, so quickly that we didn't have time to prepare the soundtrack beforehand, except for a Slim Gaillard song. So Gustavo began composing as we were shooting, before even seeing the images. This process creates a gap between the image and the music which I find more interesting. Music ceases to underline the image. When you have someone as talented as Gustavo collaborating with you, you'd better take advantage of it! For the music, Gustavo worked with brilliant musicians like Charlie Haden and Brian Blade, and the recording sessions in Los Angeles were truly blissful. I'm very fond of the Liberation Music Orchestra that Haden leads, and Charlie is a pretty incredible storyteller...

On the Road tells the story of youth burning like candles in the night – but it also encompasses moments of joy, reflected in the exuberant dance sequences. How did you make sure the actors' playing brought out these waves of energy?

Yes, the characters in the book burn, burn, burn like Roman candles... How can this energy be represented onscreen? In the characters' body language and gestures, in the constant motion that defines the film, in moments of ecstasy like the dancing scenes. But we also had to find interludes of silence and contemplation, to contrast with the sequences that were defined by a fast tempo.

How did you approach casting the film?

The cast was built over the years, starting in 2004 and 2005. Kirsten Dunst was the first actress I spoke to, with Camille in mind. I had met Carolyn Cassady and was impressed by how incredibly sharp, cultivated and luminous she was. I have always found Kirsten's acting incredibly precise, nothing is unnecessarily underlined. For Kristen Stewart, things happened in an unforeseen way. Gustavo Santaolalla and Alejandro González Inárritu had just seen a first cut of *Into the Wild* and told me, *"Don't look any further for Marylou. There's a girl in the new Sean Penn film, and she is fantastic."* I saw Penn's film, which I loved, and met Kristen just before the *Twilight* saga started. She knew the book extremely well, and she understood Marylou. Kristen stayed committed to the film during all the years of uncertainty. As for Garrett, he came in for a test. He asked to read a text he'd written while riding a bus from Minnesota to Los Angeles, stopping in nude-bars and so forth. By the time he'd gotten halfway through, I knew he would be Dean. Garrett also waited for years. Whenever he got an offer for another film, he would call first. A friendship emerged from the trust we had in each other, as it did with Gael García Bernal. Tom Sturridge also did a great test for us, reading for Carlo. I remember everyone in the room being so taken by it. When I saw *Control,* I was very impressed by Sam

Riley's performance as Ian Curtis. It was simply brilliant. He came to read with Garrett in New York, and I was profoundly moved by his humanity and intelligence, as well as his precision as an actor. These were the qualities necessary to play a writer. Closer to the shoot, Viggo joined us to play Bull Lee, as well as Amy Adams. They are both genius actors, who can morph into any character seamlessly and grant them an incredible inner life. When Viggo came to New Orleans, he brought the typing machine Burroughs was using at the time, the same guns, and he had done extensive research on what Burroughs was reading in 1949. It happened to be the Mayan Codes and the works of Celine. The improvisation on Celine in the film is a suggestion brought by Viggo. He's one of the co-auteurs of the film.

You decided to have the actors playing the leading roles gather in a "beatnik camp" prior to the shoot. Why?

It's an experiment we've been carrying out since *The Motorcycle Diaries.* The idea is to create a community before we begin creating the film.

Barry Gifford, who wrote the great *Jack's Book* and had researched *On the Road* and Kerouac's work thoroughly, came to the camp to talk to us about the book and its characters. He was extremely generous and truly inspiring. Barry had interviewed LuAnne Henderson, and listening to the recordings he made with her was a big help to Kristen. Gerald Nicosia, who wrote the Kerouac biography *Memory Babe,* also brought hours of LuAnne's interviews and introduced us to her daughter, Anne Marie Santos. Anne Marie brought a wealth of photos and information about her mother. It was very moving to see her with Kristen. Just as when Neal Cassady's son John came to see us. He was incredibly open with Garrett, and communicated something fundamental to us: *On the Road* is not a story about the Beat Generation. It's a story about young men, 18, 20 years old, mostly sons of immigrants who don't find their place in the conservative America of the late 1940s and 1950s and collide against it. *On the Road* is the moment before the eruption, the lava

forming and boiling under the surface, about to emerge… it's about the formative years of a brilliant generation. There you go: here's another parallel with *The Motorcycle Diaries*.

In your opinion, where does Kerouac's modernity lie?

In the desire to explore everything in the flesh. To feel, smell, taste, live every moment to the fullest – and not vicariously, on a screen. When I was shooting the documentary, we were driving with Lawrence Ferlinghetti around San Francisco. He looked at the jammed up Bay Bridge to Berkeley and uttered a sentence I will never forget: *"You see, there's no more away."* When *On the Road* was written, the world had yet to be mapped completely. Borges used to say that his greatest pleasure in literature was to name that which had yet to be named. Today, we get the impression everything has already been experienced or explored. Chinese director Jia Zhang-ke beautifully expresses this implosion of space and time in his film *The World*. It ends, symptomatically,

GARRETT IS ONE WITH THE CAR, SO WE WERE ABLE TO SHOOT SCENES WITH THE ACTORS MOVING AT SPEEDS THAT WERE… HOW CAN I SAY IT… NOT EXACTLY LEGAL.

with the suicide of the young hero and heroine. *On the Road* is like an antidote to this immobility. That's what fascinates me the most about the book.

The Hudson is one of the key characters in *On the Road*. It is the setting for arguments, desires, encounters, etc.

Ah, the Hudson… It really is a fully-fledged character, like "La Poderosa" in *The Motorcycle Diaries*. So many key moments in the film happen in the car, which can also be seen as a "huis-clos". We covered thousands of miles with it, nonstop, shooting first unit scenes or driving around the United States for the second unit.

People recognized the car, and came up to us to talk about it. This is when we realized that the Hudson has a cult following, and that enabled us to meet some unique individuals. Many of them were colorful mechanics, let's admit it… I've always loved Steve McQueen's films, partly because of his restraint as an actor, but also for his awesome skill as a driver. Garrett shares some of his qualities. He is one with the car, so we were able to shoot scenes with the actors moving at speeds that were… how can I say it… not exactly legal, but so much in the spirit of Neal Cassady and Dean Moriarty. ●

170 |

INTERVIEW

GARRETT HEDLUND

★

DRIVING THE FILM

AMERICAN ACTOR GARRETT HEDLUND THREW HIMSELF BODY AND SOUL INTO THE ROLE OF DEAN MORIARTY, ADOPTING HIS FEVERISH RAMBLE AND SHAMANISTIC SPEECH. AS THE HIGH PRIEST OF PARLANCE, MORIARTY, STARTER AND ACCELERATOR, DRIVES HIS DISCOURSE WITH AS MUCH EXUBER-ANCE AS HE DRIVES THE HUDSON. MEETING HEDLUND IN LOS ANGELES, WE WERE ABLE TO OBSERVE THAT THE KEROUACKIAN PEP HE'D PICKED UP AS A TEENAGER HAS AS MUCH POWER AS EVER.

BY CLÉMENTINE GALLOT, AURELIANO TONET ET LAURA TUILLIER | TRANSLATED BY ANITA CONRADE

Pure-blooded Minnesota native Garrett Hedlund has transplanted himself to the hipster district of East LA. At first, he seemed a little tense at the Four Seasons in Beverly Hills where we'd agreed to meet. But a few bottles of red wine loosened his tongue, freeing a two-hour flood of words from a veritable virtuoso of the verb. His acting debut in *Country Strong* sank his roots even deeper in Americana. But the last shot of him in *Tron: Legacy* (released in early 2011), zooming off towards California astride a dream machine, heralded the role of the roamer he'd play in *On the Road.* Dean Moriarty, pillar of the novel, Kerouac's muse and catalyst of his travels, is above all an inveterate Casanova who partakes of free love with a sassy teenager. According to Hedlund: *"They had an agreement. Marylou was his addiction."* As the driver, Garrett Hedlund delivers a full-on performance, combining joyous, jazzy virility with syncopated pelvic rolls. The 27-year-old actor seems to have absorbed Dean so thoroughly that he swamped us with a wave of words during the interview. A poet, he took up slack time on the set writing verses. He and Walter Salles actually drove the route in the novel, for the beauty of the deed and to perpetuate the spirit of the film. He talked to us about it with tears in his eyes.

Do you remember your first meeting with Walter Salles?

Yes, like it was yesterday. I remember Walter rushing in his car because he was running late and I was leaning against a brick wall, outside, trying to calm down. I was very nervous, trying to light a cigarette a hundred times. It was kind of a unique start. Then I would write to Walter about all the crazy nights, crazy ventures, crazy drives I imagined, just stories that I thought had potential. We developed a very close relationship.

How did your audition go?

In the fall of 2006 I received the script and months and months went on and they still hadn't started the casting. I went to an audition and started reading some lines that I wrote and they said *"That's beautiful, it's Kerouac isn't it?"*. And I said no, that's what I wrote. I was so passionate about the character. They got me an audition with Walter Salles in march of 2007 then we all went to New York in the summer and I found out for my birthday, in September, that I got the part.

When did you read *On the Road* for the first time?

When I first read the book, when I was 17, I went online to see who was going to direct the film. I saw Coppola and I thought *"I'm never going to be in this film"*. Seven years later I'm meeting Coppola and I'm in the film. Mind-blowing. I was never good at reading books in class. But when I got to junior year, I found out that Kerouac was being honest in the writing rather than making up some smart fashion imagination. At this point I read Kerouac, Salinger, Fitzgerald and wrote a lot, I would stay up all night and write short stories and talk about it at school. When I was working on my first film, I was in Canada and I bought Kerouac's collection of audio CD's and listening to this, I started writing in his fashion. I wanted to be him so much.

Tell us about your childhood in Minnesota.

I was a little thief, always getting in trouble. Everybody thought that by the rate I was going, by the time I was 15 I'd still be wild. I grew up in a farm, in Minnesota, I was so much in my imagination to pass time. Running into the woods, building tree houses, crawling into the fields with branches and birds as enemies...I was very energetic, always kicked out of class. I think I was very excited about life and its possibilities. Curious of everything. I always found myself as the watcher, the listener, the one across the room that

analyses everything about people. But I wouldn't talk; I was too shy for that.

How did you prepare for the role?

Once I was cast, I drove up to Frisco for the first time in my life. I went to the Beat Museum to get the feel of it. I would sit on a bench and write about the crazy cats around, I interviewed bums, and asked them what they thought about the Beat Generation. They would tell me how it doesn't exist anymore and Frisco is just full of rich kids now. The lifestyle's changed. I met Jerry Cimino who loaded my arms with everything about Neal. I read the postcards that he wrote, I understood his fast-paced style. Also he was very inspired by Marcel Proust. In my opinion, he had almost more potential

For him there was a great desire to provide for his family the way his father never did. That's why he was very proud to work on the railroad.

Kerouac's writing pulsates with jazz tempos. How much did that influence the way you played your part?

That's a tricky question: you find what drives you, and the more you live it, the more the beats that drive you come naturally. Improvising was encouraged, as long as it fitted our characters: Walter told us that we couldn't go wrong, which gave us a lot of freedom. He's not judgmental.

Give us your impressions of the shoot.

August 2nd, 2010, there we were. We started in Montreal, we shot there for two weeks, then Buenos Aires, Bariloche,

I DROVE ON ALL THE SCENES, NEVER A STUNTMAN.

than Kerouac or Ginsberg, these guys were learning from him. He was like a record player that is set up to 72. Going so fast. Also, we sat down with John Cassady and Walter in San Francisco for 6 hours, he told us more stories, I was writing and writing. We hung out with Michael McClure, a beat writer. I had time to collect all that I could because the film wasn't ready to go. All my writing would serve for improvisation. Then I had to think about Dean Moriarty and not Neal Cassady. The question was how do you say things that have been said a million times before? It was really about finding his voice, the way he would express his adventures. He was charming, persuasive, he was a man who never ceased to live. For Neal/Dean, it was always about the kicks. I'm the same, I've always been on the lookout for the greatest laugh. Neal had a fear of becoming like his father, in the book his father is a wino who abandoned him in Denver.

then some no man's land where we shot for 3 days. The rare exciting thing about this production was that it was never on a trailer, I drove on all the scenes, never a stuntman. In New Orleans we had a wonderful 2 weeks, shooting with Viggo, Amy and Elizabeth. We met new people, fanatics of the book. Then Sam and I stayed alone in a slum hotel in Mexico, eating questionable food, wondering about the ice in the water... we were exhausted actually. And only half way through the shooting! We were such a close group in terms of intellect, love and spirit. Sam, Kristen and Danny were my best friends. We were all working very hard to make Walter proud of us.

Is your relationship with Sam Riley as close as the one between Sal and Dean in the book?

We met in 2008 in New York, we had dinner very late with Walter and Jose Ribeira. Then we went to a pub, played some pool and I said *"man, you are my brother"* and he said the same. If you get that feeling, it's instinct. For the next year or two years we didn't know if the film was going to be made. But then it was so effortless, I have never met somebody like him, that has the same instinct, willpower, sense of humor, who shares my fears and my dreams.

How do you see your character?

There is always a destructive part in seeking adventure. The irony is that you always remember what goes wrong, whereas happy memories tend to be easily forgotten. Potential disasters seem to make better stories, it's a shame. I'd mortgage any house for art.

Dean is an ambiguous character: half Dionysus and half Apollo, to borrow the dichotomy Nietzsche explores in *The Birth of Tragedy...*

It's related to the way each person manages his anxiety: some people get wobbly and hide, others exude a character that seems inaccessible. They dance to release tension. It's a thirst for life: with this kind of exuberance, you bring together communities of thrilling people. It's never boring.

Kerouac calls these people *"the mad ones"...*

"Mad to live, mad to breathe, desire everything at the same time..." it's such a great description and it's on page 3, and you're hooked. You think *"I can do the same, right now".* Times have changed: there are more speed limits, more cops, gaz prices are up. It's always *"how can we get there quicker?"* and not *"how can we enjoy the landscapes around us?".* I enjoy feeling lost and technologically disconnected, taking time for a long dinner.

Are you still writing?

Yes, once I even read my own poetry at the Bowery Poetry Club in New York. We wondered with Walter: what would

I'D MORTGAGE ANY HOUSE FOR ART.

Neal and Jack be today? Would they be rappers?

Dean teaches Sal how to live, and in exchange, Sal teaches Dean how to write...

Dean has read Dostoyevsky and Proust, who inspire him, but he doesn't have the time or patience to sit down and write, or... he doesn't have a typewriter! But he never loses his sense of wonderment and curiosity.

What do you think of the inner dimension of the journey described in *On the Road*, as opposed to the geographic one?

I'm always curious to know where one's mind wanders to when one is driving. After we wrapped the film, Walter said *"How would you like to get the Hudson 4000 miles across the country?".* It was a 5 men crew, we went through the same events that are described in the book: the blizzard, the windscreen wipers not working, it was awful... We had to drive with our head outside the window. Walter had a blanket, mittends and a hat. We broke down in New York, in Kentucky and on our way to Santa Fe. We listened to jazz in Memphis and were the only white folks there, like in the book: we're dancing, we're all one. The idea was to give the film some air, a sense of space. Those 14 days on the road were the best times of my life. We were all open for adventure. *On the Road* is all about an introduction to manhood. Everybody just wants permission to go, to fall and get back up. I like this line very much: *"Growing old is mandatory, growing up is optional".* ●

INTERVIEW

SAM RILEY

★

TAKING OVER

"I WAS A YOUNG WRITER, I THOUGHT I COULD FLY". SAL PARADISE, KEROUAC'S LITERARY ERSATZ, FEEDS ON THE RECKLESS BEHAVIOUR OF DEAN MORIARTY – AN INDOMITABLE *"MYSTICAL SHIRKER,"* RUNNING AT FULL SPEED TOWARDS A LOST PARADISE. THE INTENSITY OF THEIR DUET – OR BROMANCE – COULD HAVE CRUSHED SAL, LEAVING HIM IN THE SHADOW OF HIS ECCENTRIC ALTER EGO. YET HE MANAGES TO FIND HIS RHYTHM. THIS BALANCE IS GRACEFULLY RENDERED IN THE MOVIE BY THE ELEGANT SAM RILEY, WHO EMBODIED JOY DIVISION'S FEVERISH GENIUS IAN CURTIS IN *CONTROL* (2007). AFTER THIS HEART-RENDING NOTE, 10,000 THINGS' EX-SINGER SETS OFF AGAIN AND OPENS THE FILM WITH A SONG.

BY CLÉMENTINE GALLOT | | TRANSLATED BY CATHERINE GUESDE

Acting as a counterpoint to Dean Moriarty's magnetic fury, Riley's incarnation of Sal Paradise, a discreet observer, is still very intense on the screen. Though Walter Salles' movie embodies two damned souls, this sensitive actor cleverly avoids playing the caricature of a lazy-bone, and becomes a fascinated and friendly witness of the beat way of life. Riley, a gentle Englishman intimidated by the fact that he has stolen from the US the most American of all authors, has taken Joual (a dialect from Quebec) classes for the sake of the shooting. He answers our questions from Berlin, and casts a

WHAT WAS HARD WAS TO PLAY A MIXTURE BETWEEN KEROUAC AND SAL.

passionate glance at *"two fallen angels from the western night."*

Is *On The Road* a major youth book in England?

Curiously I never read the book when I was in school, but at the time many of my friends did and went on a road trip. I've read other classics for teenagers, like Salinger's *Catcher in the Rye* – those eye-opening books. I don't know why I

missed out on this one. I only really read it for the first time after receiving the script, three or four years ago. Once I knew I had the part, I did my homework and read all the other books by Kerouac, of course.

How do you see this novel's place in American culture?

Though it was published a long time ago, *On The Road* still sells very well because young people can still identify with the characters – most of the time, these are boys. America remains a conservative country, like in the book, and young people still feel the need to rebel, to run away from their family to live their own life: it's all very modern. The book is loved so much that I felt huge pressure.

How do you regard this very masculine way of writing?

EVERYONE WAS AFFECTED BY THE SHOOTING. AT THE END OF IT, WALTER SENT US AN EMAIL EXPLAINING HOW "MAKING A MOVIE IS LIKE FIGHTING A WAR."

Speaking of the book, the actresses would say: *"it's a guy thing."* But since Walter Salles was close to Carolyn Cassady and to LuAnne Henderson's family, he tried to give them more room in the movie, so that the girls were not only left on the sideline.

How did you hear about this project?
I first met Walter Salles in Cannes. After that, I went to New York for an audition with Garrett Hedlund who had already been picked. After that, I didn't hear from Walter for a long time – apparently, there were money troubles, and they couldn't start the shooting.

As the narrator of the novel, Sal Paradise is an intermediate between Dean and the audience. In the film, the narrator's voice is replaced by the expressions on your face. Did you have very precise instructions for that?
I think it's impossible for an actor to work on his smiles or on the look in his eyes – otherwise, you start behaving in an unnatural way. Playing among good actors is what makes acting easier.

Was it a lot of pressure to embody Sal? His character dates back from the 40s, but his excitement is still very much of this time...
What was hard was to play a mixture between Kerouac and Sal. I wasn't worried about Sal, since nobody had ever acted him. But then, people tell you: *"if you play Sal, you play Kerouac."* Luckily enough, I didn't have to play the old, damaged, famous writer Kerouac was at the end of his life – only the younger one. For that, I drew inspiration from his biographies: he was warm-hearted and didn't judge people; he also fell in love with a lot of girls (young men can be so disgusting!). A lot of people adored him.

How do you perceive Neal Cassady's importance among the Beats?
The Beats were fascinated by Neal Cassady/Dean Moriarty's character. The all dreamed of being writers; they were subjugated by his freedom and his way of speaking. He was both crazy and brilliant: being next to Dean necessarily made you look very quiet.

How did you chose to embody the dynamic relationship between Dean and Sal?
It's a very profound relationship, a mix of envy, obsession and competition; it's complicated – sometimes, Kerouac and Cassady wouldn't talk for a long time, but on the other hand, there were no mobile phones at the time. Luckily, Garrett and I have a very good relationship, and we took care of each other. So much the better for us: we had to spend every single day together for six months... It's not very common for two actors of the same field (where there is a lot of competition) to get along well, so we were lucky. Nobody else could understand what we were going through. And also, I must say we were very intimidated by the long list of great actors who almost got to play our parts.

Did playing in *On The Road* change you?
Everyone was affected by the shooting.

At the end of it, Walter sent us an email explaining how *"making a movie is like fighting a war."* When you get home, it is really hard to tell other people how it felt. We were far from home for six months; the schedule was full, so that we didn't have time for anything else. At the end of it, we were all wasted. It was a relief for all of us to finish the shooting, and to have managed to do it well. After that, you feel completely empty for a while, but I suppose that's normal.

What were the difficulties for the team?
Luckily, everyone got along well during the shooting. I know that in a time of recession, nobody wants to hear an actor complain about his life, but I must confess it was especially hard for me to be far from my family. The whole experience actually was a real challenge, and it's true, the working conditions weren't that easy. To put it in a nutshell, there was a new problem every day, it was a constant struggle – it even became a joke. Tom Sturridge (who plays the part of Carlo Marx, ed.) and I were two Englishmen playing the parts of American stars, which was a lot of pressure, as you can imagine. On the first day, during the burial scene, it was raining cats and dogs – it seemed as though Kerouac and Ginsberg were pissing on us!

Were Walter Salles' working methods inspired by the Beats' free association techniques?
We did a lot of rehearsals for some scenes, and none for others. Tom Sturridge had to improvise many scenes for Walter Salles, and he had to read a lot of Ginsberg in order to be able to find his words. Walter often wanted to begin or to end a scene with improvisation, which was difficult for me since the Joual dialect is not at all my native tongue – I had a coach who helped me learn it. Walter wanted to convey the Beats' freedom, and he wanted to capture it from life. That's

APART FROM MY FACE, THERE ARE SOME LIKENESSES BETWEEN KEROUAC AND CURTIS IN "CONTROL": THEY ARE BOTH ARTISTS WHO HAVE THEIR WAY WITH WORDS, AND THEY'RE BOTH VERY SELF-DESTRUCTIVE.

why he didn't want everything to be written; he didn't want us to recite our texts like students. He wanted it to be as spontaneous and free as possible. He knows what he wants, and I don't think anyone on the film-set knew as much on that subject as Walter. He is totally responsible for the film adaptation.

How did you interact with the other actors?

I was very intimidated by Viggo Mortensen, who is very well read. I was afraid I'd have to improvise on philosophy or literature, so I read up on Wikipedia in my hotel room, in case he would ask *"so, what do you think of the Übermensch?"*. Unlike me, Viggo is a real poet.

Which stages of the trip have struck you?

I loved New Orleans, a completely crazy place with an atmosphere quite distinct from the rest of the United States. I liked San Francisco, but Garrett and I were happy to leave Mexico.

Were some parts – namely the more graphic or sensitive parts – of the book more difficult to adapt for the screen?

This is why the film is French: certain things were shocking at the time, and sometimes still are, but in fact, it's nothing compared to the reality TV shows we see nowadays. And yet, American cinema in its golden age wasn't shy.

The film really shows how the two characters break up, and tolls the bell for their friendship. How did you experience this?

It's easy to glamorize sex, drugs and be-bop, but this way of living ruined many lives. Dean is a funny guy, but he's also a heart-breaker, and he's left his kids behind. The last trip to Mexico is squalid, but it's realistic: they don't start another trip across the States, hand in hand against sunset. I like this end and I enjoyed shooting it. It was very emotional.

What similarities do you see between Jack Kerouac and Ian Curtis, the Joy Division singer you embodied in *Control*?

Apart from my face, there are some likenesses: they are both artists who have their way with words, and they're both very self-destructive.

What are your plans?

I'm currently working with Neil Jordan in Dublin on *Byzantium*, a vampire film. For the future, I don't know yet.

The movie was shot in different places. Are you now tempted to go traveling on American roads?

I had already been on tour with a band, but before playing in this movie, I had only been to New York and Los Angeles. Of course, this movie gave me an idea of what it feels like to be on the road, and it made me realize how huge that country is. ●

✦✦✦

INTERVIEW

KRISTEN STEWART

★

IT GIRL

IN ORDER TO LEAVE THE *TWILIGHT* ZONE AND VAMPIRIZE *ON THE ROAD*, THE 21-YEAR-OLD KRISTEN STEWART EMBRACED THE NOTORIOUS "IT", A TRANCE-LIKE STATE THEORIZED BY KEROUAC DURING WHICH THE MUSICIAN FILLS *"THE EMPTY OF SPACE WITH THE SUBSTANCE OF OUR LIVES."* THE CALIFORNIAN ACTRESS HAS INDEED EXPLORED DEEP INSIDE HERSELF TO EMBODY THE MYSTERIOUS MARYLOU, BOTH SHINY AND WITHDRAWN, WHO HESITATES BETWEEN TWO MEN AND TWO IDEALS – THE DANGEROUS EXCITEMENT OF FREEDOM VERSUS THE SAFE DULLNESS OF NORMALITY. WE MET KRISTEN, WHO HAS "IT" IN HER BLOOD AND BONES.

BY AURELIANO TONET | | TRANSLATED BY LAURA TUILLIER

★✦★

Do you remember what you felt when you first read *On the Road*? This book truly ignited something in me when I first read it. I was 15. I loved the manner, the story... I was so taken with the boys! It was really different from any other book I had read. It was my first favourite book. The first thing I highlighted was a description of the way Marylou's sitting in a room, like a surrealistic painting, disconnected from the boys. Thanks to Walter, we learned so much about these people – much more than what was written in the book: we knew the real story, we read the scroll version...

IT WAS REALLY DIFFERENT FROM ANY OTHER BOOK I HAD READ. IT WAS MY FIRST FAVOURITE BOOK.

How did you react when Walter offered you the part?

I was only 17. I was in my car, I was so excited that I kept switching gears. I just couldn't believe it, until the day I was on the set.

LuAnne / Marylou is described by Kerouac as a *"nymph with waist-length dirty blond hair."* How close do you feel from your character?

There's very little information on LuAnne compared to other members of the Beat Generation. Though she seemed socially friendly, she was very withdrawn from the outside world. Her life was very private. So it was hard for me to find her. Luckily, I had the chance to speak to her daughter.

What struck you the most about her?

Her incredible ability to love, her pure humanity. It's such an exceptional quality. I didn't expect it at all. She's honest, open and understanding. She's observant, but she doesn't judge anyone, and she keeps completely unaware of outside judgement. In a time like that – and even now! –, to be able to openly sleep with a man who sleeps with other men and women at the same time... And yet she stays true to the American ideals of the fifties. She travels both worlds so well! At first, I didn't understand it. LuAnne wasn't being rebellious, she was just being herself. It wasn't like

SHE WAS A BRIDGE BETWEEN THOSE TWO VERY DIFFERENT MEN. IF SHE HADN'T BEEN AROUND, THEY PROBABLY WOULDN'T HAVE BEEN SO CLOSE.

"*these times are killing me,*" she just didn't fit in them. Surprisingly, she had serious stomach problems when she was younger, but she ignored them. She was okay with her own insecurities; that's what made her able to take the trip.

During the preparation, you had the chance to listen to LuAnne's actual voice. What did you learn from those recordings?

Her voice was beautiful and it told us things and stories we didn't know. I fell in love with it. She spoke like people did in the forties, with words that we don't use anymore. She has a much more higher voice than I do. I'm clipped, I swallow everything I say... She's much more articulate.

Did Walter ask you to watch some movies before the shooting?

Shadows was the main one, especially for the New Year's Eve party scene. Walter really wanted us to feel some of that spirit. He is a very generous director. As all great artists do, he can become maniacally obsessed, in the best way.

In an interview, you said that Marylou was "*the necessary oestrogen*" between Sal and Dean. What did you mean by that?

She was a bridge between those two very different men. If she hadn't been around, they probably wouldn't have been so close. She provided harmony. She had both of them in her, and they both needed her. They had a

unique bound, which we are not used to. Everyone says that women in *On the Road* were just toys used by the guys. But she was a willing party, she was not a victim. When Neal first met her, he said: "*I've met my match!*" He was truly in love with her – maybe a little too much. She was wild and loud, she was funny, wacky and sexy. That's what he loved about her.

How intense was the shooting?

It truly was the most absolutely loaded, richest, craziest, wildest time I ever spent on a set. It didn't feel like we were doing a movie. We had the chance to spend four weeks in a boot camp before the shooting. It helped us to know each other, to feel comfortable. Though I wasn't there as long as I wanted to, we were exhausted. We didn't sleep – ever. I don't know how we did some of those scenes... Sometimes, if you're really into something, you can't sleep but you can still be be very happy with it. Walter wanted us to stop thinking about our acting. It really felt spontaneous, like *On the Road* should always feel. Our trip would have been worth doing even if we weren't filming it. The conversations that we shared, the poems that Garrett wrote...

Tell us about the New Year's Eve party scene and its impressive dancing parts...

I truly came out of every take blind. I was so dead. It was very hot in Montreal at the time, and we had 60 extras in the little room we were shooting in... I was able to shake my nerves for all the other

scenes, but for this one, I was very nervous, because I'm not a dancer. But it was my job to loose my mind. I so badly wanted to get to the point were I couldn't see. Every single time I thought I was going to fall over, someone caught me. It scared the hell out of me, but at the same time it was the most fun thing I've ever done.

Kerouac wrote his novel with jazz in mind. Somehow, did you feel like a musician on the set?

Yes. I played one other part that was based on a true person, in *The Runaways,* and it was difficult for me to put words into my character. In *On the Road,* on the contrary, we were encouraged to improvise, we wouldn't have been doing the right thing unless we stumbled onto things and lost ourselves. There is always room for freedom on a set, but in this case we had it all. We could not do wrong. In the boot camp, we worked together for four weeks, gathering all the information, preparing ourselves as much as we possibly could so we could forget it and move on. Sometimes, you're truer to the book if you don't repeat the exact line. Every single take was different. We shot so much – that's Walter's thing. He's always moving, capturing everything. The movie jumps and hops, it's sporatic, like the book. And when it stops moving, it's so apparent, oh my gosh!

Kerouac's novel is very liberal in some aspects and pretty conservative in others – it has been criticized for its misogyny. On screen, your character seems stronger than in the book...

The movie would be so different if it was true to the novel! And people wouldn't be satisfied. It would be such a shame not to tell the whole story: how many times are we going to adapt this novel? It had to be a mixture between reality and fantasy.

The Hudson is almost a character in itself. How did you fit in it?

It's a ragged boy! I always feel that my car is a girl. But the Hudson is *not* a girl! Oh God... On a road trip, you form a very particular bond to the car you're in. Interestingly, in real life, Neal didn't travel very much with this car. And the Hudson is so famous now! It's funny.

Sam Riley and Garrett Hedlund told us that they were heart-broken when you left the set. Did you feel the same way?

I couldn't believe they would carry on! Now it's fine and I know I didn't belong on the rest of the shooting, but I could have literally stayed in the hotels, just sitting and watching. I wanted to stay over so badly. LuAnne had the same feeling: she had to be gone but didn't want to. She could have stuck around a little bit longer and torture herself, but didn't.

You played in another road movie, Sean Penn's *Into the Wild.* Was it a similar experience?

Compared to all of the work that I've done, they felt the most similar. Sean and Walter are not afraid of filming landscapes that were there before them, and will still live on after them. In most movies, everyone is trying to get his own job right. With Walter and Sean, it was rather like we were all doing something together. In *Into the Wild*, my character is rooted, unlike Marylou. Had she been a little older, she may have followed him out. She could have turned into a Marylou but she was just too young.

The cinematographer Eric Gautier worked both on *Into the Wild* and *On the Road...*

You can go anywhere with him, he's going to be there for you. He has a magic power. Before you're about to move, he's already there. That's remarkable.

Like *Twilight, On the Road* is usually read during teenage. How different are these books to your eyes?

You couldn't think of more opposite novels. It stroke two very different chords in me. In *Twilight*, we tried to be

THE MOVIE WOULD BE SO DIFFERENT IF IT WAS TRUE TO THE NOVEL! AND PEOPLE WOULDN'T BE SATISFIED.

as faithful as possible to the book. In *On the Road*, freedom was welcome: it was all about finding the right tone.

Marylou is not the typical Hollywood character. After *Twilight*, most roles you chose are rough and risky: *The Runaways, Welcome to the Rileys...* What drives you towards this type of characters?

Sensitive people have more to say. They are more interesting. It's only risk to play them if you're afraid to lose vast mainstream appeal. Most actors think about how they're going to be perceived: *"This is going to get me here, this is going to make me be this type of actor!"* I don't. That's why I did *Twilight* as well. I loved it just as much as my other movies. It doesn't really matter in what capacity it's shown. What drives me is *"it"* – as Kerouac would say. Luckily, LuAnne and I have that in common.

On the Road is now finally ready. What did you feel when you first watched it?

It's hard to put it into words. It surprised me so often, it's both really sad and fun to watch. I'm so proud of everyone! Most movies try to answer all of your questions. This one just leaves you asking more. It leads you places, but it doesn't tell you where to go. Every time you watch it, you go down a different street. ❀

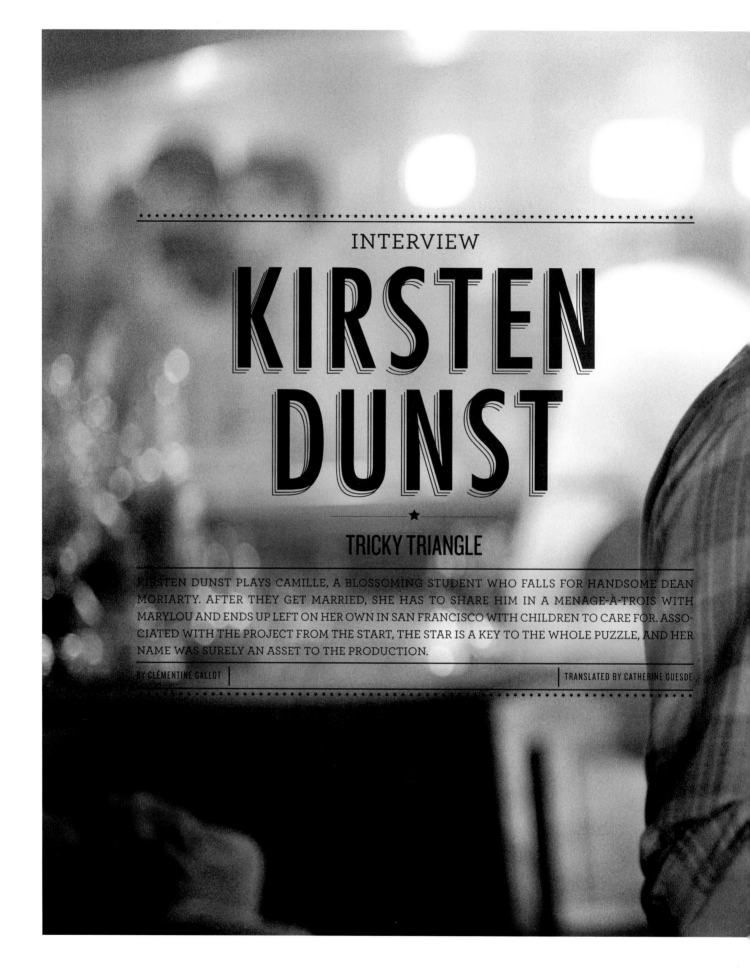

INTERVIEW

KIRSTEN DUNST

★

TRICKY TRIANGLE

KIRSTEN DUNST PLAYS CAMILLE, A BLOSSOMING STUDENT WHO FALLS FOR HANDSOME DEAN MORIARTY. AFTER THEY GET MARRIED, SHE HAS TO SHARE HIM IN A MENAGE-À-TROIS WITH MARYLOU AND ENDS UP LEFT ON HER OWN IN SAN FRANCISCO WITH CHILDREN TO CARE FOR. ASSOCIATED WITH THE PROJECT FROM THE START, THE STAR IS A KEY TO THE WHOLE PUZZLE, AND HER NAME WAS SURELY AN ASSET TO THE PRODUCTION.

BY CLÉMENTINE GALLOT   TRANSLATED BY CATHERINE GUESDE

After having graduated and become a nurse, Camille is distracted by Dean Moriarty's fiery conduct and tries to quiet down her husband's tempestuous life. The couple founds a family in the suburbs of San Francisco, but wayward Dean is constantly swerving from mariage to divorce and other misdemeanors. Kirsten Dunst looks astonishingly like surviving beat Carolyn Cassady (now 89), the real person Kerouac named "Camille" in *On the Road*. Turning 30, Dunst, the dream girl in *Spider-Man*, has often embodied restless wives or girlfriends – from the dreamy teenager in *Virgin Suicides* to *Marie-Antoinette* or *Melancholia*. Dunst – who isn't used to making such brief appearances

– only spent a few days with the team of *On The Road*, to shoot a dizzying dance scene. Then she was off to act: in *Cities*, a thriller by Roger Donaldson starring Orlando Bloom, *Red Light Winter*, a

READING CAROLYN CASSADY'S AUTOBIOGRAPHY "OFF THE ROAD" IS WHAT HELPED ME MOST BUILD UP HER CHARACTER.

family drama film based on Adam Rapp's play and featuring Mark Ruffalo, and *Upside Down* by Juan Diego Solanas – a futuristic romance with Jim Sturgess. *"I've also just played in a*

Leslye Headland comedy for girls, with Isla Fisger and Lizzy Caplan. It's called Bachelorette *and it was presented at the Sundance Festival. It should be released this year,"* she adds, over the phone from Hollywood. Interview.

Did the book *On The Road* make a deep impression on you when you were younger ?

I read it when I was a teenager; a boy I liked had given it to me – it was his favorite book. At the time, I found it hard to identify with the characters; I felt the book was more a guy thing. But when I heard I was going to play Camille, I read it again while taking a road trip myself. My father would make fun of me, saying: *"All they do in that book is do drugs and sleep together!"*

Were you a big fan of beat poetry, like Garrett Hedlund and Tom Sturridge used to be?

THE FACT THAT MY GENERATION WAS ABLE TO TAKE PART IN THE ADAPTATION MAKES ME FEEL MORE THAN HAPPY - AND NOT INTIMATED AT ALL. IT 'S A RARE, HISTORICAL FACT; IT'S AN HONOR.

I'd read some poetry by Ginsberg, but I wasn't an aficionada. I was more into female poets.

Do you find Kerouac's style in *On The Road* out of date?

Not at all! The book deals with very contemporary themes: self-discovery is something every generation has to experience in its own specific way. And no matter how old you are when you read it the book still makes sense. It raises important questions: what should I do with my life? Where should I go?

Did Carolyn Cassady (Camille, in the book) take part in the elaboration of the script?

Reading her autobiography *Off the Road* is what helped me most build up her character. Unfortunately, I wasn't able to meet her, since I had to go to New York on the day she came to visit the team in San Francisco... But Walter Salles had had long talks with her, and bits of their conversation were added to the scenario. Various scenes of the movie were also taken from her book.

In her book, Carolyn reveals that although she was married to Cassady, she actually was in love with Kerouac...

That's true. One scene of the movie refers to this in an implicit way.

Do you think that women have more room to exist in the movie than they do in the book?

Walter Salles has given more importance to every character's emotions. And for the film, he had to include female characters in the road trip – the book is written in such a fluid way... But they remain less important than men.

How do you feel about this screen adaptation of the book? Making the film took a very long time...

The fact that my generation was able to take part in that adaptation makes me feel more than happy – and not intimidated at all. It's a rare, historical fact; it's an honor.

You were one of the first actors involved in the project...

I met Walter a long time ago, maybe six years ago or so... So I was involved in the project a long before the shooting began. He had picked Kristen Stewart and I before even choosing the male actors. I may have been the first one, even though I only play in a few scenes.

Unlike the rest of the team, you only spent a few days on the film set...

I stayed two days in Montreal, and two days in San Francisco. I was never "on the road" since all my scenes were shot inside... I arrived at the end of a six-month journey. I felt a bit nervous before getting there, since I had to fit in a team where people knew each other very well, and it had been a long time since I had played such a small part. But I managed to find my place among them.

Kerouac's style in *On The Road* is influenced by jazz music. Did Walter Salles ask you to improvise?

Not really, everything was already in the scenario, and my part was more limited than others. Walter sometimes asked the others to improvise, or to sing a song immediately.

On *The Road* is an international production. Did that give the actors and the screenwriters more freedom? And did it allow things that one wouldn't necessarily show in an American movie?

Sometimes, only a foreigner can be romantic enough to look at America in a new way, from a different perspective.

On *The Road* is an American landmark book. But the production of the film and the technical team were mostly non-American. Do you think that, because of that, the American audience might reject the movie?

You know, at the time, there was some talk about Godard directing the movie! Art is art, as long as the best filmmaker makes it.

In *Marie Antoinette*, but also in *Melancholia* and in *On The Road*, you play the part of dark, surly spouses. Do you have an explanation for that?

The parts are written for me. When I decide to play in a movie, what counts is the filmmaker. I'm not particularly drawn to melancholic parts. Camille is a very lively girl, but she is a victim of her situation: she's in love with someone she cannot keep at home with her. Her melancholy is caused by the circumstances. ◉

INTERVIEW

VIGGO MORTENSEN

★

FURROWED BURROUGHS

HE SPENT ONLY ONE BRIEF WEEK ON THE SET, TO LEND HIS THREATENING FEATURES TO THE WILLIAM S. BURROUGHS CHARACTER, KNOWN IN THE BOOK AS OLD BULL LEE. AND YET IN SUCH A SHORT TIME, HIS STATUESQUE FRAME, IMPRESSIVE ACTING EXPERIENCE, OUSTANDING ERUDITION, AND AWESOME ABILITY TO GET INTO CHARACTER MAY HAVE MADE VIGGO MORTENSEN THE MOST AWE-INSPIRING OF THE VETERANS PARTICIPATING IN THE ADVENTURE, IN THE EYES OF WALTER SALLES'S YOUTHFUL CREW. AS THE LINK BETWEEN CORMAC MCCARTHY'S ROAD (HE PLAYED THE HERO IN JOHN HILL-COAT'S FILM VERSION OF THE NOVEL) AND JACK KEROUAC'S, HE FREELY ASSOCIATES HERE BETWEEN FREUD'S SOFA AND BURROUGHS'S MADNESS. INTERVIEW WITH A FORCE OF NATURE.

BY AURELIANO TONET | TRANSLATED BY ANITA CONRADE

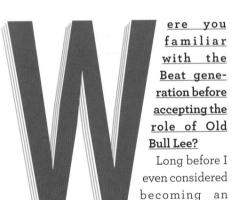

Were you familiar with the Beat generation before accepting the role of Old Bull Lee?

Long before I even considered becoming an actor, I had read *On the Road* and had become familiar with the writings and legendary personas of Jack Kerouac, William Burroughs, Allen Ginsberg, Neal Cassady and other men and women who had in some way informed the sprawling, frenzied narrative of that novel. Like others who grew up in the 1960s and 1970s, I took an interest in not only Kerouac, but also in what supposedly inspired them - apart from literature - during those post-war decades: the jazz figures (Charlie Parker, Dizzy Gillespie, Miles Davis, Thelonious Monk...), painting (Abstract Expressionism), and movies (Italian Neorealism, Nouvelle Vague,, etc.). I was excited by the energy of Kerouac's writing. I was also mesmerised by some of Ginsberg's poetry, especially by his famous long poem *Howl*. Later on, however, it was Burroughs' work that I gradually came to see as the most ground-breaking and lasting literary contribution from the Beat generation. Burroughs seemed to consistently find ways to write with beauty, humour, and a graceful inventiveness about even the most squalid and/or bizarre subjects and characters. Although his characters frequently use the argot of a specific era, he himself is not limited by it in his own descriptions. In re-reading Burroughs while preparing to play Bull Lee, and especially in listening to recordings of him reading his stories, what most struck me was the originality of his prose, his very particular sense of humour, the lack of artifice and the perverse elegance characteristic of his writing. One of the things that clearly separates his work from Kerouac's and Ginsberg's is its general lack of mysticism; to me it feels much more cold-blooded, surgical, clean.

Do you remember how you felt when first reading *On the Road*?

Reading *On the Road* made me want to travel, to see for myself and be a part of the answer to Kerouac's question in that book: "*Whither goest thou, America, in thy shiny car in the night?*" In terms of its cultural importance, I believe that for North-American and European artists and audiences of my generation Kerouac's novel provided a kind of synthesis, a loose codification of many creative, counter-cultural impulses. *On the Road* has influenced a long list of movements in art and politics that is too varied to enumerate here. I believe Jack Kerouac encouraged us to ask "*Why not do it?*".

What is Old Bull Lee's most important side to your eyes: the father, the writer, the teacher, the junkie, the lover?

All of those aspects of his character were important, but I b elieve the one we will see most clearly in the movie, and the one that to some degree includes all the rest, is that of teacher. His literary knowledge, as well as his irreverent and playful outlook on life, are important reference points for his younger fellow adventurers in *On the Road*.

The New Orleans stop is a short but crucial step in Dean and Sal's journey through America. Your character warns Sal about Dean's childish amorality and irresponsibility. Yet, Old Bull Lee is far from being moral and responsible. How did you deal with this contradiction?

In my opinion, there is a method to the Burroughs "madness". His drug-taking and other libertine interests were often based on serious study and meditation, as were, to a lesser degree, those of Kerouac. My sense about the real Kerouac is that his increasing alcohol abuse eventually diminished his creative powers and production during the 1960s, whereas Burroughs' chronic opium abuse seemed to have facilitated his literary output and experimentations.

What was the atmosphere during the shooting?

The atmosphere on the set was very relaxed, free-thinking, very conducive to exploration and risk-taking -- just as Old Bull Lee would probably have liked it to be! Although Walter Salles, unlike David Cronenberg, likes to rehearse a lot and improvise to some degree with

the script, I found that their ways of handling actors and organizing scenes were similarly well-informed and stress-free. Walter is very intelligent and kind, and seems secure in the knowledge he has gained over the years with respect to the technical skills required to make a good movie. He, like David and other extremely gifted and well-mannered directors, inspire confidence and respect.

David Cronenberg, who directed you in three movies, had adapted *Naked Lunch* in 1991. Did you speak about Burroughs together?

We did speak a little about Burroughs, which was helpful. I had seen David's movie as well as interviews he and Burroughs had done in connection with its release and promotion back in 1991, and I took another look at some of that as I went about preparing Bull Lee.

Coming out of playing Freud, how was it to play another older, "wise" figure?

My initial reaction was similar to the one I'd had when David had offered me the role of Freud -- that physically and in other ways I was perhaps not the ideal actor for the job. However, I bear more of a physical resemblance to Burroughs than I do to Freud, so less of a physical change was required. In terms of the type of person he was, and the role he played in the lives of his contemporaries, I realised that the Burroughs-based Bull Lee had much in common with Freud. Like Freud, Bull was, for example, a slightly older and more formal mentor figure. In *On the Road* he shares with Sal, Dean and others his knowledge about writing, writers, drug use, weapons and other matters -- just as Freud shares the fruits of his academic investigations and life experience with his colleagues. ❧

THE FILM
ON THE ROAD

FROM: VIGGO MORTENSEN
SENT: MONDAY, FEBRUARY 27, 7:52 PM
SUBJECT: VIGGO CAPTIONS

"I WILL SHORTLY BE SENDING YOU SEPARATELY 14 IMAGES FOR YOU TO CONSIDER. THESE ARE PHOTOS FROM A SINGLE DAY - THE LAST DAY - OF MY PARTICIPATION IN THE SHOOTING OF *ON THE ROAD* IN NEW ORLEANS, ALL ON 11 SEPTEMBER, 2010, FROM DAWN UNTIL SUNDOWN. LOVE,
VIGGO »

| 6:45 | | 7:30 |

| 9:30 | | 11:30 | | 12:00 |

| 12:30 | | 13:00 |

| 13:30 | | 14:00 | | 14:30 | | 16:45 |

| 17:45 | | 19:00 | | 19:15 |

PROFILE

TOM STURRIDGE

★

TOM THE MUSE

AS HE ENTERS A MEXICAN BAR ON HAMPSTEAD ROAD IN LONDON, A FEDORA ON HIS HEAD AND A PORTFOLIO UNDER HIS ARM, TOM STURRIDGE REMINDS ME OF THE MAGNIFICENT SCENES OF *ON THE ROAD*, IN WHICH HE PLAYS THE PART OF CARLO MARX AKA ALLEN GINSBERG. RATHER DISCREET AT FIRST, THIS PROMISING ACTOR GRADUALLY BECOMES MORE TALKATIVE, AND TELLS US EVERYTHING ABOUT HIS VOCATION, HIS WISH TO TAKE PART IN THE PROJECT, AND THE ATMOSPHERE DURING THE SHOOTING OF THE MOVIE.

BY LAURA TUILLIER | TRANSLATED BY CATHERINE GUESDE

Nearly two years after the end of the shooting, Tom Sturridge still has something of Allen Ginsberg's charismatic shyness. Or maybe it is that the British actor has managed, within a few scenes only, to impersonate the mythical American poet in an outstanding, faithful, new way. The poet – who has a high cinegenic potential – has recently been embodied in a less convincing way by James Franco in *Howl* by Rob Epstein and Jeffrey Friedman, and will soon be played by Daniel *"Harry Potter"* Radcliffe in *Kill Your Darlings* by John Krokidas, to be released in 2013. This part clearly puts Sturridge on a par with the other brilliant actors playing in *On the Road*.

IN 2008, STURRIDGE AUDITIONED TO PLAY IN "ON THE ROAD". THE TEST WENT WELL BUT HE WAS NOT CALLED AGAIN.

TEQUILA SHOT

Tom Sturridge is 26 years old and will soon become a dad. And yet, there is something extremely childlike in his way of smiling or arranging his strand of hair. No sooner is he seated than he orders tequila – as to match his character in the movie. And keeps his hat on. *"My first encounter with the book* On The Road *was more on a stylistic level than on a dramatic one. When I was 13, I read that rather than Dickens; it felt as if I was reading a song,"* he explains, smiling, more at ease already. As a teenager, this son of an artist didn't intend to become an actor. *"I was a movie buff, but I didn't want to work in the same field as my father, who is a filmmaker."* But soon, his background caught up with him. Chosen to play Jeremy Irons' son in *Being Julia* by Czech filmmaker István Szabó, he also took his first steps as a stage actor in London theatres.

In 2008, he auditioned to play in *On the Road*. Although the test seemed to go well, they didn't call back. In the meantime, we discover him as an ingenuous young man in *Good Morning England* by Richard Curtis. *"And then one day, Kristen Stewart says to me:*

'Hey, haven't I told you? I'm playing in On the Road.' *I rushed in the first plane to New York, where I pretended to run into Walter by accident."* After a long lunch together, Walter Salles reassured Tom Sturridge: he will be Carlo Marx in *On The Road.*

A GINSBERG SPECIALIST

"Since the shooting took place in Canada, we were all far from home, so we soon became a family," Tom Sturridge explains. He is now giving long answers to my questions, and even ventures to ask a few, (*"Is Walter Salles very famous in France?"*) feeling perfectly at ease. In the *"training camp"* organised by the filmmaker for the month of rehearsal, the small team watched movies, met Carolyn Cassady, dove into Kerouac and Ginsberg's poetry. Tom Sturridge became a specialist of the poet's early works (*The Book of Martyrdom and Artifice, The Denver Doldrums,* which he

"WHEN I ARRIVED ON THE FIRST DAY OF SHOOTING, I KNEW EVERYTHING ABOUT GINSBERG."

loves) and devoured his diaries. *"When I arrived on the first day of the shooting, I knew everything about Ginsberg. I could've told you what brand of tea he used to drink, and at what time of the day he had it... I had almost forgotten that I was an actor, not a History teacher."* This immersion into Ginsberg's universe was beneficial since it allowed him to embody Carlo as an oversensitive, brilliant teenager, who quivers with poetic vibrations, and is unhappy in the middle of a gang of cool guys: *"To me, Carlo represents love in the movie".*

The Tequila shots have loosened Tom Sturridge's tongue: here he is, suddenly dropping the word that he *"had lunch with Terrence Malick last week",*

before asking me what I thought about *The Tree of Life* (which he hadn't seen), about the Cannes festival (where he would love to go), about Jacques Audiard (who he follows closely), and even about my way of seeing the future (*"Would you like to direct movies one day?"*) The actor is unstoppable, and is about to order another round of Tequilas, when I point out the fact that a Eurostar train is waiting for me. That's not a problem: he shows me the way to the station, still chattering. And, before disappearing in the London fog, he adds: *"See you in Cannes!"* ◉

THE FILM
ON THE ROAD

INTERVIEW

ÉRIC GAUTIER

★

ONE-MAN BAND

CINEMATOGRAPHER ÉRIC GAUTIER, A 1982 GRADUATE OF THE ÉCOLE LOUIS LUMIÈRE AND OCCASIONAL JAZZ MUSICIAN, EMBARKED ON HIS PROFESSIONAL CAREER AS ONE OF ALAIN RESNAIS'S ASSISTANTS ON *LA VIE EST UN ROMAN*. HE THEN WORKED ON THREE OTHER RESNAIS FILMS: *CŒURS, LES HERBES FOLLES*, AND *VOUS N'AVEZ ENCORE RIEN VU*. A REGULAR ON SHOOTS WITH FRENCH DIRECTORS ARNAUD DESPLECHIN AND OLIVIER ASSAYAS, HE HAS ALSO WORKED OUTSIDE FRANCE, LIGHTING SEAN PENN'S *INTO THE WILD*, ANG LEE'S *WOODSTOCK*, AND WALTER SALLES'S *THE MOTORCYCLE DIARIES*. NOW HE AND SALLES ARE TOGETHER AGAIN FOR THE *ON THE ROAD* ADVENTURE. GAUTIER, WHO HAS NEVER CHOSEN A FILM BASED ON THE SCRIPT, HAS THE IDEAL ATTITUDE: *"MAKING A FILM IS LIKE TAKING A TRIP. WHEN YOU HIT THE ROAD, THE THING THAT MATTERS IS YOUR TRAVEL COMPANIONS, NOT THE DESTINATION."* "GETTING THERE" IS MORE THAN HALF THE FUN.

BY JULIETTE REITZER AND AURÉLIANO TONET | TRANSLATED BY ANITA CONRADE

Was *On the Road* an <u>important</u> <u>novel for</u> <u>you before</u> <u>you started</u> <u>the film?</u>

When I read the book, I had absolutely no idea that someday I'd be working on the film version of it. It didn't have that much influence on my life, because I came to it too late; I didn't read it in my youth. But I do feel comfortable with the story and its visions, because my career choices have given me an intuitive sense of what America is. The characters in the films I've shot with directors Sean Penn and Ang Lee, *Into the Wild* and *Woodstock*, were forged by Jack Kerouac's vision of America.

Tell us how you met Walter Salles. How has it been to work with him?

In 2005, he asked me to do the lighting for the segment of *Paris, je t'aime* he was directing. I had loved *Central do Brasil*, so I instantly accepted. Before he went back to Rio, he told me he was scouting locations for another film. The photographs were sensational. That's when we worked on *The Motorcycle Diaries* together.

On the Road and The Motorcycle Diaries are both about traveling. But aren't they two different types of road movies?

On *The Motorcycle Diaries*, we were scrupulous about sticking to Che Guevara's historical route through Latin America when we were filming. Che's journey was an opening to the outer world. *On the Road*, on the contrary, is an inner voyage: the destination is incidental. What counts is being on the move: the travel trance itself, its sights, sounds, smells, and tastes, its drugs, sex, and weariness. One of our objectives was to capture the sensations: the cold, the heat, the fear. That involved long lens, close-up filming of actors' faces without makeup. Hence the need to shoot under "real conditions" – in the cold, where faces almost turn blue. It's beautiful.

How did you work on the 1950s period footage?

Of course we had to use 35mm film. I brought plenty of texture and grain to

ÉRIC GAUTIER (ON THE LEFT) WITH WALTER SALLES ON THE SET OF *ON THE ROAD*

I WANTED TO KEEP SOMETHING "AMATEUR" IN THE MOVIE, BECAUSE WHAT I LOVE ABOUT KEROUAC IS HIS OCCASIONAL AWKWARDNESS WITH LANGUAGE, HIS BREAKS IN RHYTHM.

the image, so it's gritty enough to be felt as film. There are two types of period films: before and after the invention of motion pictures. If film was a part of the culture of the time, you have to imitate the style of the era. We relied on the great photographers of the 1950s, like Robert Frank, whose book *The Americans* was a vital reference to us.

To what degree did you adopt Kerouac's style?

There lies the difficulty and challenge of making the film. Five years before shooting started, I reread the novel and Walter gave me the scroll, the document the script is really based on. It was written in a three-week, 24/24 frenzy. We knew that we'd have to pick up the idea of spontaneity and run with it. Walter spent those five years doing a huge amount of research for the film. He knows the subject inside out, and I've also been doing a lot of reading about Kerouac and the Beat Generation. The two of us quickly agreed that the deeper theme of On the Road is frustration: hoping for and expecting something to happen, and then being disenchanted once the thing actually does happen. There's an idea of introspective motion along with the extroversion of the Road in the title. To render it in pictures, I did a lot of shooting with the camera on my shoulder, allowing the actors plenty of freedom of movement. I wanted to keep something "amateur" in the movie, because what I love about Kerouac is his occasional awkwardness with language, his breaks in rhythm.

After several false starts, the director tackling the adaptation of *On the Road* is a Brazilian, working with a

crew that is mainly European and Latin American...

That may be the film's saving grace. Francis Ford Coppola bought the rights to the novel in the 1970s, but I think it's hard for an American to grapple with a legend of modern literature. It was Coppola's idea to offer the project to Walter. Even though he is not a Yankee, Walter is familiar with North American "culture" and knowledgeable about it. Besides, Kerouac himself was a citizen of the world, a Francophile who cultivated his French roots. He was inspired by the great French writers like Proust and Rimbaud. His bi-culturalism partially explains his keen insight into the era. Also, Kerouac had an ear and a fondness for the great variety of North American accents, and imitated them perfectly. Walter Salles has been careful with the veracity of the accents in the film.

How did the shooting go, on the road?

Actually, much of the action in *On the Road* happens in cities. We didn't shoot anything chronologically. That's always complicated, and it generates tensions. We shot in a number of very different locations: Peru, Chile, Argentina, Canada, the United States, Mexico... That also means that in a day, we might go from a chilly 15°F to sweltering in 90°F! Louisiana, San Francisco, and Mexico are places that can't be recreated elsewhere. But the scenes that supposedly happened in Denver were shot in Montreal, Ottawa, and New Orleans. We had to pay very close attention to the continuity. A lot of times, the work was exhausting.

What's your opinion of the three leading actors, Garrett Hedlund, Sam Riley, and Kristen Stewart ?

I think they form a fantastic trio.

WORKING WITH LIGHT IS AN ATTEMPT TO CONJURE WITH TIME.

Walter Salles is especially good at creating associations between actors, like the grandmother and child in *Central do Brasil*. The one who amazes me the most is Sam Riley. He plays the Jack Kerouac character; in other words, the observer. It's a hard role to pull off: you have to be on your reserve, without being empty. Kerouac looked like a lumberjack, and Sam had to cover up his sophisticated side. He's totally credible. I knew Kristen already, from filming her in *Into the Wild*. Like many actors, when you see her off-camera, she seems a little insignificant. But as soon as the film starts to roll, there's a surge of something absolutely amazing.

Could you give us a general description of how you work with a director?

Lighting a film involves playing with contrasts, from the brightest to darkest palettes and infinite shades in between. The tools I work with are lenses, films, filters, and lighting techniques, both artificial and daylight. Once, on a set, an extra remarked, "*Actually, you're the director's assistant.*" That's exactly how I view my profession. Film is motion and duration: working with light is an attempt to conjure with time. The camera-man has to establish total rapport with the director, because light is so difficult to talk about. My work could be compared to musical arrangement: George Martin with the Beatles, or pianist Bill Evans on *Kind of Blue* by Miles Davis – artists who discreetly add orchestration and harmony to a piece they are working on. •

THE FILM
ON THE ROAD

INTERVIEW

GUSTAVO SANTAOLALLA

★

THE PASSENGER

SINCE HIS DEBUT WITH ARCO IRIS IN 1967 AND AS A MEMBER OF SEVERAL BANDS (SOLUNA, WET PICNIC, BAJOFONDO), GUSTAVO SANTAOLALLA HAS WORKED TOWARD MIXING ROCK WITH SOUTH-AMERICAN SOUNDS. THE ARGENTINIAN COLLABORATOR OF LEÓN GIECO, KRONOS QUARTET AND MORRISSEY HAS PRODUCED A VARIETY OF SOUNDTRACKS SINCE 2000, FOR DIRECTORS SUCH AS ANG LEE, WONG KAR-WAI AND ALEJANDRO GONZÁLES IÑÁRRITU. *ON THE ROAD* MARKS HIS THIRD COLLABORATION WITH WALTER SALLES, FOR WHOM HE HAS PROBABLY DELIVERED HIS BEST AND MOST INCANDESCENT SCORE. INTERVIEW.

BY AURÉLIANO TONET | TRANSLATED BY CLÉMENTINE GALLOT AND ÉTIENNE ROUILLON

Before *On the Road*, you worked with Walter Salles on *The Motorcycle Diaries* and *Linha de Passe*. What kind of director is he?

I met Walter through Alejandro Gonzáles Iñárritu, another great friend and director, for whom I scored *Amores Perros* in 2000. We immediately connected on a personal level: I already knew *Central Station*, which I loved. There is a very organic connection between us. He's a humanistic director, he brings a human aspect to the characters and he is very sophisticated. He really makes the kind of movie that I like. I haven't done that many big movies that I connect to.

The Motorcycle Diaries *and* On the Road *are two road movies which take place at the same era. In your view, how different are these two films?*

In one sense, they are very different, but in another way, part of what moves those people to get on the road is the same thing: to find their inner self. In *Motorcycle Diaries,* they try to find themselves looking at the reality of other people, they're trying to create a better world. In *On the Road*, Sal Paradise and Dean Moriarty are in a more narcissistic quest. But there is a common search for self-discovery.

Do you remember the first time you read *On the Road*?

I was a teenager in Argentina, I was younger than the Beats, but they led to the hippies so it really affected me. I also

went looking for myself, I went on a trip in Argentina with a friend and I guess I was inspired by Kerouac. Usually, you don't do it on your own but with someone else. And then, seven years ago, I went on the road with a very good friend of mine, a musician, León Gieco, and we recorded music all the way. That's also how I met my wife. At the end of *The Motorcycle Diaries*, there is a series of black and white photographs. The music in the background was composed when I was on the road with León.

On the Road *is a very musical novel. It is suffused with jazz, and it inspired many rock n'roll artists. What colors did you give to the soundtrack?*

The whole project was a big challenge. The book is iconic so bringing it on screen is already something really

EXCERPT FROM GUSTAVO SANTAOLALLA'S ORIGINAL SCORE COMPOSED FOR *ON THE ROAD*

big. As far as the music is concerned, there was a connection between bebop and these people not sleeping for days and talking, just like Charlie Parker would play the saxophone endlessly. Though I wanted to find that improvisational quality, I knew from the beginning that I didn't want a jazz score. I knew also that it would be playing in the movie in different scenes: parties, gigs in jazz clubs... I found inspiration listening to the three guys who had been on the road, each in his own way. First was Moondog, a street musician from New York, who played with explosives as a kid, which left him blind. He is the father of minimalism, he used primitive but classical percussions, he was a friend of Charlie Parker. I also thought about Harry Partch who was obsessed with language, he would record people from all over the U.S.A, he became a vagrant and lived in trains, he was on the road until he got a record deal. My third source of inspiration was John Cage.

Did you compose the score with the images of the movie in mind?

No, most of it, no. That's how I usually work. I write from the script and from my discussion with the director. I did the same thing for *Brokeback Mountain*. In the case of *On the Road*, I wanted to keep some elements that connect with jazz.I worked with a friend, the double bassist Charlie Haden, who truly comes from that generation – he worked with Ornette Coleman, among others.

You played live with the musicians?

I recorded some of it live, and I assembled the rest in studio. I had to keep in mind that the soundtrack had to sound as if it had been written at the time of *On the Road*.

Have you seen the movie?

I've seen it several times, and I love it. It's such a Walter way of telling the story: he humanizes his characters, he gives them a soul. It's one of his trademarks.

Your score is very percussive. It perfectly suits the hectic rhythm of the movie. I thought about *Shadows* by John Cassavetes.

It's the best compliment I could get, you've made my day! We wanted that immediacy. I wanted lots of percussion, to connect with African sounds and different ethnicities. Something like urban tribal. ●

SHOOTING

DIARIES

WITH: **SAM RILEY | TERRENCE HOWARD | KRISTEN STEWART GARRETT HEDLUND | DANNY MORGAN | STEVE BUSCEMI VIGGO MORTENSEN | AMY ADAMS | ELISABETH MOSS**

As a set photographer, Gregory Smith followed Walter Salles' team; with his camera he captured fragments of a long cinematographic journey going from the smoky student rooms and jazz clubs in New York — all pieced together in Montreal — to the sunny outdoors of New Orleans, through Mexico and the Argentinian pampa. In order to be able to embody the mythical characters of Kerouac's gang, the actors had to dive deep in that universe, surrounding themselves with typical objects of that era (typewriters, cars, musical instruments...), so that their expressions could embody the emotions of a whole generation. Looking at the faces of Sam Riley, Kristen Stewart and Garret Hedlund — at the height of their skills, backed by five star actors playing secondary parts (Kirsten Dunst, Steve Buscemi, Viggo Mortensen, Elisabeth Moss) — gives us a privileged access to Walter Salles' universe. We enter his world through the main gate: where journey is seen as a sensorial experience and as a spiritual and aesthetical quest. Snapshots on the road.

BY LAURA TUILLIER

TRANSLATED BY CATHERINE GUESDE – PHOTOS BY GREGORY SMITH

ROAD BUDDIES

"THE ONLY THING I REMEMBER ABOUT THE BEAT GENERATION WRITERS IS THAT THEY GOT ME HOOKED ON WEARING SANDALS," DIRECTOR MONTE HELLMAN TOLD US. SOMEWHAT TAKEN ABACK BY THIS NON SEQUITUR FROM THE MAN WHO MADE THE 1971 ROAD MOVIE *TWO LANE BLACKTOP,* WE WENT OFF IN SEARCH OF OTHER VOICES – THOSE OF FRIENDS, CONTEMPORARIES, SPECIALISTS, OR HEIRS TO THE DHARMA BUMS. THEY FRANKLY ADMITTED THEIR ADMIRATION FOR THE BEATS, AND THEIR DEBT TO THE MOVEMENT. *"THE POET IS THE ONE WHO INSPIRES, MUCH MORE THAN THE ONE WHO IS INSPIRED,"* PAUL ÉLUARD WROTE. THE TESTIMONIALS BELOW ARE PROOF THAT KEROUAC, GINSBERG AND THEIR FRIENDS WERE INDEED POETS, AND NOT MINOR ONES.

TRANSLATED BY ANITA CONRADE

SAUL WILLIAMS
MUSICIAN, POET AND ACTOR

"What excites me about the Beat Generation is how they ignited the Hippie movement, in the same way the poets of the Harlem Renaissance ignited the Civil Rights Movement. When it comes to Kerouac, I'm influenced most by the *"boppity bop bop"* of his language. It's as if he had fireworks going off in his mouth, in his brain, and I'm a fan of all the little explosions... The run on sentences, the internal rhythm and overall nuance of it all. It's like reading Mingus... I like to feel the rhythm on the page and he did a great job of imitating those rhythms. I did a poetry reading with Allen Ginsberg, three weeks before he died. He read *Howl*, sitting down. I read my poems *Ohm* and *Untimely Meditations*. When I got off the stage, he kissed me on the mouth, told me he didn't understand all of my references -they were mostly hip hop based-, and then proceeded to teach me about the benefits of chanting *Ohm*: "*It connects the heart and crown chakras.*" And I learned what it felt like to be kissed on the mouth by a man who had a way with words." **É. V.**

" IT'S LIKE READING MINGUS... I LIKE FEELING THE RYTHM ON THE PAGE. "

SAUL WILLIAMS

DANNY MORGAN
ACTOR, PLAYS ED DUNKEL IN ON THE ROAD

"For me it was the biggest thing in my life, everything after that is going to be a bonus. Growing up ginger haired you don't think you're going to be on the big screen. In the film they actually dyed it jet black. My favorite part was the amazing house in New Orleans, even though there were bugs the size of cricket balls. Also, the New Year scene with a hundred people in a room going mental for 2 straight days, just drenched. When you stepped into the locations, you didn't feel like you were doing a period piece. Some strange things happened to me while we were shooting: the running joke when we travelled anywhere was that I would get lost along the way. Somehow we (the cast) became a really close group of friends traveling around together. For Walter it was a labor of love, he would tell us about the Beat generation and Garrett would be completely immersed in Dean. I got to meet Al Hinkle, the only guy still alive, and Carolyn Cassady - she looks so upbeat! I thought that if we met the universe would implode, but he was really sweet." **C. G.**

" FREEDOM WAS WORTH CELEBRATING. "

AL HINKLE
FRIEND OF NEAL CASSADY, CAROLYN CASSADY AND JACK KEROUAC

"Jack had moved to Berkeley in 1955. One day I went there with Neal and LuAnne. Neal jumped out of the car and walked right in the front door of the house, startling Jack, who was just opening a package that contained eight advance copies of On the Road. He tried to hide them from us, but Neal grabbed a copy and started reading from different parts of it, jumping around and dancing in excitement. Jack asked, "You guys won't hate me for what I wrote, will you?" We assured him we loved it, and he said, "I'm very happy to hear that, because I have seven more books ready to go!" You know, it's a good thing Jack was a successful writer, because he wasn't a very good brakeman!

The Beat Scene in San Francisco was pretty wild! Most of the bars that we hung out in didn't have liquor licenses, so they only sold wine and beer. They had sawdust or peanut shells on the floor, and provided chess sets so the regulars could play. One of our favourite places was actually called "The Place". It had a balcony inside, and people stood up there and read their poetry. The winner won a 49-cent bottle of wine. Of course, you had to share it with everybody, but you were honored with a title, like "Winner-Most Original Work". The police presence got really heavy at the time the Beat Scene was emerging. In 1958, Neal got into trouble by sharing a joint with an undercover policeman, and

was sentenced to San Quentin for three to five years. The one thing that I regret most is not being more influential on Neal after he got out of prison. I had known him since we were twelve years old; he was barely forty two when he died. I often wonder what he was thinking of while he was walking all alone on that railroad track. I wish things had turned out differently for him. That's probably my worst memory – that I wasn't able to save his life. If there's anything worth remembering and understanding about the Beat lifestyle, it is that they celebrated freedom in all its aspects. To my friends, freedom was worth all they went through to celebrate it." **J .R.**

ROAD BUDDIES

ROMAN COPPOLA
CO-PRODUCER OF *ON THE ROAD*, FILM DIRECTOR

"It's amazing to discover the legends that were produced by this book and its adaptation on screen. There's the rumor that my father, Francis Ford Coppola, wanted to direct it in Russia, in the early 1990s. It was a joke during a dinner. One of his associates drew parallelism between the U.S.A. from the 1940s-1950s, *On the Road*'s years, and post-U.S.S.R. Russia: the same cultural state of mind after a very oppressed time. An interesting concept, but nothing more." **É. R.**

CHARLES CARMIGNAC
GUITAR PLAYER FOR THE BAND MORIARTY

"We love the intensity and frenzy of *On the Road* character Dean Moriarty, the namesake of our band. He crosses the United States with the pedal to the metal, eating up experiences, encounters, and miles with the car radio blaring, until the road burns him up. The tempo he gives off is speedy and alert. He lives inside music you would play in a hyper-energetic rush, but in an easygoing, laidback way – and that's really hard to do!" **É. V.**

BERNARD BENOLIEL
CULTURAL DIRECTOR OF THE CINEMATHEQUE FRANÇAISE AND CO-AUTHOR WITH JEAN-BAPTISTE THORET OF *ROAD MOVIE, USA*

"AN ESSENTIAL MOMENT THAT HAS DEFINED AMERICA."

"*On the Road* is simultaneously momentum and getting stuck, steering and disorientation, euphoria and depression, a trip across country and an inner journey, the certainty the wilderness is still out there, and the conviction it's already spoiled. In this sense, Kerouac's novel prefigures or sums up all the Utopias in the "glorious" road movies of the 1970s. The presence of *On the Road* is so strong, no one even has to cite it. At the same time, even though it's a monumental novel, American history and geography are even more monumental. Their dimensions came before it, and obviously survive it. Hence Kerouac's despair: from one page to the next, he dreams of embracing an expanse, and then it slips out of his grasp. *On the Road* is an essential moment, but only one moment, of a drifter spirit that has defined America since covered-wagon times, back when the "asphalt" was still just a dirt trail or a river." **L. T.**

JERRY CIMINO
FOUNDER AND CURATOR OF THE BEAT MUSEUM IN SAN FRANCISCO

"I first got the idea for creating the Beat Museum while walking through Amsterdam. I passed by the Hemp Museum and realized, *"If they can have a Hemp Museum in Amsterdam why can't I create a Beat Museum in San Francisco?"* For 25 years I worked for two major corporations and it was like I was a cog in the wheel. I wanted to do something that would have a lasting impact on the world. The Beats weren't out to change the world. They simply followed their own passions and desires and by doing so they did, in fact, change the world. I knew we were on to something the very first day we opened up our doors. A man came in and handed me a record album, a very rare album of Lawrence Ferlinghetti and Kenneth Rexroth reading poetry to jazz music at the Cellar. I looked at the man and said, *"This is worth a few hundred dollars and I don't have the money to give to you for that."* The man said, *"I don't want money. I want you to put it on the wall and tell the story. People need to know this history."* **Q. G.**

FRANCIS FORD COPPOLA
DIRECTOR, CO-PRODUCER OF *ON THE ROAD*

"Thirty years ago, I had a protégée, she loved *On the Road* so I bought it. But I was never as crazy about it as she was: I thought it was a piece of literature that got a very lucky break thanks to a review in *The New York Times*. But the Whitman love of America and the country is a real thing. The trouble with *On the Road* is that the book has a crazy non-plot, so it was very difficult to do a film adaptation. I couldn't figure out in my own head how to do it. Jerry Garcia from the Grateful Dead, who knew Neal Cassady once told me that Woody Harrelson at 22 would have been perfect for the part. But Garrett Hedlund has the right kind of maniac craziness. Sam Riley is convincing: he's not American, so what? Those guys seem too young? But they were! I read people complaining that the movie is shot in Canada, so what? Movies are illusions, there is no America from the 1940s anymore. I'm glad because Walter Salles worked so hard on it and I want it to be successful." **C.G. & J.R.**

RAY CARNEY
PROFESSOR OF AMERICAN STUDIES AT BOSTON UNIVERSITY

"Many of the impulses that animated the Beat Movement have corollaries in the myths of the American West and the frontier, but their real starting point is much further back in the 18th century myths of the founding of America, as expressed in the Federalist Papers, The Declaration of Independence, and The Constitution, and in the 19th century writings of Ralph Waldo Emerson, Henry David Thoreau, and Emily Dickinson." **L. T.**

JEAN-JACQUES BONVIN
SOCIOLOGIST AND NOVELIST

"Refusing to submit, denying authority, glowing with the beauty of endless self destruction - that's always existed. The Beats simply gave shape to a movement that includes François Villon, Arthur Rimbaud, and Georg Trakl. My book *Ballast* centers on the Neal Cassady figure. I pruned that fantasy down to the minimum, limiting myself to a brief sixty-four pages. It was a question of rhythm: I had to run alongside Cassady and fall on the track ballast early, with him." **Q. G.**

CARLOS CONTI
ON THE ROAD PRODUCTION DESIGNER

"I'd worked with Walter Salles on *The Motorcycle Diaries*. For *On the Road*, I went to the US alone to scout locations. At the beginning, the whole film was supposed to be shot there, and then MK2 made it possible to travel elsewhere, to Canada, Mexico, or Argentina. The road movie is a difficult genre. The crew is always on the move, and you have to be flexible enough to adapt to anything. We opted for natural settings, as close as possible to the locations in the novel. I wanted to avoid the "period film" look because the characters and book are so modern, so I based the design on imagery from the early 1950s instead of the 1940s. We found Denver's red bricks at a location near Ottawa. Because the roads in Quebec were in bad shape, we shot some of the driving scenes in Calgary. Physically, the shoot was harsh. We'd switch from sweltering Louisiana weather to polar Argentinian chill, followed up by three days of pouring rain in Mexico. It was sheer hell!" **C. G. & A. T.**

> ## "THE BOOK IS SO MODERN, I WANTED TO AVOID THE "PERIOD FILM" LOOK."
> CARLOS CONTI

"JACK WAS DROP-DEAD HANDSOME."
CAROLYN CASSADY
NEAL CASSADY'S SECOND WIFE, JACK KEROUAC'S FRIEND AND LOVER, AUTHOR OF *OFF THE ROAD: TWENTY YEARS WITH CASSADY, KEROUAC AND GINSBERG*

"At that time I never thought that *On the Road* was a misogynist novel, nor do I agree. I don't know why people make these judgements—unless from envy. It was written by a man about a man's thoughts. The men were always perfect gentlemen. They pulled out chairs, opened car doors. Of course, when Neal was so intimate with LuAnne, some of that declined... Now then, LOVE. Jack was romantic and fell in love with every woman he met. He was very lonely and wanted a partner. I don't think Neal could ever love or be in love, as we usually think of it. I've known others who had horrible childhoods. They built up defense mechanisms then, and kept them—that is, they could never surrender themselves to another. Neal was driven by sexual desire. He admired and respected me -I was his passport to respectability, the great motive in his whole life. As for me, I truly completely loved the man Neal showed to me when wooing me, and I could never get over the fact that that man was in him no matter how he later behaved. Jack was drop-dead handsome with the black hair and big blue eyes as well as the perfect male physique. Then, my being so educated, his knowledge of literature was a bonus. Although Neal and I had far more intense discussions -so much so that Jack complained no one could interrupt us—meaning himself. Neal had a genius mind and a photographic memory. Jack was extremely sensitive and paranoid. Nobody loved him; they wouldn't publish his "great" books. When he was so misunderstood by the media and the hippies, he vowed to kill himself—and he did. I think Neal did influence Jack the most. But they had so much in common, and Neal hoped Jack would help him write "properly." As it was, Neal's spontaneous letters were the catalyst for Jack's change in style and his future success. Neal said he wished no one would read *On the Road*—he hated it. It emphasized the wild side of his nature, not his brilliant mind. I couldn't read it until many many years later-I didn't want to know about that trip." **J. R.**

ROAD
BUDDIES

GORDON BALL
FILMMAKER AND
PHOTOGRAPHER OF THE BEAT GENERATION

"I came to the United States to go to college. I already had on my mind to go on the road before reading Jack Kerouac's book. Reading it certainly didn't discourage me. In a way On the Road is an elegy to the two-lane blacktops, which were about to disappear to put interstates to facilitate military progress. That changed the landscape of America, not only physically but spiritually. When I was hitchhiking in 1968, there was a growing sense of paranoia." **L. T.**

BARRY MILES
COUNTER-CULTURE SPECIALIST,
AUTHOR OF *BEAT HOTEL*

"I took over as manager of the Better Books bookstore in 1965. Allen Ginsberg moved in with me. I met Burroughs and became one of the Beats' main advocates. Their legacy is that they gave rise to the hippies and counter-culture, the ecology movement, the gay liberation and women's movement... *On the Road* was a celebration of the size, the magnificence of America. Kerouac didn't even drive. It was about the enthusiasm and the excitement that he generated in his prose." **C. G.**

JOYCE JOHNSON
POET, JACK KEROUAC'S PARTNER FROM 1957 TO 1959, AUTHOR OF A BIOGRAPHY
ON KEROUAC TO BE PUBLISHED, *THE VOICE WAS ALL: READING JACK KEROUAC'S LIFE*

" KEROUAC FELT LIKE AN OUTSIDER. "

"I was particularly interested in dealing with him as a bilingual American writer. The fact that he was French Canadian had a tremendous impact on his life. He really felt split between his French Canadian side of himself and the American side of himself. He called himself a half American and I think he always had that feeling. He wrote about a culture that was not totally his and that he admired. *On the Road* is a book by someone who felt like an outsider in America. When I look at Jack's English prose I see a lot of French in the sound of it. Although he is credited with just sitting down and easily writing *On the Road,* tremendous amount of work had preceded that and in his own way he was a perfectionist. But his way of revising was to start something then say "no" it's not it, throw it out, start all over again. The writing of On the Road was preceded just a month or so before by the writing of a wonderful little novella in French that has never been published. It was based on all the different lousy jobs he had to take, before becoming a writer." **L.T.**

HETTIE JONES
BEAT GENERATION WRITER

"It was a very small bohemia, not only writers but also painters, musicians, dancers. There were lots of parties at our house. Our friendship was based on our desire to change the way people thought about art in the United States. In New York and San Francisco, we were redefining art. I didn't want to go on the road because New York was the best place in the world. I drove across the country ten years later with my two daughters. I was not conscious of being part of a generation, I just felt I finally escaped my bourgeois world and was with people that interested me. I was able to do an interesting job instead of just marrying and going in the suburbs to have children. The fun part is that now the new bohemia lives in Brooklyn and that's my neighborhood, that's the place from which I so much wanted to escape!" **L. T.**

CHRISTOPHE COUSIN
ADVENTURER, WRITER-TRAVELER AND
FILMMAKER, AUTHOR OF
DANS LES ROUES DE JACK KEROUAC

"Basically, here's what I got from *On the Road.* Kerouac has not yet entered upon his mystical phase. He's still a kid. He has some fancy education polish on him, but he's unsure of the course he should set for his life. And then he figures, *'let's go, I'm going to tell this story.'* It's about having the courage to take off. I started by reading *The Dharma Bums* when I was 16 or 17 years old. With that behind me, I did like everyone else and tackled *On the Road.* I stopped halfway through. I just couldn't get into it. *Visions of Cody, Satori in Paris...* I read all of Kerouac, but couldn't finish *On the Road.* I finally read it in 2003, the night before I was leaving for a two-year, round-the-world solo bicycle ride. Finally, I understood how Kerouac's free-fall writing style reflects a philosophy about travel. You hit the road, without a direction; you find your rhythm, you abandon yourself to the weariness, the litany of the asphalt under your tires, and finally, you find yourself." **É. R.**

JEFFREY LEWIS
COMIC BOOK ARTIST AND MUSICIAN

"The Beats had a big influence on the Fugs and the Velvet Underground who had a big influence on so many bands since then. Jazz in the fifties found powerful new ways to express creativity and freedom, but the Beats tried to find ways to do this with words. The sixties rock bands tried to mix both forms, and that's the kind of music that I'm drawn to, with sounds that can go further outside and words that can go further inside." **É. V.**

ISAAC GEWIRTZ
CURATOR AT THE NEW YORK PUBLIC LIBRARY

"Universities tend to look down on Kerouac. It has to do with his alcoholism, and there was the racism issue. His own statements about the way he wrote also have influenced the opinion of critics and scholars toward him, like his principle that one should not revise. For *On the Road* he did revise but also he prepared very carefully. Many of the lyrical descriptive passages that you find in the novel have their genesis in Kerouac's *Rain and Rivers* notebook, sometimes word for word." **J. R.**

PHILIPPE DJIAN
NOVELIST AND SONGWRITER

"When I was 14, I worked at Gallimard [the publishing house]. I used to see Paul Morand with his walker, and had absolute no desire to look like that. I read Kerouac, who taught me reading isn't enough. You have to take your backpack and go see what's happening in Japan, go learn Oriental philosophy. Kerouac set me off. When I was twenty, a buddy and I wanted to go to the United States. We'd never been. But we didn't want to be like all the corny tourists who take a plane. We wanted to crew on a freighter, so we got longshoremen's papers in Le Havre. For two months, we got up at three in the morning, hoping to sail the open sea that day. Finally, we took a plane, like everybody else. The Kerouac-style road trip didn't fit with the times. From a practical point of view, it's behind me, but I did learn a valuable lesson. Kerouac taught me to cross the street. You jaywalk. Once you've absorbed all these characters and their visions, you'll never again use the crosswalk like a common banker." **Q. G.**

> ## "KEROUAC TAUGHT ME THAT READING ISN'T ENOUGH."
> PHILIPPE DJIAN

YVES SIMON
SINGER AND WRITER

"When I was 20, I worshipped the Beat Generation writers. I loved the way they refused to sit placidly at home writing, confined to a study. They had to zoom across the continent from coast to coast, picking up on the effervescence of the others. They took pride in being "dharma bums," writers whose primary purpose was to live life to the max, and then write. Beat literature feeds on everything that makes noise and moves the soul from joy to despair: chipped-tooth smiles, creaking jalopies, truck stops, macadam, sweet Moroccan breath and New York fracas. The Beats traveled the planet as verbal conquerors. Banging out my second and third novels on my Brother Deluxe, I kept thinking of them, crazy about mandalas and tantrism, mystical ecstasies blooming from their sick skulls, as starved for the abyss as they were for satori. Self-fulfillments." **Q. G.**

> ## "BEAT LITERATURE FEEDS ON EVERYTHING THAT MOVES THE SOUL."
> YVES SIMON

ANNE WALDMAN
WRITER, POET AND EDITOR. FRIEND OF THE BEATS

"I never knew Kerouac personally. I am somewhat the next generation, born in 1945. I grew up in Greenwich Village, and used to see these "guys" as a teenager. I met the poet Diane di Prima when I was 17 years old and she was an inspiration and goad. Kerouac's writing was a huge inspiration to my generation and a whole community of experimental writers. I was into the literary work-Burroughs' cut-up methods, Kerouac's spontaneity and energy, Ginsberg's political consciousness. The Jack Kerouac School of Disembodied Poetic was founded by myself and Ginsberg in 1974, the first Buddhist-inspired university in the west. Allen insisted on reading *Howl* to the Dalai Lama. The Beat legacy is enormous: the sense of camaraderie, a continuation of "*candor*" as an artistic aesthetic, close observation of the rhythms and nuances of language, the ongoing possibilities with an experimental poetics for younger writers... I think the Occupy Movement is influenced by the values of the Beat ethos and the sense of inquiry." **C. G.**

ROAD BUDDIES

MICHEL BULTEAU
POET AND FILMMAKER

"I met Williams Burroughs in London in 1972. Then, in 1974, Henri Michaux introduced me to Allen Ginsberg and Gregory Corso, who were in Paris. They were hanging out with French artists like Jean-Jacques Lebel and Alain Jouffroy, authors of *La Poésie de la "Beat Generation"* published by Denoël. The Beat poets left an imprint on my writing. They were a combination of Rimbaud and Charlie Parker, two artists who always believed art can change life." **Q. G.**

PIERS FACCINI
MUSICIAN AND PAINTER

"Like many musicians of my generation, I feel a strong kinship with American and Canadian songwriters, who in turn owe a lot to Kerouac and the Beat poets: Bob Dylan, Tim Hardin, Fred Neil, Tim Buckley, Joni Mitchell, and Neil Young. Today's songwriters are inspired by them without even knowing it. Kerouac was an indirect influence on me. His writing style opened horizons for me. I also love Ginsberg's poetry, and I've read everything Burroughs wrote." **É. V.**

PETER COYOTE
ACTOR, CO-FOUNDER AND MEMBER OF THE DIGGER GROUP

"THEY HAD THE COURAGE TO BE MARGINAL AND OUT-OF-FASHION AND SIMPLY TO PURSUE THEIR DEEP INTERESTS."

"Even before I was a Digger, I was inspired by the Beats as far back as 1954, when I was 13; fascinated by these men and women who talked openly about social problems my family and friends had already experienced. They were part of a general exodus from the majority culture, joining forces with folk music. I think it was the sense of autonomy and personal authority that struck me about them. They had a world view to which they were completely faithful. They had the courage to be "marginal" and "out-of-fashion," and simply to pursue their deepest interests and intentions. Among the Diggers, we felt in direct continuity with the Beats. We knew, as Bob Dylan said, *"something's happening,"* and we had a clear sense of it. One of the great nights of that time was a poetry reading where the Diggers presented their ideas and philosophies. Gary Snyder and Allen Ginsberg were in the audience, and there was a clear sense from Allen and the elders that they were *"passing the mantle to us"*." **L. T.**

PHILIPPE GARNIER
JOURNALIST, WRITER, AND TRANSLATOR

"In the 1950s, it was common for a truck or car to pull over and pick up a hitchhiker. In the 1960s, young travelers with backpacks thumbed rides all over the world. But by the late 1970s and early 1980s, things had changed. Hippie youth had been demonized by the Manson murders. Fear and paranoia ruled. The few hitchhikers on the roads weren't usually doing it for fun. But I remember when I lived San Francisco in 1976-77, I didn't have a car, and I traveled all over the Bay Area hitching rides. Either way on the Bay Bridge was a piece of cake. What I mean is that when Kerouac thumbed his way across the country, it wasn't an amazing feat. Hitchhiking was a common, everyday means of transportation. He may already have had a romantic vision of the phenomenon. And he certainly did a lot to immortalize that romance." **Q. G.**

F.J. OSSANG
POET, MUSICIAN, AND FILMMAKER

"The chorus of Richard Hell's song *Blank Generation* is inspired by a much earlier cheer: *"I belong to the Beat Generation."* The first punks were the natural allies of the Beats, and quickly made friends with veteran nihilists like William S. Burroughs, who was nicknamed "Daddy Punk." Richard Hell, Joe Strummer, and later Kurt Cobain maintained close ties with Burroughs. In 1982, British performance artist Genesis P-Orridge released an anthology of the darkest Beat's sound archives called *Nothing Here But the Recordings.* In my opinion, William S. Burroughs is among the essential writers of the second half of the 20th century. In fact, in 1979, we published his essay *Le Temps des assassins* in the magazine *Cée* (of which I was then editor). It is a study of how drugs, money, organized crime, and political power are intertwined, a plea for the liberalization of drug laws." **Q. G.**

BARRY GIFFORD
POET, SCRIPT WRITER, CO-AUTHOR OF *JACK'S BOOK: AN ORAL BIOGRAPHY OF JACK KEROUAC*

"*On the Road* is all about the search for the missing father. Jack Kerouac had a difficult, troubled relationship with his, and Cassady's went missing. *On the Road* is also about the changes in America following World War II. It's really a book about the late 1940s in America. The first road novel was *Don Quixote* by Cervantes, followed by *Joseph Andrews* and *Tom Jones* by Henry Fielding. It's a long literary tradition which Kerouac followed. Kerouac and Allen Ginsberg were great inspiration for me and many others of my generation. My favorite books of Kerouac's are his first novel *The Town and the City,* and *Doctor Sax,* which is the one I would have made into a movie were it up to me. The so-called Beat Generation produced a lot of very bad writing, as does any movement. Kerouac was an individual. His major influences were Melville, Celine, etc. Other than being a great writer, Kerouac struck a literary chord that is still being heard. It's a tragedy that he died young, drunk, and broke." **A. T. and L. T.**

> "GINSBERG WAS NOT ONLY A GREAT POET AND TEACHER: HE WAS A CATALYST."
>
> JEAN-JACQUES LEBEL

JEAN-JACQUES LEBEL
VISUAL ARTIST, WRITER, TRANSLATOR AND PUBLISHER

"Ginsberg was not only a great poet and teacher; he was also a catalyst. He proclaimed himself his friends' agent, and he was the one who finally found a publisher for Kerouac. When Ginsberg sent Ferlinghetti the manuscript of *Naked Lunch* by Burroughs, he rejected it, because of all the homosexuality and violence. What a mistake! He regretted that decision for years. In Paris, I got together with Ginsberg, Corso, and Gysin, to offer the manuscript to Maurice Girodias. I can assure you, as an eyewitness, he didn't want to touch it. He thought it was outrageous, unbearable. We put pressure on him a little by locking him in his office – we told him we wouldn't let him go until he signed a contract. After three hours, when we'd drunk all the alcohol and smoked all the joints on his side of the door, he changed his mind. And after that, he claimed that he was the one who had discovered Burroughs." **Q. G.**

JOHN SAMPAS
JACK KEROUAC'S BROTHER-IN-LAW AND COPYRIGHT HOLDER

"In the spring of 1964 Jack Kerouac had come to Lowell to visit my brother Anthony and sister Stella. He asked me to drive him back to New York which I was happy to do and so we jumped into my old Pontiac and drove directly to Allen Ginsberg's apartment on the Lower East Side. Ensconced at Allen's were Peter Orlovsky and Gregory Corso. Apparently, Jack hadn't seen them for some years, at least that's the impression I gathered as Allen went on to describe his years spent in India. After a while Allen suggested we all go and visit Lucian Carr. We arrived to find that Lucian was in Florida but his wife invited us in for what turned out to be a long afternoon visit. After a while Gregory opened up his pack of cigarettes which turned out to be a pack of rolled up marijuana sticks. I was offered one, I had never smoked this weed before and so I gave it a try. It was a bit too much for me and soon I felt somewhat discombobulated. I remember saying to Jack that the effect made me feel that I was hovering in the room next door." **J. R.**

MARIE-LAURE DAGOIT
AUTHOR AND PUBLISHER

> " THE FACT THAT ALL THESE AUTHORS HUNG OUT TOGETHER IS INCREDIBLE!"

"Claude Pélieu turned me on to the Beat Generation. I'd heard the authors' names, but I hadn't read them. Claude Pélieu had notebooks full of facsimile editions of American underground publications and fanzines. I used to go see him every day, and we'd talk. He gave me the texts, telling me thousands of stories, true and false. It was intensely absorbing. That's how I discovered *On the Road*, jazz, rhythm, Buddhism. The beat. I love groups of individuals, artist collectives. The fact that all these authors hung out together is incredible! Pélieu gave me a few addresses, in particular contacts with Allen Ginsberg and William S. Burroughs. I wrote to them as a friend of his, and they sent texts. In 1995, I settled in Rouen and founded Les Editions Derrière la Salle de Bains (Translator's note: Behind the Bathroom). Since then, I have moved all the operations to my home, where I work while humming *This is my Beat Generation*." **Q. G.**

GLOSSARY

KEROUAC'S WAY OF WRITING IS BOTH ORAL AND INTROSPECTIVE; IT BORROWS ELEMENTS FROM THE JOUAL DIALECT BUT ALSO HAS SIMILARITIES WITH EUROPEAN LITERARY MASTERPIECES. ALTERNATELY SLANGY, INCORRECT, LYRICAL AND JERKY, HIS LANGUAGE STRIKES US BY ITS BOLDNESS AND IRREVERENCE. HERE IS A COMPENDIUM FOR NEOPHYTES.

BY QUENTIN GROSSET | TRANSLATED BY CATHERINE QUESDE

BEAT

"Guys, I'm beat!" Herbert Huncke – one of Kerouac and Ginsberg's friends – cries, as they are getting high on Benzedrine. The word that will become the seal of a whole generation means "tierd out," "worn out," "tired," "poor," and "dead-beat" at the same time. It also refers to the heart-beat, to its rhythm, linking the "beat" movement directly to jazz music. The novelist John Clellon Holmes, following a discussion with Jack Kerouac, made the expression "Beat Generation" popular in a manifesto published in *The New York Times* in 1952.

BEATNIK

"I'm a catholic, not a beatnik," Kerouac said at the end of his life. The journalist Herb Caen tagged the term in 1958 using the word "beat" and the Russian satellite's name "Sputnik", referring to the concentration of stereotypes relating to the Beat Generation: young, long-haired and neglected bohemians. Ginsberg, who also rejected this unflattering image, wrote: *"(beatniks) have been created not by Kerouac but by industries of mass communication which continue to brainwash man."*

BENZEDRINE

A psychoactive substance put on the market in 1932, Benzedrine (or "speed") is one of the commercial versions of amphetamine. It can be swallowed, smoked, sniffed or injected in the veins. It has stimulating effects such as euphoria; sensations like tiredness and hunger disappear, and intellectual capacities seem to increase. The Beats used this substance through 98 cents inhalators.

DHARMA

This word, originating from the root *"dhar"* – meaning "carry" or "support" – embraces numerous meanings and was first used in Indian philosophies and religions. In Hinduism, it refers to the universal, cosmic order, that is, the "eternal law" governing the world, from microcosm to macrocosm. In *The Dharma Bums*, the hero Ray Smith searches for his soul with the help of Japhy Ryder, a character inspired by the poet Gary Snyder, who introduced Kerouac to introspection and meditation.

HIPSTER

Originally, in the 40's, the term "hipster" referred to American amateurs of jazz and bebop music, who favored a cool attitude, carelessness and free love. Hipsters are mostly young Whites imitating the style of urban Blacks of the time, using jazz slang, and doing the same drugs as the jazzmen. The term is now revived and refers to the urban young people keen on alternative cultural movements, and wearing a whole range of retro clothes.

HOBO

"Hobo" was first used at the end of the 19th century to refer to itinerant workers, without home or family, who would travel through the United States by foot or by freight trains, looking for seasonal work. The Beats considered themselves hobos, since they worked from time to time in order to travel during the rest of the year. In a text entitled *The Vanishing American Hobo*, Kerouac evokes the hardships of such a way of life, at a time when people on the road were checked more and more often.

IT

Supreme level in jazz music; moment when the music acquires a literally ontological value, that is, when the musician manages to blend with the Being and when, in the middle of an improvisation, he tries with all his heart to reach a state of trance. For Dean Moriarty in *On The Road*, the jazzmen reaches "it" when he's *"filling the empty of space with the substance of our lives, confessions of his belly button strain, remembrances of ideas, rehashes of old blowing."*

JOUAL

Sociolect from Quebec originating from French, and borrowing various terms from English. It was Kerouac's mother tongue, the only language he spoke until the age of 6. Even though Joual is an oral tongue, Kerouac tried to use it for written language several times, notably in a version of *On The Road*. A work entitled *La Nuit est ma femme* (1951), entirely written in Joual, was discovered in 2007. A year later, another short novel using Joual and entitled *Sur le chemin* (1952) was found.

HITCHINGS LIFTS

On The Road has become a manifesto of hitchhiking and has encouraged several generations of rovers to hit the road and hitchhike. Hiking through the States from lift to lift, Kerouac moves forward on his road making various and unlikely encounters. Although hitchhiking was much more common in the 50's than it is now, this activity remains unalterably linked to the mythology of the road.

MÉMÈRE

Nickname of Gabrielle-Ange Lévesque, Kerouac's mother. He regularly came back to her house, and he spent the end of his life with her. An orphan at the age of 14, sanctimonious and possessive, she was apparently also a tattler since that's what "mémère" means in Joual. Kerouac was proud of his mother's so-called Iroquois origins, thinking of himself as half-Indian, half-Canadian. In the June 1971 issue of *Actuel,* Jean-François Bizot used the cheeky headline: *"Would you have hit the road if you'd known that Kerouac lived with his mother?"*

SPONTANEOUS PROSE

Literary style initiated and theorized by Jack Kerouac in a list of thirty "principles" (*"wild typewritten pages for your own joy,"* *"be in love with your life"* etc.) Spontaneous prose recommends rhythm and immediacy in literature, and is inspired on the one hand by the "stream of consciousness" technique used by James Joyce and Virginia Woolf, and on the other by the way bebop uses improvisation. Later on, the singer-songwriter Bob Dylan was to be influenced by this way of writing.

ROAD

Factual and symbolical term referring to the road, but also to everything connected to it: travelling, nomadism, searching, wandering, adventure, unworldliness, freedom... Taking a road trip (across the United States) is a traditional American experience. *"Our battered suitcases were piled on the sidewalk again; we had longer ways to go. But no matter, the road is life,"* Kerouac writes in *On The Road.*

SATORI

A Japanese word from Zen Buddhism, literally meaning "comprehension" and regularly used by Kerouac to describe a kind of spiritual awakening. In *Satori In Paris,* evoking his stay in France searching for his ancestors, Kerouac has a *Satori* and describes it as *"a sudden illumination, a sudden awakening or a kick in the eye".* Zen Buddhism considers it as a transient experience of life, comparable to what Westerners call an "epiphany."

SCROLL

This is the famous 36 meters long typewriter paper roll, on which *On The Road* was written. Kerouac wrote more than a hundred words a minute and putting new sheets of paper in the typewriter interrupted the flow of his spontaneous prose. The end of the scroll of *On The Road* was eaten by Lucien Carr's dog. It had to be rewritten and Scotch-taped to the rest. The original 1951 scroll, much modified by Kerouac after the editors refused it, was eventually published – uncensored – in 2007.

TEA

One of the various nicknames the Beats used for cannabis. In *The Dharma Bums,* Kerouac writes how he later discovered the virtues of tea (the actual tea) which is part of the Buddhist way of life. *"The first sip is joy, the second is gladness, the third is serenity, the fourth is madness, the fifth is ecstasy,"* he writes. From there follows *"teaism,"* a Japanese cult based on the idolization of the beautiful, and inculcating values such as harmony, purity and charity.

VISION

When he meets his fellow Beats, Jack Kerouac is trying to develop a *"New Vision."* Through various excesses and experimentations, he aims to reach superior levels of poetic awareness. This quest had already been initiated by William Blake and Arthur Rimbaud, the former through his *"vision"* resulting from a disorder of the senses in his *Illuminations,* the latter through his *"doors of perception."* Kerouac's *Visions of Cody* and *Visions of Gerard* carry the term in their title.

WILDERNESS

For Kerouac in his Buddhist period, urbanity and modernity rhyme with the middle-class way of life he despises. In order to reach inner peace, he decides to give the wilderness a try. *"No man should go through life without once experiencing healthy, even bored solitude in the wilderness, finding himself depending solely on himself and thereby learning his true and hidden strength,"* he writes in *The Lonesome Traveler.*

BIBLIOGRAPHY

AS SOON AS *ON THE ROAD* WAS PUBLISHED, KEROUAC, THE BEAT GENERATION'S STAR WRITER, BECAME THE SOURCE OF A PLETHORA OF WORKS THAT ARE CRITICAL AND REVERENTIAL, PERSONAL AND INTELLECTUAL, VISUAL AND LITERARY. AMONG THE COUNTLESS BIOGRAPHIES, ESSAYS, NARRATIVES, COFFEE TABLE BOOKS AND EVEN GRAPHIC NOVELS PUBLISHED TO DATE, HERE IS A LIST OF THOSE THAT HAVE ACCOMPANIED US THROUGHOUT THE MAKING OF THIS SPECIAL ISSUE.

| TRANSLATED BY ALEX WYNNE HAUET

ON THE ROAD
(Jack Kerouac, 1957, re-issued 1999, Penguin Books)

As soon as it was published, *On the Road* entered the realm of cult books, a standard bearer for the Beat Generation and a bible for many teenagers in search of a guide. Fleeting relationships, drugs and jazz clubs, the adventures of Sal Paradise and Dean Moriarty, sharing a friendship that Kerouac had dreamed of for Neal Cassady and himself, are transcribed in ebulliating language: from slang to lyrical to spasmodic, a *"vast, misty epic,"* somewhere between vision and reality. **L. T.**

THE HORN
(John Clellon Holmes, 1958, re-issued 1988, Thunder's Mouth PR)

A friend of Kerouac, Ginsberg and Cassady's and a jazz fanatic, John Clellon Holmes (1926-1988) is the forgotten player of the Beat Generation, despite having included the expression in 1952 in an article for *The New York Times*. His masterpiece, *The Horn,* is the quintessential jazz novel, telling the story of a black musician's decline directly inspired by Charlie Parker and Lester Young. It is essential reading in order to understand the artistic atmosphere of the 50s, even though Kerouac found his style a little too safe. **B. Q.**

KEROUAC
A BIOGRAPHY
(Ann Charters, 1973, re-issued 2009, St. Martin's Press)

The first biography on Kerouac is also the only one the author contributed to while he was still alive. Ann Charters met Kerouac in 1956 at Berkeley, then again in Hyannis, Massachusetts, not long before his death. Since its publication, this personal text has been questioned because of inaccuracies (Kerouac was, after all, a revisionist of his own story), and also because Charters did not have access to the original manuscript of *On the Road.* It nevertheless remains a reference in the realm of Beat studies. **C. G.**

LES ÉCRIVAINS DE LA BEAT GENERATION
(Jacqueline Starer, 1977, re-issued 2011, Éditions d'écarts, in French only)

In the late 1960s, Jacqueline Starer wrote her thesis about a literary movement that was little known in France. Based on her meetings with Burroughs, Ferlinghetti, Ginsberg and Snyder in California, she wrote a reference work published in 1977, *Les Écrivains beats et le voyage.* Reprinted in 2011 without its valuable photos, this book sounds out the very essence of the movement and questions the irrepressible desire to travel the roads of America, Morocco and Europe. **G. M.**

JACK'S BOOK
AN ORAL BIOGRAPHY OF JACK KEROUAC
(Barry Gifford and Lawrence Lee, 1978, re-issued. 2012, Penguin Books)

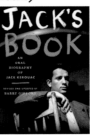

Built like a *'book movie'*, a mixture of documentary and fiction, *Jack's Book* is a collection of testimonies by those close to Jack Kerouac. Barry Gifford (the screenwriter for David Lynch's *Sailor & Lula*) and Lawrence Lee met the writer's friends, starting with Allen Ginsberg. The poet allegedly cried out upon reading *Jack's Book,* "My god, you would think we were in Rashōmon, everyone tells lies and the truth comes out!" **L. T.**

OFF THE ROAD

20 YEARS WITH CASSADY, KEROUAC AND GINSBERG
(Carolyn Cassady, 1990, re-issued 2007, Black Spring Press Ltd.)

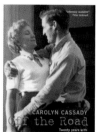

How did the women involved in *On the Road* feel about Dean Moriarty? In this tome, Carolyn Cassady, his second wife, puts pen to paper to give us an account of a marriage bleak with absence and infidelity, but also coloured with passionate discussions about art, literature and religion. Between visits from Ginsberg, Corso or Kerouac, whose mistress she was and whom we discover as a fiery romantic, Carolyn also tells of her struggle to keep her family afloat, despite the stormy weather. **J.R.**

WOMEN OF THE BEAT GENERATION

THE WRITERS, ARTISTS AND MUSES AT THE HEART OF A GENERATION (Brenda Knight, 1996, re-issued 1998, Conari Press)

Under the auspices of Anne Waldman and Ann Charters, Brenda Knight's book is a portrait of the women that made a name for themselves in the Beat Generation's masculine world. Rich with anecdotes and extracts of works by Joyce Johnson, Diane di Prima and Jan Kerouac (the writer's only daughter), *Women of the Beat Generation* nevertheless fails to free itself completely: the women are mainly envisaged in the context of their relationships to the men they frequented. **L.T.**

THE BEAT BOOK

WRITINGS FROM THE BEAT GENERATION
(Anthology edited by Anne Waldman, 1996, re-issued 2007, Shambhala Publications)

Edited by Anne Waldman, poet and specialist of the Beat movement, which she considers *"an artistic and social revolution,"* this anthology compiles the most essential extracts and texts by the poets on the periphery of the movement: John Wieners, Charles Olson and Robert Creeley. With an introduction by her friend Allen Ginsberg, highlighting younger generations' attraction for *"the exuberance, humour and frankness"* of the Beats. **C.G.**

BEAT HOTEL

BURROUGHS AND CORSO IN PARIS, 1958-1963
(Barry Miles, 2000, Grove Press, out of print)

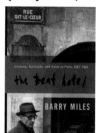

"The international aspect of the Beat Generation is underestimated" by historians, according to the author. Nevertheless, the Beats' Parisian sojourn was one of the movement's most intense ones. Barry Miles, friend and biographer of Ginsberg and Burroughs revisits "The Beat Hotel", a filthy boarding house at 9, rue Git-le-Coeur in Paris's Latin Quarter where poets slept and partied. The proximity Miles enjoyed with the Beat players is the source of intimate anecdotes about their Parisian years. **Q.G. & C.G.**

ARDOISE

(Philippe Djian, 2002, re-issued 2010, 10/18, in French only)

A tribute by the novelist Philippe Djian to his 10 favourite authors, *Ardoise* elaborates at great length on Kerouac's spontaneous prose. Djian definitely does not wish to be considered as an heir, but since *Ardoise* exists, he admits to owing something to Kerouac: *"The writing incites you, aged 20, to get away and hit the road – it imparts a melody and rhythm through which the sentences unfold, giving a certain vision of the world."* **Q.G.**

KEROUAC

(Yves Buin, 2006, Gallimard, in French only)

"The only people for me are the mad ones, the ones who are mad to live, mad to talk, mad to be saved, desirous of everything at the same time, the ones who never yawn or say a commonplace thing, but burn, burn, burn like fabulous yellow roman candles exploding like spiders across the stars," Kerouac wrote. This outburst, so typical of the writer's spontaneous prose, had everything needed to attract the psychiatrist and jazz specialist Yves Buin who, in this concise yet complete biography, establishes a subtle portrait of the raving poet. **Q.G.**

BIBLIOGRAPHY

BEAT SOUND, BEAT VISION

BEAT SOUND, BEAT VISION – THE BEAT SPIRIT AND
POPULAR SONG

(Laurence Coupe, 2007, Manchester
University Press)

Beat Sound, Beat Vision is not a book about musicology, history or rock criticism. The ambition of Laurence Coupe, a senior lecturer in English at Manchester Metropolitan University, is to articulate reflections about the thoughts of 60s songwriters through the fruitful link between Kerouac and Bob Dylan, the influence of the Beats on the Beatles and John Lennon, and also on Jim Morrison and Nick Drake. In other words, how literary counter-culture infused the spiritual basis of pop music. **É. V.**

BEATIFIC SOUL

JACK KEROUAC ON THE ROAD

(Isaac Gewirtz, 2007, The New York Public Library/Scala
Publishers)

An important documentary and reconstructive work, *Beatific Soul* is the first biography to take reference in Kerouac's own archives, until now unknown to the wider public. In this coffee table book, Isaac Gewirtz, curator of the Henry W. and Albert A. Berg Collection of English and American Literature at the New York Public Library, explores and reproduces Kerouac's journals, notes, manuscripts and sketches, retracing his chaotic path by concentrating on the creative process he used in his work. **I. P.-F.**

RIDING TOWARD EVERYWHERE

(William T. Vollmann, 2008, Ecco)

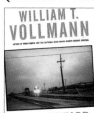

The genius novelist, essayist and journalist William T. Vollmann delves into the American myths of freedom, the road and the conquest of the West. For several years, he sneaked free rides on freight trains in the steps of Thoreau, London and Kerouac, the vagabonds of yesteryear, to meet today's Dharma bums. Somewhere between an investigation and a personal quest, this is a beautiful, intelligent essay that puts travel as a way of life – on the road, the rails, or within the self – on a pedestal. **G. M.**

NOIR C'EST NOIR

(Tim Lane, 2009, Delcourt, in French only)

"Step right this way! Enter a world of madness! It will be lots of fun!" cries a circus tout caustically on the first page of *Noir c'est Noir*. Adapted from his own short stories and full of Dharma bums, Tim Lane's graphic stories are direct descendents of the Beats' aesthetic heritage. A recurrent character in the midst of a crowd of magnificent pariahs, Spirit (a tribute to Will Eisner's hero and his chiselled black and white art) takes the train, following Kerouac's path. **É. V.**

BEAT MEMORIES

THE PHOTOGRAPHS OF ALLEN GINSBERG

(Sarah Greenough, 2010, Prestel)

This work is a collection of some 80 black and white photos taken by Allen Ginsberg between 1953 and 1963, and more from the 80s and 90s. We meet at random Neal Cassady beaming behind the wheel, Jack Kerouac smoking on the balcony, Bob Dylan in a New York park, William S. Burroughs wearing a floppy hat and various self-portraits of Ginsberg at different ages and in various stages of undressing. This casting call is a luxury, allowing us to dive into the Beat Generation with exuberance and nostalgia. **J. R.**

SAN FRANCISCO
L'UTOPIE LIBERTAIRE DES SIXTIES
(Steven Jezo-Vannier, 2010, Le mot et le reste, in French only)

Focused on the West Coast, Steven Jezo-Vannier's essay takes as its starting point the Haight-Ashbury district of San Francisco, the true birthplace of the hippie movement. From the publication of *Howl* by Allen Ginsberg to the psychedelic road trip taken by the Merry Pranksters (of whom Neal Cassady was a member), the author retraces the sociological and political lines of a liberation movement that was as explosive as it was short-lived: the utopia did not survive the Nixon era. **L. T.**

DANS LES ROUES DE JACK KEROUAC
(Text by Christophe Cousin, photos by Matthieu Paley, 2011, Éditions de La Martinière, in French only)

To hit the road again, without it being an obsessive pilgrimage or a vain imitation, is the promise kept by these two hunters of the nomadic lifestyle, the writer Christophe Cousin and the photographer Matthieu Paley. In this travel diary we see a procession of tightrope-walking hobos and silent cowboys, *On the Road* is brilliantly summoned, not as a literary standard but as a manifesto, the source of a thirst to make oneself scarce, each in our own way, even if it means leaving the beat(en) track and finding one's own road. **É. R.**

LA COMPAGNIE DES FEMMES
(Yves Simon, 2011, Stock, in French only)

"These alchemists of travel have taught me migration, the happiness of being a small dot in the world without any attachments," Yves Simon tells us of the Beat poets. In his latest novel, *La Compagnie des femmes*, an aging writer leaves the daily gloom of Paris and the woman he loves in order to write a travel journal. Through one night stands and meetings with hitchhikers, the writer renews his love for the books of his youth in a very French road trip. **Q. G.**

BALLAST
(Jean-Jacques Bonvin, 2011, Allia, in French only)

In this condensed work of 64 pages, Jean-Jacques Bonvin assumes the frenetic lifestyles of Kerouac, Ginsberg, Burroughs and especially Neal Cassady. By car, by train and in love, the life of this unpublished poet accelerated towards the railway lines in Mexico, where he collapsed, aged 42. In a feverish style, Bonvin rids himself of biographical details *à la Wikipedia* to marvellously reproduce the intensity of the journeys specific to the Beat Generation. **Q. G.**

PHOTOGRAPHS – 1961-1967
(Dennis Hopper, 2011, Taschen)

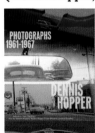

A worthy heir to the Beat Generation and *On the Road* because of its appetite for wide open spaces and long journeys, the road movie *Easy Rider* came out in 1969. Dennis Hopper, who directed and starred in the film, had a habit of taking his camera everywhere with him. The result is Jane Fonda, Paul Newman and Andy Warhol mingling with an eclectic bunch of bikers and figures from Beat art like Bruce Conner, his feet up in a bath tub surrounded by girls in their panties with 60s hairdos. What an era! **J. R.**

ROAD MOVIE, USA
(Bernard Benoliel and Jean-Baptiste Thoret, 2011, Hoëbeke, in French only)

More than a cinematic genre, the road movie is defined here by the authors as a motive intrinsically linked to the American imagination. The successor of the western, the road movie allows us to continue exploring the founding myths of an America that the movie directors (notably in New Hollywood) are demystifying little by little. A beautifully illustrated essay, the work of Benoliel and Thoret happily combines solid theoretical analysis and a true love of images. **L. T.**

DISCOGRAPHY

WITH THEIR RARE MUSICALITY, THE WRITINGS OF KEROUAC FORM A BRIDGE BETWEEN THE TWO MOST IMPORTANT STYLES OF THE 20TH CENTURY: JAZZ, PULSING THROUGHOUT KEROUAC'S LANGUAGE, AND ROCK, ALL OF WHICH'S MAJOR NAMES HAVE AT LEAST READ *ON THE ROAD*. WHAT FOLLOWS IS A LIMITED, BIASED OVERVIEW OF UNCLE JACK'S MUSICAL HERITAGE.

| TRANSLATED BY ALEX WYNNE HAUET

1. THE JACK KEROUAC COLLECTION
(Jack Kerouac, 1990, Rhino)

Bringing together Kerouac's three albums – *Poetry for the Beat Generation* (1959), *Blues and Haikus* (1959) and *Readings by Jack Kerouac on the Beat Generation* (1960) –, this box set offers the opportunity to discover the author's own interpretation of his major texts. Accompanied by the pianist Steve Allen on the first record and the tenor saxes Zoot Sims and Al Cohn on the second, Kerouac also reads passages from *On the Road* in a jazzy stream of consciousness that evokes improvisations of bebop. **É. V.**

2. HIGHWAY 61 REVISITED
(Bob Dylan, 1965, Sony BMG)

With its travel theme as a metaphor for poetic escape and spiritual quest, *Highway 61 Revisited* is without a doubt Dylan's album that was most influenced by *On the Road*. Traveling across the United States from Minnesota (Zim's native region) to Louisiana, the young songwriter's *Highway 61* opens with *Like a Rolling Stone*, a tale about the decline of a "princess" who discovers the reality of an America that has been abandoned. Liberated from bourgeois comforts, she can free herself. **É. V.**

1.

2.

3.

4.

5.

3. THE DOORS
(The Doors, 1967, Warner Music)

In response to the call of Aldous Huxley, who was an amateur of mescaline trips, and especially William Blake, one of the major poetic influences of the Beat Generation, Jim Morrison invites the listener to open the *"doors of perception"*, to break down the deceptive veil over reality and *Break on Through (To the Other Side)*. His shaman-like incantations aim at spiritual revelation via Dionysian rites and psychotropic drugs. **É. V.**

4. SONGS OF LEONARD COHEN
(Leonard Cohen, 1968, Sony BMG)

When Bob Dylan was still an adolescent, at the beginning of the sixties, Leonard Cohen was already a successful poet. After breaking with jazz poetry, which he wrote in Montréal and then in New York, following the tracks of the Beats, the Canadian released his first album at the same time as another record that was decisive in rock's entry into the adult world: *The Velvet Underground & Nico*. Carried by a mystical force, his dark, romantic folk songs mix the profane and the sacred to attain the beatitude aspired to by Kerouac. **É. V.**

5. THE SMITHS
(The Smiths, 1984, Rough Trade)

"Pretty girls make graves," Kerouac wrote in *The Dharma Bums*. Some 25 years later, the Englishman Steven Patrick Morrissey embraced the phrase and made it the title of one of the songs on the first album by his band, The Smiths. With his latent homosexuality, dark romanticism, chiselled literary scansion, taste for paradox and provocation, the popstar carved his path from the start as Kerouac's most insolent offspring. Pretty boys make flowers. **A. T.**

6. RAIN DOGS
(Tom Waits, 1985, Universal)

The cornerstone of Tom Waits' most beautiful triptych (with the 1983 and 1987 albums *Swordfishtrombones* and *Franks Wild Years*), *Rain Dogs* is a bust-up musical comedy that tells the story of a worthless middle class man who decides to do away with his repetitive consumer lifestyle. Zigzagging from one style to the next (tango, rumba, polka), the crooner, supported by Marc Ribot and Keith Richards, delivers a blues-jazz-rock tribute to leaving the beaten track behind. **É. V.**

7. POP SATORI
(Étienne Daho, 1986, EMI)

In 1986, the Beats are no longer in France. Paris is depressed, but Saint-Germain lights up with the suave voice of Étienne Daho. On one of the most touching albums in French pop, the Breton innovates with the flash of spontaneous prose, here applied to the synths of modern youth. *Satori Pop Century*, *Paris*, *Le Flore* and *Soleil de Minuit* are all references to American myths, from James Dean to Edie Sedgwick as well as Kerouac with his *Satori in Paris*, and a Beat credo: to hang around without a purpose... **Q. G.**

8. GEE WHIZ BUT THIS IS A LONESOME TOWN
(Moriarty, 2008, Naïve)

The name of this French-American band is a direct tribute to Dean Moriarty, the colourful young man who fascinates Sal Paradise so much in *On the Road*. Moriarty's members all read Kerouac's novel the same year, and recognised themselves in the intensity of the character and his taste for adventure. On this first LP marked by travel and bohemian motifs, the sound of typewriters and church bells mix with those of the kazoo and the Jew's harp in an elegant country-folk escape. **É. V.**

6.

7.

8.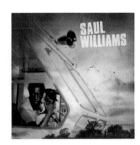

9.

10.

9. SAUL WILLIAMS
(Saul Williams, 2004, Fader)

Saul Williams grew up in New York surrounded by beatniks and hippies. The folk pioneer Pete Seeger sang regularly in his father's church. In 1997, Allen Ginsberg names him in person. On his second album, Saul Williams makes tonic slam spin around, inherited from the jazz poetry of the Beats, against rock riffs and hip-hop rhythms. Williams' hybrid style is particularly inspired by Bob Kaufman, a mixed-race provocative poet known for his anti-racist punchlines. **É. V.**

10. KEROUAC: KICKS JOY DARKNESS
(Compilation, 1997, Rykodisc)

A tribute album to Jack Kerouac, *Kicks Joy Darkness* places the word at the centre of the musical plan to make it "jazz." Mythical voices from the rock and literary worlds followed one another at the altar: John Cale from the Velvet Underground, Michael Stipe from R.E.M., Eddie Vedder from Pearl Jam, Lee Ranaldo from Sonic Youth, Steven Tyler from Aerosmith, Jeff Buckley, as well as punk legends Patti Smith, Lydia Lunch, Jim Carroll and Joe Strummer from The Clash. Members of the Beat Generation are also present: Allen Ginsberg, William S. Burroughs, Lawrence Ferlinghetti and even the pope of gonzo journalism, Hunter S. Thomson. Half the pieces on this spoken word record are taken from the compilation *Pomes All Sizes* (poems written between 1954 and 1965 about drugs, meditation and car trips), the rest being sourced in his letters and novels. At times slightly artificial, this tribute is nevertheless a moving testimony to the impact Kerouac had on the rock culture he rejected. **É. V.**

FILMOGRAPHY

LONG BEFORE WALTER SALLES ADAPTED *ON THE ROAD*, THE WRITINGS OF THE BEAT GENERATION INSPIRED GENERATIONS OF FILMMAKERS, SCREENWRITERS AND DOCUMENTARY MAKERS. SOME BELIEVE THEY ARE EVEN AT THE ROOT OF A CINEMATIC GENRE IN ITS OWN RIGHT, THE ROAD MOVIE. FAST REWIND.

TRANSLATED BY ALEX WYNNE HAUET

SHADOWS
by John Cassavetes (1959, 1h 21)

PULL MY DAISY
by Robert Frank et Alfred Leslie (1959, 30 min)

John Cassavetes' first film, *Shadows*, was shot in 16mm in the streets of New York and financed on a tight budget thanks to a call for funds launched on the radio by the director. The film was almost completely improvised by John Cassavetes' class mates (he was studying theatre at the time). He directs Benny and Lelia, a mixed-race brother and sister, in their beatnik existence: jazz, hanging out, crazy parties as well as racial discrimination and boredom. A first version was presented in New York (Cassavetes would later put significant extra work in it) at the same time as *Pull My Daisy*, the ultimate Beat film because it was written by Jack Kerouac and the Beat poets acted in it. In this unpretentious short, Allen Ginsberg, Gregory Corso and Peter Orlovsky create havoc around a bishop who understands none of it. Kerouac's voice-over contributes to the charm of this liberating pleasantry. This double bill, presented two years after the publication of *On the Road*, confirmed the emergence of the Beat Generation as an artistic movement that mixed spontaneity, protest and a joyful team spirit. This was nothing less than the birth of American independent film. **L. T.**

SHADOWS IS AVAILABLE ON DVD (CRITERION COLLECTION)

THE WILD RIDE
by Harvey Berman (1960, 59 min)

THE BEATNIKS
by Paul Frees (1960, 1h 18)

Surfing on the beatnik trend, Paul Frees and Harvey Berman made their only films. In *The Beatniks*, Eddy Crane is spotted by a major company and prepares to become a singing star of the small screen. But this is without counting on his beatnik friends who, during an alcoholised evening, commit a crime...In *The Wild Ride*, Jack Nicholson succumbs to the debaucherous life of beatnik·. These two B movies caricature the Beat Generation and are of little interest. **L. T.**

EASY RIDER
by Dennis Hopper (1969, 1h 35)

The road movie's birth certificate, Dennis Hopper's humming classic has lost none of its superb appeal. Wyatt (Peter Fonda, magnificent as the pacifist rider) and Billy are traveling across the southern states (from Los Angeles to New Orleans) searching for a mythical country that they will find nowhere. On the contrary, the further they go, the more the United States reveal themselves as they were at the end of the sixties: violent, reactionary and deadly. A special mention goes to Jack Nicholson, idealistic lawyer and collateral victim. **L. T.**

AVAILABLE ON DVD (SONY)

TWO-LANE BLACKTOP
by Monte Hellman (1971, 1h 42)

An absurd counterpart to *Easy Rider*, Monte Hellman's film recounts the voyage on the mythical route 66 of the Driver, the Mechanic and their Girl. The two friends are mad about cars, obsessed with the speed of their engine. At a gas station, they meet G.T.O. (Warren Oates), a compulsive liar against whom they decide to race to Washington. This cult movie ends with the film roll catching fire, as if to say the road was only a dead end after all. **L. T.**

AVAILABLE ON DVD (THE CRITERION COLLECTION)

HEART BEAT

by John Byrum (1980, 1 h 50)

Adapted from the memoirs of Carolyn Cassady, *Heart Beat* is centred on the *ménage à trois* formed by Neal and Carolyn Cassady (very successfully played by Sissy Spacek) and Jack Kerouac. From their first encounter to Neal's prolonged disappearances via Kerouac's sudden success and its repercussions, this psychological drama nevertheless does not manage to attain a higher status than that of a made-for-TV movie. Carolyn Cassady hates the film, which she says debases the relationship she had with both men. **L. T.**

AVAILABLE ON DVD (WARNER BROS.).

JACK KEROUAC – KING OF THE BEATS

by John Antonelli (1985, 1 h 18)

This docufiction retraces Kerouac's life thanks to a mixture of archive images, interviews with close friends (including John Clellon Holmes, William S. Burroughs, Allen Ginsberg, Carolyn Cassady and Edie Parker), readings of the writer's works and reconstruction (with Jack Coulter as Kerouac and David Andrews as Neal Cassady). Difficult to find today, the main appeal of *King of the Beats* is the first-hand memories shared by those who are no longer of this world. **I. P.-F.**

DRUGSTORE COWBOY

by Gus Van Sant (1989, 1 h 42)

The director's second movie *Drugstore Cowboy* finds in Matt Dillon (the teen star of Coppola's dark movies *Outsiders* and *Rumble Fish*) a new version of the 70s beatnik figure 20 years on. Bob and Dianne, a young junkie couple on the West Coast, live off petty theft. One evening, Bob leaves Dianne on her own, and she dies of an overdose. This is a dark account of the drowning of a generation by the grand master of films about confused youth. It includes a cameo appearance from William S. Burroughs. **L. T.**

AVAILABLE ON DVD (MGM/UNITED ARTISTS)

NAKED LUNCH

by David Cronenberg (1991, 1 h 55)

Taking the title of William S. Burroughs' novel, Cronenberg – in his experimental period – offers up a very free interpretation of the drugged, hallucinating, neurotic Beat author. Bill Lee kills his wife by playing at William Tell (an unfortunate episode in Burroughs' life) before taking exile in Tangier where he types away frantically in the muggy atmosphere of a seedy hotel. Soon enough, his typewriter morphs into a disgusting (but often hilarious) cockroach that gets him running around in circles. **L. T.**

AVAILABLE ON DVD (THE CRITERION COLLECTION)

MAD MEN – SEASON I

series created by Matthew Weiner (2007, 612 min)

Don Draper, the dashing ad man hero of AMC's cult series, is a contemporary of the Beat Generation. From the opulent Madison Avenue to The Village, there is but a single step, which Don takes happily to go to see Midge, his very own free woman. Through the season, the hero's incursions into the beatnik world become darker: Don disapproves of the behaviour of these anti-establishment artists, and their ending up as junkies proves him right. From now on, everyone stays on their own side of the fence. **L. T.**

AVAILABLE ON DVD (LIONSGATE)

FERLINGHETTI, LE DERNIER DES BEATNIKS

by Laurent Perrin (2011, 52 min)

Open doors, books, minds and hearts: that is the credo of the City Lights bookshop and publishing house, opened by Lawrence Ferlinghetti in 1953. When he learnt that the poet and editor was still alive, Laurent Perrin hurried to San Francisco to take down the statements of the last protagonist of the Beat Generation. This exercise in admiration recalls the appearance of Ginsberg's *Howl*, whose success allowed Ferlinghetti to continue publishing what was important to him. **Q. G.**

KEY HANG-OUTS

"WHITHER GOEST THOU, AMERICA, IN THY SHINY CAR IN THE NIGHT?" SAL PARADISE ASKS HIMSELF IN ON THE ROAD. THE ULTIMATE INCARNATION OF THE WRITER-ADVENTURER, TRAVELLING ALONE OR SURROUNDED BY HIS BEAT FRIENDS, KEROUAC IS THE AUTHOR OF A WORK HAUNTED BY SPACE AND GEOGRAPHY. THESE 10 PLACES STILL HOLD THE MEMORY OF HIS JOURNEYS.

| TRANSLATED BY ALEX WYNNE HAUET

SHAKESPEARE & COMPANY
(Paris)

On the banks of the Seine, this is an Ali Baba's cave where books are piled from floor to ceiling in a marvellously cramped space. You can stay until late in the evening, and fun-loving travellers can even sleep upstairs (beware of the lice). Since its opening in 1951, this English bookshop has been working on spreading Beat culture through events and publications as well as by welcoming its protagonists. Its founder, George Whitman, died in December 2011 at the age of 98. **C. G.**

THE "BEAT HOTEL"
(Paris)

From 1957 to 1963, Allen Ginsberg, William S. Burroughs and Gregory Corso took refuge at 9 rue Gît-le-Cœur in Paris to escape post-war American conformism. In this shabby hotel, the owner Madame Rachou let them indulge in drugs and free love. Burroughs finished Naked Lunch here, while Ginsberg wrote Kaddish and Brion Gysin invented the famous cut-up technique. The address is now occupied by a four-star auberge, a world apart from the old Beat hideaway. **Q. G.**

THE BEAT MUSEUM
(San Francisco)

Unhappy in his role as a businessman at IBM, Jerry Cimino decided in 2003 to return to the readings of his youth by creating a place of worship dedicated to Kerouac, Ginsberg, Burroughs and the rest. Initially situated in Monterey, California, the Beat Museum moved to San Francisco to be as close as possible to the City Lights bookshop. As soon as it opened, fans turned up in droves to enrich the collection of objects having belonged to the Beats: first editions, paintings, drawings and even number plates on which groupies have inscribed the name "Kerouac". The only thing missing is the famous 1949 Hudson driven by Kerouac and Cassady and featured in *On the Road*. The car was sold off only three months after Cassady bought it, and disappeared without a trace: no registration number, no photos, no purchase documents. This has now been rectified as Walter Salles has given the car driven by Sam Riley and Garrett Hedlund in the movie to the museum. **Q. G.**

VESUVIO CAFE
(San Francisco)

Separated from City Lights by Jack Kerouac Alley, the dark and elegant Vesuvio is the historic café of the Beat Generation. Founded in 1948 by Henri Lenoir, it was Jack Kerouac and Neal Cassady's local. You can come here for a glass of wine at 11 am and stumble across a maker of *"poetic fiction and real catastrophe"* who will take you around the bars and introduce you as his daughter to his friends, old beat poets who enjoy reciting their texts to you. **G. M.**

THE CITY LIGHTS BOOKSHOP
(San Francisco)

A place of mythical literary encounters and the temple of beat poetry, the famous bookshop founded by Lawrence Ferlinghetti in 1953 has without a doubt lost some of its edge. Situated in San Francisco, it welcomed (and sometimes published) the group of penniless writers. Some even had bedrooms and offices there. Even if you can no longer sleep, drink or smoke there today, its poetry and paperback departments (its specialties at the time) are still among the most discriminating and well stocked in America. **G. M.**

LOWELL, MASSACHUSETTS

It is here, in this industrial city built in the 1820s along the river Merrimack, north of Boston, that Kerouac was born and buried. Red brick factory buildings sit alongside painted wooden Victorian houses, and wandering around, you find Kerouac's school, the premises of the daily newspaper *The Sun,* where he worked, and the altar of the French-American orphanage, where his mother took him to pray. A few personal objects are on display at the local museum – books, socks (!) and rucksack. **J. R.**

THE JACK KEROUAC SCHOOL OF DISEMBODIED POETICS
(Naropa, Colorado)

Founded as part of the Buddhist University of Naropa in Colorado, The Jack Kerouac School of Disembodied Poetics was created by Anne Waldman and Allen Ginsberg in 1974. By doing so, they wanted to pay tribute to Kerouac – the first, according to Waldman, *"to understand the noble Buddhist truth of suffering"* – as well as to teach *"poetry to those who meditate, and meditation to poets."* William S. Burroughs, Gregory Corso, Diane di Prima, Gary Snyder and Lawrence Ferlinghetti have all given lectures there. **I. P.-F.**

NEW YORK PUBLIC LIBRARY

Two sculptured lions guard the entrance to the New York Public Library, founded in Manhattan in 1895. You have to show your credentials to get through the little wooden door of the Berg Collection, on the third floor, and view the 150,000 original English and American literary documents kept there – manuscripts, letters and personal papers having belonged to Dickens, Byron and Kerouac. The latter's archives are the fourth most consulted after those of Woolf, Nabokov and Burroughs. **J. R.**

MINTON'S PLAYHOUSE
(New York)

Founded by the sax player Henry Minton in 1938, this famous Harlem club welcomed the jazz virtuosos of the era (Thelonious Monk, Charlie Parker, Dizzy Gillespie...). For the duration of a session, they would free themselves of their respective groups and, alone or in pairs, embark on feverish improvisation sessions. That is how bebop, the supreme form of jazz according to Kerouac, was born. He become a regular at Minton's from his arrival in New York in 1939. **I. P.-F.**

THE CHELSEA HOTEL
(New York)

Situated at 222 West 23rd Street in New York, this imposing red brick hotel was home, from 1905 to 2007, to a breathtaking number of artists (from Frida Kahlo to Henri Cartier-Bresson), musicians (Edith Piaf to Jimi Hendrix...), writers (of which all the Beats of course), filmmakers (Dennis Hopper, Ethan Hawke...) and cranks (gurus, prophets, muses...). Guests for a night or long-term residents, most of the time they paid with their works – if they paid at all, that is. **I. P.-F.**

AMONG HIS EARLY INFLUENCES WAS THE NOVELIST THOMAS WOLFE. JACK WAS AN AUTODIDACT WHO HAD READ ASSIDUOUSLY SINCE HIGH SCHOOL.

THOUGH KEROUAC GOT GOOD GRADES AT HORACE MANN AND COMPLETED HIS CREDITS, HE WAS ABSENT FROM CLASS OFTEN, CHECKING OUT THE JUNKIES AND PROSTITUTES IN TIMES SQUARE.

HEY, HOW MUCH YOU CHARGE?

HE QUICKLY BECAME A JAZZ FAN, AND ATTENDED THE LEGENDARY UPTOWN JAM SESSIONS AT WHICH CHARLIE PARKER, DIZZY GILLESPIE, AND THELONIOUS MONK AND OTHERS BEGAN INVENTING BEBOP.

YEAH, MAN, GO !!!

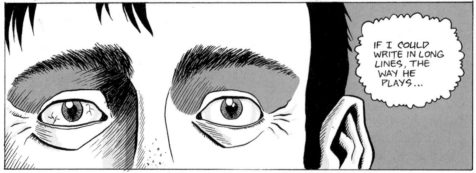

THE LONG MUSIC PHRASES OF THE BOPPERS HAD AN INFLUENCE ON KEROUAC'S PROSE.

IF I COULD WRITE IN LONG LINES, THE WAY HE PLAYS...

THE BEAT GOES ON

The large, contrasting features of the character drawings in the collective work *The Beats*, are without a doubt influenced by Burroughs' benzedrine-fueled eyes and Ginsberg's shaggy beard. Edited by the late Harvey Pekar, writer of the cult *American Splendor* comic books, the project brought together a dozen or so illustrators from different horizons, including famous veterans (the feminist Trina Robbins and *Mad* contributor Peter Kuper) and promising newcomers (the unknown Jerome Neukirch and the anti-folk musician Jeffrey Lewis). Far from confining itself to the holy trinity of Kerouac-Burroughs-Ginsberg, this generational portrait retraces the trajectory of a group in a hurry to enter American mythology. **Q. G.**
THE BEATS: A GRAPHIC HISTORY (HARVEY PEKAR, PAUL BUHLE, ED PISKOR…, HILL AND WANG, 2010)

Go
on the road
with Penguin

On the Road

KEROUAC

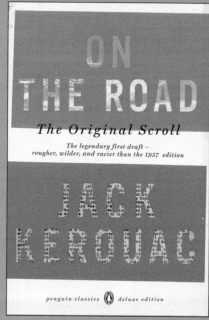

ON
THE ROAD
The Original Scroll

The legendary first draft –
rougher, wilder, and racier than the 1957 edition

JACK
KEROUAC

penguin classics deluxe edition

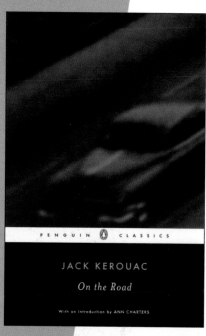

PENGUIN CLASSICS

JACK KEROUAC
On the Road

With an introduction by ANN CHARTERS

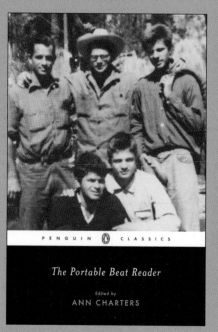

PENGUIN CLASSICS

The Portable Beat Reader

Edited by
ANN CHARTERS

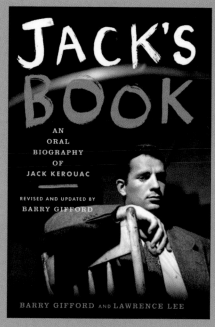

JACK'S
BOOK

AN
ORAL
BIOGRAPHY
OF
JACK KEROUAC

REVISED AND UPDATED BY
BARRY GIFFORD

BARRY GIFFORD AND LAWRENCE LEE

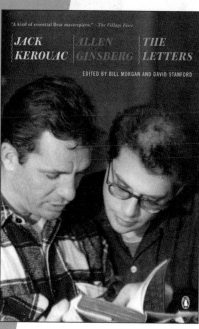

"A kind of essential Beat masterpiece." —*The Village Voice*

JACK
KEROUAC   ALLEN
GINSBERG   THE
LETTERS

EDITED BY BILL MORGAN AND DAVID STANFORD

Penguin Books
Penguin Classics
Members of Penguin Group (USA)
www.penguin.com

BEAT QUIZ

BY CLÉMENTINE GALLOT | TRANSLATED BY LAURA HUGO WESTERHOUT

1. WHAT HAPPENED TO THE END OF THE 1951 VERSION OF THE MANUSCRIPT OF "ON THE ROAD"?

A/ A DOG ATE IT. B/ A SMOLDERING ROACH REDUCED IT TO SMOKE AND ASHES. C/ ALLEN GINSBERG SPILLED BEER ON IT.

2. WHAT WAS JACK KEROUAC'S NICKNAME?

A/ KK. B/ JACKY. C/ TI-JEAN.

3. NEAL CASSADY HAD SO MUCH FUN, HE LOST THE TIP OF HIS...

A/ EAR. B/ LIVER. C/ THUMB.

4. WHICH ARTIFICIAL PARADISE DID THE BEATS PREFER?

A/ BENZEDRINE. B/ REEFER... TEA, THAT IS. C/ WHISKY.

5. WHERE IN MEXICO CITY DID KEROUAC WRITE "DOCTOR SAX"?

A/ IN BILL BURROUGHS'S BED. B/ IN A WHOREHOUSE. C/ IN THE TOILET.

6. WHAT EXTRACURRICULAR ACTIVITY DID KEROUAC EXCEL AT, AS A COLUMBIA UNIVERSITY UNDERGRAD?

A/ HORN PLAYING. B/ FOOTBALL. C/ CHESS.

7. WHAT GAME WERE WILLIAM S. BURROUGHS AND HIS WIFE, JOAN VOLLMER, PLAYING WHEN HE KILLED HER?

A/ COPS AND ROBBERS. B/ WILLIAM TELL. C/ LEAPFROG.

8. JACK KEROUAC KEPT NOTEBOOKS OF THE NAMES OF THE WOMEN HE'D SLEPT WITH. HOW MANY ENTRIES ARE THERE?

A/ 0 – NICE TRY! B/ 250. C/ 3800.

9. WHAT UNLIKELY JOB DID KEROUAC TAKE IN SAN FRANCISCO?

A/ BRAKEMAN. B/ CHOIRBOY. C/ CABLECAR DRIVER.

10. WHAT WAS JACK'S NICKNAME FOR HIS DEAR MOTHER, GABRIELLE?

A/ GABY. B/ MÉMÈRE. C/ BRENDA.

11. HOW MUCH TIME DID JACK KEROUAC ACTUALLY SPEND HITCHHIKING?

A/ A WEEK. B/ A MONTH. C/ A YEAR.

12. HOW LONG DID IT TAKE HIM TO WRITE "ON THE ROAD"?

A/ THREE WEEKS. B/ THREE YEARS. C/ NINE YEARS.

ANSWERS (1. A / 2. C / 3. C / 4. A,B,C / 5. C / 6. B / 7. B / 8. B / 9. A / 10. B /11. B: CHICAGO TO DENVER IN JULY 1947 – OTHERWISE, NEAL USUALLY DROVE / 12. A,B,C: SCHOLARS DISAGREE)